THE HUMAN RESOURCE FUNCTION IN EDUCATIONAL ADMINISTRATION

EIGHTH EDITION

THE HUMAN RESOURCE FUNCTION IN EDUCATIONAL ADMINISTRATION

EIGHTH EDITION

I. Phillip Young
College of Education
University of California-Davis

William B. Castetter
Professor Emeritus
Graduate School of Education
University of Pennsylvania

PEARSON

Merrill
Prentice Hall

Upper Saddle River, New Jersey
Columbus, Ohio

Library of Congress Cataloging-in-Publication Data

Young, Ila Phillip
  The human resource function in educational administration / I. Phillip Young, William B.
Castetter.–8th ed.
    p. cm.
  William B. Castetter named first on previous ed.
  Includes bibliographical references and indexes.
  ISBN 0-13-048404-0
  1. School personnel management–United States. I. Castetter, William Benjamin, 1914-
II. Title.
  LB2831.58.C37 2004
  371.2'01'093–dc21   2003052706

Vice President and Executive Publisher: Jeffery W. Johnston
Executive Editor: Debra A. Stollenwerk
Associate Editor: Ben Stephen
Editorial Assistant: Mary Morrill
Production Editor: Kris Robinson-Roach
Production Coordination: Carlisle Publishers Services
Design Coordinator: Diane C. Lorenzo
Cover Designer: Jason Moore
Cover Image: SuperStock
Production Manager: Pamela D. Bennett
Director of Marketing: Ann Castel Davis
Marketing Manager: Darcy Betts Prybella
Marketing Coordinator: Tyra Poole

This book was set in Photina MT by Carlisle Communications, Ltd. It was printed and bound by R.R.
Donnelley & Sons Company. The cover was printed by The Lehigh Press, Inc.

Earlier editions, entitled *The Personnel Function in Educational Administration*, © 1992, 1986, 1981, 1976, and 1971
by William B. Castetter.

Pearson Education Ltd.   Pearson Education Australia Pty. Limited
Pearson Education Singapore Pte. Ltd.   Pearson Education North Asia Ltd.
Pearson Education Canada, Ltd.   Pearson Educación de Mexico, S.A. de C.V.
Pearson Education—Japan   Pearson Education Malaysia Pte. Ltd.

10 9 8 7 6 5 4 3 2 1
ISBN: 0-13-048404-0

To my wife, Karen
My daughter, Rebecca
and my son, Phillip
—I.P.Y.

To Roberta, with affection
—W.B.C.

PREFACE

Every employee of an educational organization is influenced by the human resource function. This influence begins prior to employment through recruitment and selection processes and continues throughout the employment period of an individual. Whether or not this influence is positive depends on how well the human resource function is managed by those responsible for making important decisions about individuals as employees and about the overall operation of the human resource function in the educational setting.

Some of the decisions involve old issues ever new, while other decisions involve new issues yet to be broached by many educational organizations. Within this edition, both types of issues are addressed. Issues that have been and continue to be a mainstay of the human resource function are examined from both traditional and novel perspectives. Emerging human resource issues are introduced, and best practices relating to these issues are examined.

This edition, like the seventh edition, is organized into three parts. However, some of the chapters from the previous edition have been deleted, and other chapters have been combined. Most importantly, each chapter has been revised, and each chapter contains web links.

The three parts of this edition reflect pre-employment considerations from a strategic planning perspective, core human resource functions common to every organization, and continuity of employment considerations pertaining to enhancing the employment life of individuals as employees. Considerable emphasis is placed on the readability of these parts from a student perspective.

Part I introduces the human resource function and places the human resource function within the strategic planning context. Informational needs for linking human resource functions and strategic planning processes are examined from a policy perspective.

In Part II, core human resource functions associated with recruitment and selection, induction, development, performance appraisal, and compensation are addressed from several perspectives. Emphasis is placed on policy decisions and administrative decisions relative to these different human resource functions, and current research is brought to bear on these topics.

The focus of Part III is on the employment continuity process and benefits associated with continued employment. Attention is afforded to collective bargaining within the school setting, and the role of human resources as related to collective bargaining.

What's New in This Edition

In maintaining its signature orientation among competing textbooks, this eighth edition follows the general systems approach to the human resource function from a strategic management perspective as set forth in previous editions and expands current knowledge in this area from several viewpoints by drawing from emerging research, by expanding current knowledge about human resource practice, by addressing new systemic reform efforts confronting public school districts, and by linking recent Web-based information illustrating current practice of the human resource function in each chapter. Again, as with past editions, attention is devoted to the concerns of those administrators responsible for administering the human resource function in the educational setting and to those employees subjected to the human resource process in fulfilling job assignments. Both perspectives are addressed in this new edition by the following:

- Clarifying the role of strategic planning and identifying systemic reform efforts pertaining to competency-based testing and institutional report cards that impact the operation of the human resource function
- Illustrating the importance of mission statements for shaping the direction of human resource functions and supplying on-line working examples from exemplary public school districts
- Providing a mosaic depiction of the human resource components emphasizing the interrelatedness among planning, recruitment, selection, compensation, appraisal, development, and other continuity processes necessary for a competent work force
- Exploring fundamental components of the intra structure necessary for developing and maintaining an information system that can be used to inform those responsible for administrating a human resource process
- Examining proactive policy issues bearing on the recruitment and selection of employees and differentiating between the equal employment opportunity perspective and the affirmative action perspective as related to the procurement of employees
- Including Web-based references for legislative acts governing the employee procurement process and linking these acts to practice in the field setting
- Viewing recruitment and selection both from an organizational (employer) and from an individual (applicant) perspective and including emerging research findings addressing the recruitment and selection from both perspectives
- Offering methodologies for assessing selection practices as related to both legislative mandates (disproportional impacts) and practical utility that can be tailored to and performed by an individual school district
- Exemplifying different quantitative and qualitative models that can be used to evaluate the internal consistency of a compensation system used by a school district for paying nonunionized employees

- Presenting criteria for defining a relevant labor used to establish salaries based on common educational practices and alluding to specific economic principles such as ability to pay, cost-benefit, scale of economy, and supply and demand
- Advocating specific experimental designs and planning techniques that can improve the assessment and development of staff improvement programs for all groups of employees
- Differentiating among different types of performance assessment systems and providing a decision matrix for choosing among performance assessment systems according to purposes(s)
- Dissecting fringe benefits according to entitlements and privileges within the employment continuity process and explaining differences between defined contribution and defined benefit plans
- Classifying contractual items and proposals within a master agreement according to legislative definitions (mandatory, permissive, and illegal) and to personal preference (person concerns, organizational concerns, and general concerns)

Finally, by addressing past practices, examining present practices, and suggesting future practices, the eighth edition offers those responsible for, and those subjected to, the human resource function in the school setting with viable options. Underlying the philosophy of this textbook is that a singular approach to human resource management in the school setting fails to exist and that knowledgeable choices must be made by all the stakeholders. If easy answers and fixed solutions existed for most human resource issues, then many of the current educational problems would have been resolved decades ago.

Acknowledgments

We would like to acknowledge the following practicing professionals from the public school setting for their efforts and insights relative to the eighth edition of this text. They took time from their busy schedule and administrative responsibilities to provide a much needed service without the benefit of any compensation: Paul Chounet, Director of Information–Dos Palos, CA; Xavier De La Torre, High School Principal–Portersville, CA; Todd Oto, Assistant High School Principal– Visalia, CA; and David Waggener, Director Finance–Morganfield, KY.

We also wish to thank those who reviewed the manuscript in its early stages and offered their comments and suggestions: Richard Bartholome, Whittier College; Ira Bogotch, Florida Atlantic University; Gary D. Brooks, University of Texas at El Paso; Robert Decker, University of Northern Iowa; Margaret Grogan, University of Virginia; and Carleton R. Holt, University of Arkansas.

I.P.Y.
W.B.C.

EDUCATOR LEARNING CENTER: AN INVALUABLE ONLINE RESOURCE

Merrill Education and the Association for Supervision and Curriculum Development (ASCD) invite you to take advantage of a new online resource, one that provides access to the top research and proven strategies associated with ASCD and Merrill—the Educator Learning Center. At **www.EducatorLearningCenter.com** you will find resources that will enhance your students' understanding of course topics and of current educational issues, in addition to being invaluable for further research.

How the Educator Learning Center will help your students become better teachers

With the combined resources of Merrill Education and ASCD, you and your students will find a wealth of tools and materials to better prepare them for the classroom.

Research

- More than 600 articles from the ASCD journal *Educational Leadership* discuss everyday issues faced by practicing teachers.
- A direct link on the site to Research Navigator™ gives students access to many of the leading education journals, as well as extensive content detailing the research process.
- Excerpts from Merrill Education texts give your students insights on important topics of instructional methods, diverse populations, assessment, classroom management, technology, and refining classroom practice.

Classroom Practice

- Hundreds of lesson plans and teaching strategies are categorized by content area and age range.
- Case studies and classroom video footage provide virtual field experience for student reflection.
- Computer simulations and other electronic tools keep your students abreast of today's classrooms and current technologies.

Look into the value of Educator Learning Center yourself

Preview the value of this educational environment by visiting **www.EducatorLearningCenter.com** and clicking on "Demo." For a free 4-month subscription to the Educator Learning Center in conjunction with this text, simply contact your Merrill/Prentice Hall sales representative.

BRIEF CONTENTS

CONTENTS

10   Unionism and the Human Resource Function   264

NOTE: Every effort has been made to provide accurate and current Internet information in this book. However, the Internet and information posted on it are constantly changing, it is inevitable that some of the Internet addresses listed in this textbook will change.

THE HUMAN RESOURCE FUNCTION IN EDUCATIONAL ADMINISTRATION

EIGHTH EDITION

PART I

FOUNDATIONS OF THE HUMAN RESOURCE FUNCTION

Chapter 1
The Human Resource Function in Perspective

Chapter 2
Strategic Planning and the Human Resource Function

Chapter 3
Information Technology and the Human Resource Function

Part I introduces the reader to the content and context of the human resource function as applied to educational organizations. The intent of Part I is to

- Provide an overview of the human resource function, link the human resource function to other organizational functions, and illustrate how the human resource function is a vital part of the overall operation of an educational organization.
- Describe strategic planning from a human resource perspective and discuss ways in which it can be employed to enhance attainment of the strategic objectives and goals of an educational organization.
- Emphasize the vital importance of the information–communication connection and its power to affect the efficacy and efficiency of human resource outcomes.

1 The Human Resource Function in Perspective

CHAPTER OBJECTIVES

Place in perspective the nature, dimensions, and significance of the human resource function for an educational organization.

Establish the purposive nature of educational institutions as related to the human resource function.

Stress the impact of social change and examine the role of the human resource function in resolving the challenges that social change represents.

Support the proposition that the human resource function is a vital part of every educational organization.

Identify current and emerging problems confronting school systems that hinder or enhance educational change within the human resource context.

Provide a foundation for improving the system's ability to close the gap between the actual and desired states of individual, work unit, and system effectiveness.

CHAPTER CONCEPTS

Affirmative action	Human resource function
Culture	Internal environment
Ethics	Organizational structure
External environment	Values

This book addresses the human resource function in educational institutions, primarily within the public school setting. The aim is to bring a broad perspective to the human resource function—to provide insights into the purposes, policies, plans, procedures, and projects, and the impact of these human resource aspects on work, working arrangements, and work motivation of school administrative, teaching, and support personnel. The intent of this book is expressed through a framework that includes

- Placing, in perspective, significance, scope, and dimensions of the human resource function within the context of educational organizations.
- Emphasizing the purposive aspects and potential power of school systems by internalizing application of the human resource function.
- Considering the interlocking triad of three organizational variables—social change, education reform, and the human resource function—as factors either hampering or enhancing the process of school improvement.
- Identifying six dimensions of the human resource function and their potential for affecting individual, work unit, and system performance.

Goals and Objectives of the Human Resource Function

Within the educational setting, the human resource function has several goals that facilitate the effective and efficient operation of a public school district. Major goals of the **human resource function** are to attract, select, induct, develop, retain, and motivate personnel to achieve the system's mission; assist members in obtaining position and work unit standards; maximize career opportunities for employees; and coordinate organizational and individual objectives. These goals must be translated into operational objectives to give direction to those responsible for achieving the overall intent of the human resource function.

As school districts enter the 21st century, many of the goals have yet to be realized fully within the education setting. Impediments to realizing these goals include rigidity of individuals responsible for administering the school district and reluctance or inability of these persons to apply emerging new knowledge about human resource practices. Compounding these impediments are, in many instances, internal and external political constraints on the school system over which little discretion can be afforded.

Goals and objectives defining the human resource function are interrelated, rather than stand-alone events. Relationships exist both *within the human resource function* among goals and objectives and *between other organizational functions* comprising a public school system and the goals and objectives of the human resource function. Figure 1.1 depicts the centrality of the human resource function in a hypothetical school system.

As Figure 1.1 shows, the human resource function contains 10 different objectives or processes. When fulfilling the human resource function, designated personnel within the public school setting should perform each of these objectives or

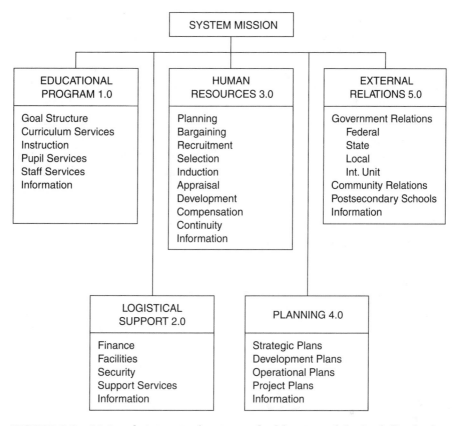

FIGURE 1.1   *Major administrative functions and subfunctions of the Goodville school system.*

processes. Failure to perform or at least tend to any one of these processes will limit substantially the effectiveness and the efficiency of a school system in our modern-day society.

Within small school districts, responsibilities for the human resource function may be delegated among several different position holders. The superintendent may perform some responsibilities associated with the human resource function, whereas building-level administrators within the school district may perform other responsibilities. In large school systems, specific personnel or entire departments may be assigned all human resource functions.

Our purpose of depicting the relationships, as found in Figure 1.1, is to identify, classify, and relate major functions and subfunctions of human resource management that must be performed within a school system if the mission of a school system is to be fulfilled. The human resource function, it should be noted, is divided into 10 areas: planning, information communication, recruitment, selection, induction, development, appraisal, compensation, justice, employment continuity, and unionism. These processes form the foundation of subsequent chapters addressed in this book.

From the preceding introduction of the human resource function, one can examine the significance of this important subsystem of a school organization. For example,

- In contrast to some other major functions, human resource is concerned with activities related primarily to people in different stages of their careers.

The scope of the human resource function, as can be judged from the activities listed in Figure 1.1, is extensive. These functional activities exercise a pervasive influence on system personnel throughout their employment careers.

- Design and operation of the human resource function can have either positive or negative effects on the individual, the work unit, and/or the system at large. Individuals' behaviors influence organizational effectiveness. A proactive role of the human resource function is to develop a structure within which individuals and work units are able to work cooperatively and perform productively when fulfilling assigned job requirements.

- With the maelstrom of contemporary challenges posed by external and internal governmental, political, educational, economic, and social change, the human resource function must be shaped so that human resources occupy a pivotal position to link system purposes to human resource practices. These points provide a prelude to the forthcoming discussion on the purposive aspects of the human resource function in the school setting.

Purposive Aspects of the Human Resource Function

The school system is one of the most important social institutions in today's society. Interestingly, the school system is the largest employer in most communities across the United States and is one of the most influential institutions found in America. Although there are contrasting views on the school system's role as a social institution, a statement by Counts (1952) regarding public education in the United States represents a mainstay for the purposes of education in a democracy:

Education for individual excellence.
Education for a society of equals.
Education for a government of free men.
Education for an economy of security and plenty.
Education for a civilization of beauty and grandeur.
Education for an enduring civilization.

In a distant call for a thorough reexamination of what schools are about in the United States, Goodlad (1994) echoed Counts's statement of purposes. According to Goodlad, the goals of schools are to develop the following:

- Mastery of basic skills or fundamental processes
- Career or vocational education

- Enculturation
- Interpersonal relations
- Autonomy
- Citizenship
- Moral and ethical character
- Self-realization

The statements of Counts and Goodlad are illustrative of what should be considered for meaning, significance, and implications in educational practice as it relates to human resource activities within the school setting. In subsequent chapters, one of the objectives is to consider ways in which the mission of a school system is converted into functional goals, programs, processes, practices, and projects that reinforce these statements with potential for enhancing the growth and development of human beings for whom school systems are created. If one accepts the proposition that a school system is a purposive organization whose members seek through common effort to attain goals such as those just cited, then it becomes clear that the long-range strategy of human resource administration is to help the school system attract, retain, and develop the kinds of human resources needed to achieve a school system's overall goals.

Personnel needed by a school system are those who will have the ability, motivation, and creativity to: (a) enable the system to surmount its infirmities; (b) adjust the educational program continually to the needs of individuals living and competing in a dynamic society; (c) provide leadership that shapes the human organization in such a way that there will be congruence between the individual and the system; (d) create a climate conducive to maximizing voluntary growth and individual effectiveness; and (e) influence ordinary personnel to perform in an extraordinary fashion. This kind of human resource strategy calls for a leadership focus that is intent on achieving the goals of the organization; that provides opportunities for its members to bring initiative and creativity to their tasks, which will result in both individual satisfaction and effective position performance; and that will mesh administrative processes so that greater congruence between organizational ends and individual efforts becomes a reality.

Educational organizations, like all organizations, are created and maintained to achieve specific purposes. It is important that the reader understands the significance of the relationship between organizational purposes and the human resource function. Figure 1.2 will enable the reader to visualize the interaction among three types of goals and the human resource function within a productive school setting.

System Purposes and the Human Resource Function

Contemporary thought about organizations in general and educational organizations in particular emphasizes the human resource function as a vital part of system operation. Human resources are the basis for addressing problems encountered

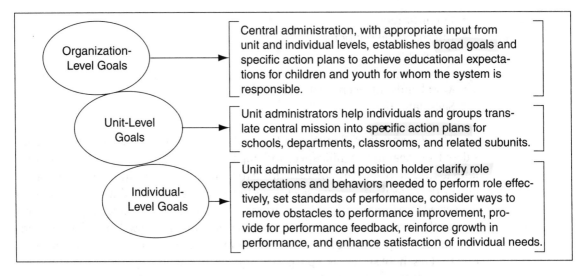

FIGURE 1.2   *Trilevel interlocking goals: antecedents to the human resource function.*

within the work setting. This viewpoint includes, among other values, careful attention to formulation, clarification, adherence, and internalization, as well as development of plans within the human resource function for improving interpersonal relationships, seeking better methods of resolving conflict, and increasing mutual understanding among system personnel.

Goal setting and goal achieving are emerging as significant organizational activities within the human resource context (House, 1971). A growing acceptance of these activities is the result of a number of factors, which include the need for greater unity of direction in all organizations, the pressure to clarify system and individual roles, and the importance of feedback to reduce gaps between both individual and organizational needs and actual performance expectations of on-job behaviors.

Considerably less attention has been devoted by the human resource function within the public school setting, however, to the behavioral aspects of the goal-setting process as they apply to members of a school system. Although it is clear that numerous benefits can be derived from goals established at the top level of the system, it is equally true that unless members of the system are committed to general organizational goals and specific position objectives as established, the intended outcomes will fail to be realized. As will be stressed in subsequent chapters, setting organizational goals involves consideration of the impact of this process and of the outcomes on the people it will affect when it comes to internalizing organizational goals as part of the individual's value system as a member of the school community.

One of the major tasks of human resource administration is to understand employees' reactions to system processes designed to achieve organizational goals. By understanding employee's reactions to system processes and to expected outcomes, it is possible to modify those processes and expected outcomes when it is apparent that there is incompatibility between goals/outcomes and human reactions to mechanisms for attainment. Goal acceptance, commitment, and internalization are behavioral aspects involved in and essential to the outcomes of the goal-setting process when utilized as part of the human resource function.

There is a kernel of truth to the often-stated criticism that educational establishments suffer from "purpose ambiguity" within the human resource function. Not only does clarification of organizational expectations for the individual contribute to security and to position satisfaction, but achievement of both organizational and individual goals also gives the individual a significant sense of accomplishment. The more clearly individuals understand what they are expected to do, the more likely they are to achieve expectations and goal obtainment.

In fact, other objectives of the human resource function (see Figure 1.1) indicate that the clearer the organizational expectations on behalf of individuals as position holders, the easier it is to evaluate their progress in attaining the goals established by the organization. Individuals cannot know where they are going or what they are doing until the school system defines clearly where the district is going. If the goals of the system are known and the individual has an opportunity to participate meaningfully in meeting these objectives through activities contributing to self-actualization, then attainment of both system and individual goals will be enhanced through an effective human resource strategy.

Defining and Articulating Strategic Goals and Objectives

Part of the human resource leadership responsibility of a school system involves defining, articulating, and assisting with the attainment of strategic goals and objectives of the district for employees through induction and staff development activities. Explicating and implementing these intentions begins with ongoing staff development programs for system members that explain the mission, purposes, goals, aims, objectives, strategies, and values. These components are defined in the following sections.

Mission

The mission statement for a school district reflects the philosophy of the school board by capturing the ultimate goals of the district in a succinct manner. A mission statement provides a background for assessing current programs and activities within the district and offers a measuring stick for choosing among potential programs and activities for a district.

Purposes and Goals

Within the present context, both purposes and goals are used interchangeably in the planning process. Purposes and goals attach means and methods to the mission statement by describing such matters as what work and what work activities are to be undertaken and what competencies are needed to accomplish the core activities. In addition, purposes and goals lead to consideration of performance requirements for the work and for determining a structure appropriate to facilitate achievement of core tasks.

Aims and Objectives

Specific targets for purposes and goals are defined by aims and objectives. Aims and objectives are time referenced. The latter focuses on what is to be accomplished, by whom, and during what time period.

Strategies

Plans of action are encapsulated with an overall design or strategy. Strategy is considered to be a technique of total planning that encompasses the overall purposes of the system and establishes functional strategies (e.g., educational program, human resources, logistics, and environmental relations) to achieve these purposes. Each of the functional human resource areas is cast into individual modules to create an overall plan for guiding the system's future direction in a proactive rather than reactive manner.

Values

Every school system has a culture, and this culture is defined by values. Values form the framework for a school system's culture, beliefs, and operational style. As such, values temper all aspects of the planning process within a particular school system.

The Power and Promise of System Purpose

The foregoing delineation of the purposive aspects of school systems leads to the realization that planning goals are to be accomplished more likely when human resource plans and practices are focused on critical issues and problems to be solved. Attainment of strategic outcomes is enhanced when human resource practices are focused on strategic intent, prioritized, and translated into plans of action. Plans of action must be capable of being assessed in terms of their outcome.

In sum, it can be said that careful attention to the purposive aspects of a school system may be viewed as having a rippling effect across all human resource functions. It would be senseless, for example, to make decisions about recruitment, selection, induction, compensation, appraisal, and tenure of system members without connecting these planning components to the mission, purposes and goals, aims and objectives, strategies, and values of the system. Listed here are some reasons to support the contention that purposeful planning is an empowerment tool for meeting some novel as well as traditional human resource challenges:

- School system goals are arranged hierarchically.
- Goals define the final purpose and direction of members' activities.

- Goals create unit, system, and individual subgoals.
- Goals affect virtually all types of plans relating to system membership, from the quantity and quality of personnel to their recruitment, selection, and related processes identified in Figure 1.1.
- Goals provide the basis for coordinated effort.
- Failure to achieve individual objectives adversely affects unit and system objectives.
- Human beings are goal directed. Clearly established goals provide meaning for work and workers throughout the organization.
- Goals provide standards against which to evaluate not only system parts but the total system as well.
- Goals are conducive to self-regulated behavior.
- Goals set the tone of members' behavior.
- Goals are antecedents to human resource policies, procedures, rules, methods, and strategies.
- Organizational effectiveness is enhanced when individual, system, and unit goals are compatible.

Social Change, Education Renewal, and the Human Resource Function

In the dawn of the new millennium there are numerous concerns, expressed in various ways, regarding the quality of public education in the United States. As reported in various media, there are both challenges and problems in our schools (Graham, 1997). These criticisms are less than surprising in view of the changes that have and continue to occur in a modern-day society.

It is said that the only certainty in life is change, and education is no exception to this adage. One very important factor creating both problems and challenges in educational systems is contemporary social change. Figure 1.3 lists a host of external environmental factors over which educational institutions can exert little control but that pose extensive challenges for education reform in order to improve what is deemed to be wrong and unsatisfactory in both the system and human resource management.

Whether school officials favor or oppose emerging social developments is largely irrelevant for the operation of public school systems. Public school administrators must operate within parameters not of their own making and not necessarily to their own liking. What is equally evident is that if the viewpoint is accepted that effective human resource management is the foundation of any well-managed organization, then educational institutions must face the reality of change by strengthening those entities designed to aid the system to move from where it is to where it should be.

Those responsible for managing school systems in the 21st century face many human resource pressures. Pressures will originate from school report cards, competency-based testing, union activism, regulatory controls, personnel litigation, competition for qualified personnel, career development issues, and changes in

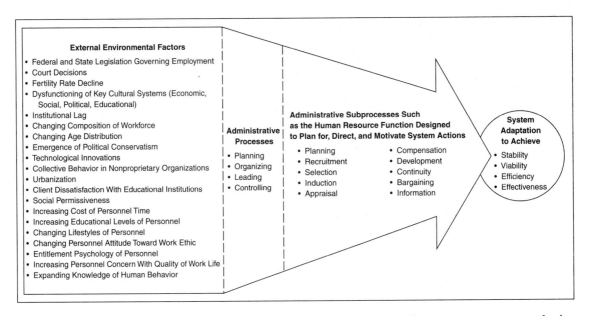

FIGURE 1.3   *Illustration of the relationship among environmental factors, administrative processes and sub-processes, and school system adaptation.*

the work, the worker, and the work environment. Tomorrow's school officials, regardless of district size, will face additional challenges as they confront pressing social needs related to schooling. Judging from current indications, the 21st century is emerging as a time when educational systems will be forced to address problems that have extensive implications for the human resource function.

Some of the hypothesized influences suggested to impact the human resource function in the schools have come to fruition (Nelan, 1992), whereas other hypothesized influences suggested to impact the human resource function are emerging. Sharp and Sharp (1995) listed 10 such influences for human resource management. These influences include decentralization of power and shared decision making, increased demands on schools, ambivalent or hostile publics, altered school structures and programs, a diverse school populace with a variety of needs, the concept of choice in education, the further expansion of technology into schools, increased emphasis on member performance, and early retirement of teachers and administrators.

Influences, as listed, are among many others cited within the education reform literature. What is important is that these influences provide a point of departure for: (a) understanding the forces, factors, and conditions involved in giving direction to the human resource function; (b) emphasizing the importance of appreciating the nature, extent, and causes of workplace problems; and (c) establishing a supportive framework on which to fashion strategies, policies, and processes that enable the human resource function to contribute more effectively and efficiently to a school system's established purposes.

Social Change and the Human Resource Function

Consideration of social change helps to illustrate that the challenges are compelling and warrant redesign of human resource strategies directed toward greater resource productivity within the school setting. Among various criticisms leveled at management of a school system is that traditional models have failed to develop comprehensive approaches to cope satisfactorily with changing internal and external environments. In large measure, present models have failed to reflect the degree to which emerging developments are shaping the nature and needs of a human resource function whose force is vital to achieving organizational purpose.

For example, changes in the internal and external environments have exceeded, in many instances, our full understanding of their organizational implications for managing school systems. Most current models have yet to bring together two elements critical to improving the human resource function. The first element consists of plans to cope with political, economic, and technological forces; regulatory provisions; accountability issues; unionism; and an increasingly litigious society. The second element includes incorporation of new ideas, strategies, policies, and processes generated by academicians from a variety of disciplines, as well as those developed by practicing school administrators.

Adding to the present dialogue are comments by McAdams (1997). McAdams, in a review of reform literature, indicated that different models are needed to engage the challenges of school reform.

> Repeated failed attempts at reform suggest that our standard approach to reform is fundamentally flawed. Substantive reform in a complex system such as a school district requires a level of sophistication and unity of purpose that is seldom attainable under our prevailing model of school governance. Moreover, leading educational researchers and theorists typically focus on narrow slices of the reality of school systems and ignore the relationships between their area of expertise and other relevant phenomena in school district operations. (pp. 139–142)

Successful reform, according to McAdams, requires the understanding of interplay among five factors and the ability to integrate this understanding into a systemic reform effort. These factors are leadership theory, local politics and governance, state and national politics, organizational theory, and change theory. In capsule form, the characteristics of a school system that would be amenable to reform are an effective superintendent, a politically stable school district, a long-term relationship between the superintendent and the school board, ongoing state-level reform initiatives, understanding of change theory, and knowledge of school systems as loosely coupled systems.

An important message can be derived from the foregoing discussion of social change and its relevance to the management of school systems and human resource functions within school systems. The world, in total, is undergoing change—governmentally, technologically, socially, legally, economically, politically, morally, and ethically. Therefore, challenges are presented to all types of organizations, are highly complex, and will tend to require concentrated planning efforts over time, ultimately impacting school systems.

School systems in the United States are one of our most valued social institutions. If we are determined to pass on to future generations a better country and better school systems, and to achieve the general purposes of education, then continued improvement of educational institutions—public, private, and parochial—is central to the task. In the section that follows, six dimensions of the human resource function will be discussed to provide foundation for understanding the challenges of social change, the need for a systems approach to substantive management of the interaction between processes and functions, and the need to forsake the myth that government must guarantee the right of all school systems to stay in business, regardless of ineptness and ineffectiveness.

Dimensions of the Human Resource Function

Any attempt to understand the scope and the significance of the human resource function and the role of human resources for facilitating individual, group, and system effectiveness requires some understanding of *dimensions* impacting the human resource function. The text that follows highlights key dimensions of the human resource function and their implications for designing, implementing, controlling, and correcting courses of action so that desirable results are achieved within the bounds of established standards. Figure 1.4 identifies major dimensions that have an impact on the operation of the human resource function.

An examination of these dimensions indicates that management of a school system involves many interdependent activities, the governance of which is influenced by various forces, factors, and conditions. Because each of these forces has

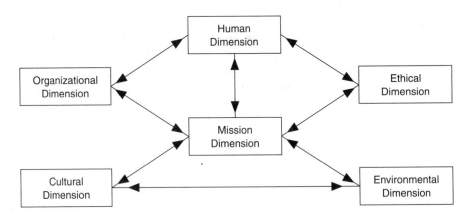

FIGURE 1.4   *Dimensional elements that define and influence the design and operation of the human resource function.*

the potential to affect organizational performance, each must be understood to appreciate fully how they pervade the decision-making process. In the context of decision making, the dimensions noted in Figure 1.4 can be considered as a framework for bringing about school system improvement in a mission-oriented and *ethically appropriate* manner.

Mission Dimension

The mission of a school system identifies the purposes for which it has been created, its boundaries, and its activities, as well as its governmental and collateral purposes. A mission statement represents the foundation for providing an educational program and supporting services that will enhance the mental, moral, social, and emotional development of children, youth, and adults served by the school district. Following are examples of mission statements from two separate school districts:

> The Mission of the Upper Arlington City School District is to provide each student with an innovative and superior education that instills integrity and promotes personal achievement in an ever-changing society (Upper Arlington School District, n.d.).

> To educate and empower our students to reach their potential as productive citizens through a unified commitment to excellence (Clarksville County School System, 2002).

To some board members and to some educators, developing a mission statement to guide school system planning and selecting from among the multitude of underlying choices that must be made to coordinate diverse system activities represents a meaningless exercise in academic nonsense. As we examine mission statements, however, such as those listed previously, the mission statement is arguably the most basic property of a school system, and one possessing considerable practical utility. The mission statement is the system's overarching plan from which a set of subplans is derived.

Subplans include definitions of the types of work to be done, the division of labor, the specification of the number and kinds of jobs needed and how the jobs are structured, how resources are allocated, and articulation of system **values** and their content through such processes as personnel involvement, goal acceptance and commitment, as well as member induction and socialization. Examination of the mission statements provided leads to the realization that they embody the potential for the following

- Clarifying the core purpose of school system existence
- Identifying services that the public expects the system to deliver in exchange for financial support
- Providing a framework for judging the extent to which the mission is being realized
- Creating a focus for defining the scope and limitations of the system's endeavors
- Establishing a point of reference for deciding which key activities need to be performed

- Deciding how financial, technical, human, and organizational resources will be allocated
- Focusing on the end state rather than on the means of getting there
- Developing a frame of reference by which controls are generated to implement the mission (strategies, policies, programs, projects, rules, and regulations)

Another important value of a clearly defined mission statement is that it serves as a boundary guide, determining what the school system should not do as well as stating what the school system should do. There is, for example, a hierarchy of laws, rules, and decisions in each state that have operational meaning for school systems. These include such elements as the state constitution, statutes, state board of education rules, department of education regulations, court decisions, and system policies, contracts, and rules.

Consequently, these governing influences eliminate discretionary consideration of certain decisions while also leaving important permissive decisions to the school system. A reality-based mission statement serves as an important contemporary base for defining the scope of acceptable choices regarding such current education issues as integrating religion into the public schools, sex education, preschool day care, pressures for extensive extracurricular programs, the extent of special education and pupil disability arrangements, various types of age-group plans, continuing education classes for pregnant teenagers, desegregation, bilingual education, and issues relating to cultural diversity, quality of work life, and restructuring the system. Viewed in the context of this discussion, the mission plan is important because it provides a focal point for debating, discussing, and arriving at a consensus among system members concerning their expectations and beliefs, as well as to their expressed wishes about what the organization's common purpose should be.

For all of these considerations, the system mission, if clearly understood, can be conducive to internalizing commitment and dedication to an explicit set of values. The school system is ill served when officials fail to appreciate the interactive potential of a system mission and to use it consistently as a standard in making decisions regarding transformation from the present to a desired state. However, the creation and the application of a unified purpose through a mission statement is frequently hindered by short-term perspectives and obscured by the business at hand.

Human Dimension

The *human dimension* of a school system pertains to all individuals who contribute to the operation of the district. Included within this definition are those involved directly and indirectly with the instructional process. Contributions of both types of individuals are required for an effective and efficient school system.

Individuals execute the schooling process; they decide what is to be done, when it is to be done, and how it is to be done. Given these decisions, one actuality is worth recognizing: *Individual performance is the core element fundamental to any organizational endeavor.* To ensure that individual performance is aligned with the mission statement of a school system, considerable attention must be afforded to the procurement, selection, development, contentment, and retention of personnel.

Procurement has become a major issue for many school districts during the 21st century. Large pools of applicants are more the exception than the rule for most public school districts. Recruitment, considered a luxury not so long ago, has become a necessity for most school districts during the current decade.

Because of labor shortages for many positions in the public school setting (Haselkom, 1996), employee selection plays a critical role in fulfilling the mission of a school district. Without exception, school districts must select employees every year as the result of resignations and retirements associated with existing positions and as the result of new positions being created in light of emerging demands. To consummate the selection process, both applicants and employers must agree. However, in the past, public school districts have largely ignored the concerns of the former.

Employees entering the school system or employees moving within the school system to a new assignment cannot be expected to realize immediately their full potential in the newly assigned position. They encounter, in most instances, a new work environment, a different set of colleagues, and a novel set of job demands. Integrating these experiences and linking these exposures to the mission statement are major human resource activities.

After employees become acclimated in their new work environment, many may lose sight of the encapsulating mission of the school district over time. Without a broad perspective on which to cast their immediate work demands, these employees are prone to burnout and general position dissatisfaction (Faculty of Education, n.d.). Realigning position demands and expectations with the mission of the school district requires continued effort on the part of the human resource function.

Indeed, if the ideals of human dignity and worth are to permeate the organizational culture, then it is clear that these principles must have a significant role in the conduct of the human resource function. Adoption of and adherence to a set of guidelines that are ethically oriented to the mission statement is a way of committing system authorities to a philosophy for enhancing individual–organization relationships.

Organizational Dimension

The formal organization, as represented collectively in Figure 1.1, is one of the forces in a school district's infrastructure influencing the design and operation of the human resource function. As noted previously within this chapter, a well-developed and extensively promulgated sense of common purpose is fundamental to unification of the talents, education, experience, and motivation of individuals and groups to achieve the goals of the school system. Because a mission statement represents the system's strategic aim and provides a means of establishing the outcomes it intends to achieve, the educational impact it intends to create, and the client expectations it aims to satisfy, articulation and communication of the mission statement are important for an effective and efficient public school district.

In keeping with the organizational dimension found in Figure 1.4, every organization has a structure—a plan for linking positions and people to purposes. The structure may be one that has been adopted formally by the board of education and described by **organizational charts,** position guides, and **organizational manuals.** On the other hand, the structure may be informal, without documentation or evidence of any kind to describe specific characteristics of alignment. In both cases, organizations are composed of people who occupy positions, interact with each other, and are vitally concerned that they be compensated, both for responsibilities inherent in the work they perform and for their individual contributions to organizational effectiveness.

As illustrated in Figure 1.5, elements of **organizational structure** should include purposes, people, activities, and relationships. One of the inferences that can be drawn from an analysis of an organization's structure is that its design and implementation involve individual and group participation through which system purpose is transformed into policies, functions, processes, activities, operations, and control mechanisms aimed at achieving perceived organizational outcomes. Another inference is that there are compelling questions to be answered about the design of the organization's structure such as these:

- What are the key activities that need to be performed to serve the interests of our students, human resources, regulatory agencies, community groups, parents, and the school system?
- What is the most appropriate way to group these key activities into positions?
- How should positions be grouped into attendance units, departments, administrative and supervisory groups, support services, and temporary personnel requirements?
- What number of positions should be in the structure? What major tasks, authority relationships, and performance criteria should be established for each position?
- To what extent should the system be decentralized or centralized for decision-making purposes?
- What integration devices such as communication and coordination are most suitable for bringing together positions, position holders, and work units into a cohesive whole for system betterment?
- What chain of command should be established? How many levels of management are needed in the system? A few? A moderate number?

Structural questions such as these force designers to focus on how to utilize best the structure, choosing from among the feasible options the ones most likely to im-

Purposes	Every organization has a structure—a plan for linking positions and people to purposes. The purposes of an organization form the starting point of structural planning because all activities flow from purpose.
Activities	Activities are divided into positions; positions are grouped into major functions; functions are grouped into organizational units.
Superior–subordinate	Every structure has a hierarchy to coordinate organizational activity. The essence of a hierarchy is the superior–subordinate system in which certain positions are granted authority to direct the work of subordinate positions. The number of subordinates reporting to a superior is referred to as the span of control. Degrees of responsibility and authority are referred to as levels or layers of administration in the hierarchy.
Line and staff relationships	Most organizations have line and staff positions. Line positions are those that have the authority to initiate and carry through the basic activities of the organization that are essential to goal attainment. Collectively, line positions form the chain of command in an organization through which decisions are made, information communicated, and activities coordinated and controlled. Staff positions are those responsible for rendering advice, service, and counsel to individuals and groups within the organization.

FIGURE 1.5   *Elements of organizational structure.*

prove individual, group, and system performance. An inescapable circumstance of school management in the early years of the 21st century is that the complexity, as well as the politically and intellectually demanding tasks associated with school restructuring, requires an appreciation of a host of factors. These factors must be taken into consideration when designing an organizational structure for a school system. Failure to consider these tasks defeats many of the concerns associated with a sound mission statement.

Despite all the criticism about school system structures that has surfaced in the long-running debate about restructuring schools, especially regarding hierarchies, levels of management, close supervision, and top-down decision making, some mode of procedure, of fusing human and nonhuman resources into a cohesive effort toward purpose attainment, is inescapable. An arrangement of authority is essential to implement system improvement through direction and coordination. Without a chain of command, power becomes unbridled.

To balance power in a school system, control mechanisms are essential to any and all forms of human resource planning. At least two kinds of control mechanisms should be discussed: (a) system and (b) functional. System controls are focused on the total organization and include policies, position descriptions, strategic plans, and mission statements, whereas functional controls pertain to those measures that guide the human resource function, such as the 10 human resource processes identified in Figure 1.1.

Several compelling reasons exist as to why control mechanisms are essential to any and all forms of human resource planning. One compelling reason is that every plan that the school system initiates and allocates resources for should have built-in means for judging its effectiveness. There are numerous other justifications for control mechanisms, such as preventing and correcting deviations from standards as in curbing turnover, absenteeism, sick leave, and other benefit abuses and minimizing behaviors that are anti-organizational, self-serving, defiant, rebellious, or in violation of the system's culture.

Cultural Dimension

Every organization has a culture, and school districts are no exception to this generality. The **culture** of a school district is defined by several constructs including norms, values, expectations, and ideas. As such, the culture of a school system is rooted within local traditions and community expectations.

According to Smithers (1988), an organization's culture can serve a variety of useful functions. For employees new to a school system, the system's culture provides a range of behaviors that the employees must exhibit before becoming fully assimilated within the work environment. Existing employees rely on their knowledge of a school system's culture to help them select behaviors in uncertain situations.

The culture of a school system is difficult to observe directly but is recognizable by astute employees. Culture is something that is felt and that renders a particular school district unique. It is "the ways things are done" in that school district.

What might be appropriate behavior for employees in one school district might be entirely inappropriate in another school district. Appropriateness of behavior for employees, in many instances, may depend more on the culture in which behavior occurs than on the behavior itself. This explains, at least in part, why different school districts can adopt similar mission statements but utilize quite different procedures and processes to implement the intent.

A school district's culture has important implications for most of the human resource functions listed in Figure 1.1. Although a school district's culture is ever present, it is not beyond change. Indeed, many of the planning techniques used within the human resource function are designed to alter a school system's culture.

Cultural factors in the human resource function that can be changed by those in leadership positions include envisioning, bringing to life, reinforcing, rewarding, and embedding constructive behavior. Beyond helping members to understand their culture, leaders create means to enhance its positive features and this aids in neutralizing tendencies toward system instability. Leaders can use their knowledge of a school district's culture to enhance the performance of several other human resource functions.

For example, research addressing the recruitment of educators has revealed the importance of culture for the recruitment process (Winter, Newton, & Kirkpatrick, 1998). Several studies have shown that many applicants are more interested in the cultural aspects of a school system than the economic rewards provided by school systems (see Young, Place, Rinehart, Jury, & Baits, 1999). Applicants for teacher positions were more likely to pursue job offerings when recruitment interviews with the school district's representative focused on the work and the work environment than on salaries and fringe benefits.

Selection of employees has been expanded to incorporate issues related to an organization's culture within the assessment process. Traditional selection paradigms focused almost exclusively on person–position fit. More recently, organizations have begun to examine selection from a person–organization fit perspective (see Parsons, Cable, & Liden, 1999).

For many school districts, the format for induction and development activities and programs can be quite similar, but the content of these activities and programs should vary considerably because of a district's unique culture. Culture of a school district comes into play even in those economic activities performed by the human resource function. Often, the pay rate for employees of a public school district is influenced by a district's culture as well as by a district's ability to pay.

One of the continuing questions about school system culture is, what is its relationship to the human resource function? One response is that to a considerable extent culture is tied to the impact of change in the workplace. There are shifting human values and changes in the demographics of the workforce (in ethnic background, in cultural diversity, and in graying of the instructional cadre), and these changes alter existing culture for a school system.

There is another set of culture-driven forces with the potential to affect individual and group behavior—the environmental dimension. The environmental dimension includes regulatory agencies, community groups, boards of education, school management, unions, standing committees, work units (such as elementary schools), and support groups (maintenance, operation, clerical, food service, security, and transportation). In one way or another, each of these system entities and their constituents is affected by changes that have personal, organizational, legal, state, national, and international causes.

Environmental Dimension

School systems are created by and are intended to serve our society that sustains education. Those persons performing or aspiring to managerial roles in school systems need an effective working knowledge of the relationship of the environmental dimension to the operation of the human resource function. Consequently, a model for understanding the interaction of the school system environment and the influence

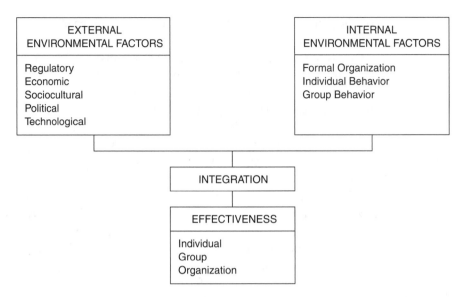

FIGURE 1.6   *Environmental interactions that influence performance effectiveness.*

of the environment on individual, group, and organizational behavior is presented in Figure 1.6.

This schematic portrayal of the environmental dimension consists of two types of environments: external and internal. Much of the evolution of the human resource function, in both the public and private sectors, has been brought about more by the **external environment** than by the internal environment. Major external forces that affect the human resource function have been grouped arbitrarily into five clusters (as outlined in Figure 1.6) in order to establish a framework for analyzing the complex interaction between environmental factors and the human resource of a school system.

Environmental–organizational interaction suggests that there are constraints, forces, and options to which a system must respond to achieve stability and viability. The human resource function plays a vital role in helping the system to operate within economic structures, meet legal mandates, honor contractual obligations, address pressures of special-interest groups, adapt to emerging technologies, and uphold ethical standards while maintaining centrality of purpose. Striking this balance between the external environment and the ongoing operations of a school system requires considerable organizational effort on the part of the human resource function.

Contextually, education in the United States operates within a framework of regulatory controls of varying degrees. As indicated in Figure 1.7, these elements include the Constitution; federal laws; state, county, and municipal laws; court decisions; executive orders; administrative agency rulings; legal challenges; and employment contracts. It is generally agreed that provisions governing employment in both the public and private sectors have far-reaching influence on the operation of the human resource function. Each state system controls the school curriculum

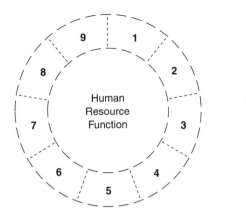

FACTORS

1. Constitutional Guarantees
2. Federal Laws
3. State Laws
4. Court Decisions
5. Executive Orders
6. Administrative Agency Rulings
7. County-Municipal Laws
8. Legal Challenges
9. Employment Contracts

FIGURE 1.7   *Regulatory environment of the human resource function.*

and supporting services, who shall teach, how schools are financed, and school board policy-making authority. In addition, there are regulatory controls governing taxation limitations, salaries, benefits, collective bargaining, performance appraisal, tenure, grievance procedures, and budgetary requirements.

Because school systems operate within an external environment over which school districts exercise little control, knowledge of the present environment, especially its direction and organizational impact, is an essential aspect of human resource management. In addition to the regulatory factor, there are four other factors noted in Figure 1.6 (economic, sociocultural, political, and technological) that affect conditions in the workplace. Following are some indicators illustrating the external environmental impact on people, positions, and direction of human resource affairs.

Economic factors are variables that influence the human resource function within the public school setting because most of the costs associated with operating a public school district are related to human resource expenditures. Public school districts, as nonprofit organizations, depend on the ebb and flow of available funds to operate. Although there are recent efforts to reduce the dependency on public funds through school–business relationships, only a minute portion of the funds necessary to operate a public school district come from private sources.

Most of the funds needed to operate a school district are derived from public coffers. Federal funds are awarded usually through entitlements for ongoing programs or through grants for new initiatives. State monies, the largest contributor to public school districts, are generated through some type of formula funding process designed to provide a minimum level of acceptable education for the students. Public school districts use local revenues to supplement outside sources of income and to provide services beyond those funded by external sources.

All sources of revenue for public school districts are subject to political agendas shaped largely by social–cultural phenomena. As the political climate changes, funding sources and funding amounts can also change. Among many recent factors influencing the political climate fueled by social–cultural phenomena are testing, teacher certifications, AIDS, and drug/alcohol testing.

Last, but by no means least, of the external influences on the operation of a school district is technology. Technology within the present context refers to the sum of ways in which the school system attains the material means needed to carry out the processes, mechanisms, and techniques it employs to deliver educational services. Among the emerging challenges for the human resource function created by the advent of modern technology and the quickening pace of its development are these pressing agenda items:

- *Technology assimilation*—Ensuring that technology is available for and used to the best advantage by the system and its members.
- *Comprehensive information system*—A modern, systematic plan designed to acquire, store, maintain, protect, retrieve, and communicate data in a valid and accurate form, sometimes employing computerized approaches.
- *Staff development*—With widespread adoption of electronic technology, a critical shortage of computer-literate support staff has developed. Programs for assisting personnel, especially those in the temporary category, are necessary to acquire the skills needed to satisfy burgeoning demands for information.
- *Office operations*—An information-driven school system requires application of new technology to increase the efficiency and effectiveness of office operations.
- *Computer applications*—Examples of computer applications to the human resource function include recruitment and selection tracking, attendance tracking, training and development management, position control, compensation (including benefits), regulatory adherence, payroll, forms management, record center operations, and computer-assisted instruction.

The second environmental dimension portrayed in Figure 1.6 is the **internal environment** of a school district. A school district's internal environment interacts with the external environment to change almost every aspect of schooling. Interaction of these influences creates administrative challenges, especially concerning their impact on individual and group behavior, as well as the need for strategies to cope with the inexorable tendency toward environmental change.

An internal factor that has changed the ways school districts operate in recent years is the formal organization of a school district. To meet emerging needs, some of which have been imposed by the external environment, school districts have created new positions. These new positions alter the formal structure of the organization.

One of the new positions created by many school systems is for testing and/or accountability. This position is designed to address accountability issues related to proficiency test scores. Not long ago, responsibilities associated with student achievement would have been subsumed under curriculum but have more recently assumed an independent status with direct reporting relationships to the superintendent.

Another new position that has altered the formal structure of school systems pertains to technology. Technology, as initially conceived within public school districts, was viewed as an operational position responsible for the business functions of the school district. In recent times, technology has expanded to cover educational as well as operational concerns and commands a prominent place within the educational hierarchy.

Group behavior within public school districts has changed due largely to collective bargaining. Since the first public law was passed by Wisconsin in 1959, many states have followed in the adoption of public sector laws. What was once entirely a management decision regarding the educational process has become a bilateral decision that requires the concurrence of union leadership.

Individual behavior, like group behavior, has changed within public school districts during recent times. Different populations are seeking and acquiring positions in the educational setting. Changes in employment populations for individuals are due to several external and internal causes.

Certificated personnel, at one time, entered the ranks of educators fresh out of college. Because of certification requirements and entrance requirements being lessened, many individuals now enter the certificated ranks in nontraditional ways. Alternate certification routes have allowed individuals to become teachers and administrators without following traditional career progressions, and these individuals have different human resource needs than traditional educators.

Many changes may be observed concerning noncertificated employees in school systems during the 21st century. For example, not so long ago, most bus drivers were males seeking merely to supplement their incomes. Today, most bus drivers are females who rely on the position as a major, if not sole, source of income.

Collectively, these changes in the internal environment of a school district alter substantially the way school districts operate. In response to these changes, the human resource function must make certain adaptations to ensure the effective and efficient operation of a school district. To guide many of these changes are ethical considerations.

Ethical Dimension

It is an inescapable fact that decisions give life to a school system and that most decisions are permeated by **ethics.** Following this stream of thought, exercise of authority through the decision-making process includes consideration of ethical implications for the operation of a school district. *Ethics,* according to most definitions (see the National Education Association Web site at **http://www.nea.org/aboutnea/ code.html**), refers to the rightness or wrongness of certain actions and to the goodness or badness of the motives and ends of such actions.

What is or is not ethical, in many instances, is a matter of personal interpretation. Because ethics are a matter of interpretation, ethical standards to which a school system is committed need to be clearly and extensively communicated. Mechanisms for clarifying and communicating ethics include personnel handbooks, policy manuals, and a code of ethics adopted by the school system.

A broader understanding of ethical behavior in the workplace, especially as it applies to the human resource function, is an important step in dealing with personnel problems and enhancing system betterment. The relationship between ethical sensitivity and the human resource function is an intimate one, as the following concepts demonstrate:

- Leadership is involved with decisions about such matters as organizational purpose, goals, objectives, strategies, and their implications.
- Ethical considerations, when factored into the decision-making process, uphold human dignity as a contributor to positive personal and organizational behavior.
- Decisions made by leaders have a direct impact on both the internal and external environments.
- The task orientation of individuals and groups is influenced by ethical sensitivity to their expectations, aspirations, well-being, conditions of work, compensation equity, and the reward system.
- Decisions and power are inseparable. Those who have authority to make decisions are able to exert control over others, either directly through position power or indirectly through various forms of expertise.

Issues of ethical concern for the school system include obligations as well as various kinds of responsibilities. For example, system and member obligations, such as those following, have the inherent potential for unethical conduct when behavioral obligations and responsibilities are unfulfilled:

- Member ethical obligations to the school system
- Personnel obligations to the profession
- System and personnel obligations to adhere to the psychological contract
- Teacher ethical obligations to students
- System and member commitment to professional employment practices
- System and member obligations and responsibilities to *claimants* in the external environment such as taxpayers, creditors, suppliers, governments, unions, accrediting agencies, and recruitment sources (colleges and universities, other school systems, and placement agencies)
- System ethical obligations to its members and the public

From the foregoing points, it may be assumed that power to decide can influence member behavior. As we examine the 10 personnel processes in forthcoming chapters, attention will be focused, in part, on decisions with ethical connotations, especially in such areas as recruitment, selection, appraisal, compensation, development, and justice.

Review and Preview

One of the main purposes of studying the human resource function of a school system is to develop a broader understanding of the forces, factors, conditions, and circumstances that shape its role as a contributor to organizational effectiveness. The intent of this chapter is to convey the viewpoints that follow.

Evolving models of the human resource function extend well beyond traditional tasks of record keeping, social work, and collective bargaining. Today's designs consider the human resource function to be a vital unit in any organization. The organized and unified array of system parts interact through human performance to establish a productive public institution. The 10 personnel processes within the human resource function (Figure 1.1) are linked to the organization infrastructure (Figure 1.4). Dimensions of the infrastructure include system mission, human resources, regulatory requirements, environmental factors, and ethical presence.

The chapter that follows examines the planning process as a component of the human resource function and its linkage to the elements in the organizational infrastructure.

Social change and educational reform movements brought about by a combination of sociological, political, economic, regulatory, technological, and human resource forces require changes in models for enhancing the potential of the function to clarify problems and to develop plans for their solution.

Discussion Questions

1. Identify one change-related issue facing your school organization. (1) What factors from the *external* environment influence how the organization responds to that issue? (2) What factors from the *internal* environment influence how the organization responds to that issue? (3) How can the organization assess these factors comprehensively in developing a solution to the issue?

2. Consider a change or school organization improvement issue. (1) How can this issue be addressed through the *mission dimension* of the human resource function? (2) Through the *organizational dimension?*

3. Identify three *system ethical obligations* of your school organization to the public. Identify three *system ethical obligations* of your school organization to its members.

4. Educational organizations often suffer from "purpose ambiguity" as a result of poor clarification of organizational expectations and goals. Identify one example of this ambiguity within your school organization. What could be done to eliminate or minimize this ambiguity?

5. Organizational efficiency can be measured by the amount of effort it takes the organization to accomplish its work. (1) What is the impact of organizational structure on organizational efficiency? (2) How can control mechanisms influence organizational efficiency?

References

Clarksville County School System. Retrieved August 29, 2002, from the Clarksville County School System Web site: **http://www.cmcss.net/**

Counts, G. S. (1952). *Education and American civilization* (pp. 311–430). New York: Bureau of Publications, Teachers College, Columbia University.

Faculty of Education–The Chinese University of Hong Kong. (n.d.). *Studies on teacher burnout.* Retrieved August 29, 2002, from the Faculty of Education Web site: **http://www.fed.cuhk.edu. hk/fllee/AppOfComp/WebResource Rep/burnout.htm**

Goodlad, J. I. (1994). *What schools are for.* Bloomington, IN: Phi Delta Kappa Educational Foundation, Chapter 3.

Graham, E. (1997, March 14). What's wrong—and right—with our schools? [American opinion]. *Wall Street Journal,* p. R1.

Haselkorn, D. (1996, August 7). Breaking the class ceiling. *Education Week on the Web,* 15. Retrieved August 29, 2002, from the *Education Week on the Web* Web site: **http://www.edweek.org/ew/vol-15/ 41hasel.h15**

House, R. J. (1971). A path-goal theory of leader effectiveness. *Administrative Science Leadership Review, 16,* 321–339. Retrieved August 29, 2002, from the College of St. Scholastica Web site: **http://www.css.edu/users/dswenson/ web/LEAD/path-goal.html**

McAdams, R. P. (1997, October). A systems approach to school reform. *Phi Delta Kappan, 79,* 138.

Nelan, B. W. (1992, Fall). How the world will look in 50 years. *Time Magazine, Special Issue: Beyond the Year 2000,* 36–38.

Parsons, C. K., Cable, D. M., & Liden, R. C. (1999). Establishing person-organization fit. In R. W. Eder & M. M. Harris (Eds.), *The employment interview handbook.* Thousand Oaks, CA: Sage.

Sharp, H. M., & Sharp, W. L. (1995). Preparing for the future in the next stage. *National Forum of Educational Administration and Supervision Journal, 13*(1), 25–33.

Smither, R. D. (1988). *The psychology of work* (p. 363). New York: Harper & Row.

Upper Arlington School District. (n.d.). *Strategic plan.* Retrieved August 29, 2002, from the Upper Arlington School District Web site: **http://www. uaschools. org/strateg.htm**

Winter P. A., Newton, R. M., & Kirkpatrick, R. L. (1998). The influence of work values on teacher selection decisions: The effects of principal values, and principal–teacher value interactions. *Teaching and Teacher Education, 14*(4), 385–400.

Young, I. P., Place, A. W., Rinehart, J. S., Jury, J. C., & Baits, D. F. (1999). Teacher recruitment: A test of the similarity–attraction hypothesis for race and sex. *Educational Administration Quarterly, 33*(1), 86–106.

Supplementary Reading

Arenofsky, J. (1997, March). Information age: How it affects the way we work. *Career World, 25,* 6–11.

Consortium on Productivity in the Schools. (1998, April). *Using what we have to get the schools we need.* New York: Author.

Digh, P. (1998, November). Coming to terms with diversity. *HR Magazine, 43*(12), 117–120.

Education Commission of the States. (1993). *Education accountability systems in the fifty states.* Denver: Author.

Education Commission of the States. (1993). *The New American Urban School District.* Denver: Author.

Galphin, T. (1995, June). Connecting culture to organizational change. *HR Magazine, 40,* 98–104.

Greene, R. J. (1995, June). Culturally compatible HR strategies. *HR Magazine, 40,* 115–123.

Kaplan, R. D. (1998, August). Travels into America's future. *Atlantic Monthly, 282*(2), 37–61.

Kreyche, G. F. (1997, July). Public education's intractable problems. *USA Today, 126,* 82.

Kritsonis, W. (1997). The psychology of leadership in educational institutions. *Record, 17*(172), 11–14.

Ladenson, R. R. (1996). *Ethics in the American workplace: Policies and decisions.* Horsham, PA: LRP Publications.

Leider, R. J. (1997). *The power of purpose.* San Francisco: Berrett-Koehler.

Morgan, G. (1998). *Images of organization.* San Francisco: Berrett-Koehler.

Pell, T. J. (1998, November 24). Does 'diversity' justify quotas? The courts say no. *Wall Street Journal,* p. A22.

Schuler, R. S. (1998). *Managing human resources* (6th ed.). Cincinnati, OH: South-Western College Publishing.

Sheridan, J. E. (1992). Organization culture and employee retention. *Academy of Management Journal, 36,* 1036–1056.

Shlaes, A. (1997, February 6). The saving grace of school reform. *Wall Street Journal,* p. A14.

Steinhauser, S. (1998, July). Is your corporate culture in need of an overhaul? *HR Magazine, 43*(8), 87–91.

Stutz, J., & Massengale, R. (1997, December). Measuring diversity initiatives. *HR Magazine, 42,* 85–90.

Terry, C. C. (Ed.). (1990). *Dictionary of principles in the workplace.* Chicago: DeAcklen-Terry.

2

Strategic Planning and the Human Resource Function

CHAPTER OBJECTIVES

Introduce the concept of strategic planning and discuss its relationship to the human resource function.

Emphasize the importance of developing system visions, values, goals, ideas, and initiatives to implement human resource plans.

Highlight key stages of the strategic planning sequence, major components, and their linkage.

Stress that strategic plans are temporary and subject to change as internal and external challenges emerge.

Gain greater understanding of the need to motivate all personnel, from the top to the bottom of the system, to perform their roles effectively in the interests of strategic expectations.

CHAPTER CONCEPTS

Effectiveness	Policy
Goal structure	Position guide
Organizational chart	Program structure
Organizational manual	System
Organizational structure	Work analysis

Organizational Change Within a Strategic Planning Context

This chapter introduces the reader to the broad framework around which a human resource planning system is developed to influence personnel behavior toward achievement of system, work unit, and individual goals. The focal point of analysis is the family of plans employed to make the human resource function an effective part of the entire school system. In subsequent chapters, the primary intent of each of the human resource processes is to emphasize plans for employing people most efficiently and effectively in the pursuit of the system's strategic goals.

Every school system, regardless of size or organizational structure, must perform certain basic human resource functions to maintain the ongoing operation. At minimum within every school system, personnel must be recruited, selected, inducted, compensated, appraised, developed, and supervised. These human resource tasks are always ongoing and reoccurring due to the fluidity of school systems as dynamic organizations.

In small school districts, human resource tasks may be decentralized and may be shared among position holders as a complement to their regular job assignments. In large school districts, on the other hand, human resource tasks may be centralized and may be performed by a designated department or unit. In either situation, these tasks are performed most successfully when guided by systematic plans of actions. Devising systematic plans of action to guide the execution of human resource functions is essential if an organization is to capitalize on environmental changes that can afford limited windows of opportunity.

Throughout history, the concept of systematic planning has been an intellectual luxury rather than an organizational necessity for many public school districts. Since the last half of the 20th century, the complexities of organizational demands and environmental changes have changed planning from a luxury to a necessity for an efficient and effective school district. In fact, instances of the lack of planning in educational institutions relative to the human resource function are abundant within the professional literature. Examples from the literature include the following:

- Failure to incorporate the human resource function effectively within the total **organizational structure**
- Absence of administrative rationality in planning for the human resource needs of public school districts
- Failure to link organizational expectations to human resource needs of public school districts
- Viewing personnel needs as ends rather than means for managing public school districts
- Failure to staff the function adequately within a public school district (numerically and qualitatively)
- Failure to develop accurate and realistic staffing specifications

- Failure to maintain aggressive, imaginative, and well-designed recruiting programs to attract new personnel to a public school district
- Creation of psychic anxieties in personnel as a result of ineffective ideologies, plans, procedures, and rules when managing a public school district
- Failure to use collective bargaining positively to resolve human problems in the operation of a public school district
- Persistent adherence to obsolete performance appraisal systems lacking reliability and validity for a designated purpose
- Failure to anticipate personnel shortages and surpluses in specific target areas
- Unresponsiveness to legislation governing fair employment, compensation, and related conditions of work affecting the operation of a public school district

Mandated competency-based testing for students and the advent of report cards for school districts illuminate the importance of human resource functions and the strategic planning process. For high-performing districts, maintenance of current performance is not assured; for low-performing districts, change in existing performance is not guaranteed. Systematic planning on the part of all stakeholders involved in the education process is required for maintaining and building a competent staff of administrators and teachers for educating America's youth.

The following section examines the relationship between the planning process and the behavior of system members. In setting forth these ideas we will do the following:

- Consider the relationship between planning and the resolution of human performance problems in the school setting
- Examine human resource planning in the context of educational system planning as it relates to overall objectives and goals of a school system
- Review the system's approach to human resource planning as applied to students
- Identify the elements of a human resource planning process that must be addressed by efficient and effective school districts
- Portray planning outcomes as a system of plans rather than as an isolated event
- Analyze the interrelationship among system, unit, and position plans and the personnel function within the public school setting
- Review the connection between planning and the time dimension necessary for executing human resource plans in a systematic manner
- Depict the significance of planning to individual and organizational change necessary in the new millennium

Human Resource Planning in the Context of Educational System Planning

Planning is a methodological mechanism for projecting intentions and actions rather than reacting to causes and events. Because planning addresses the future, planning is a challenging endeavor. It is the antithesis of expediency, laissez-faire, and indirection. As such, planning is an effort to set a course of action and to guide it toward a set of expectations that align the school district with objectives and goals.

The general notion of planning within organizations is less than novel. Some time ago Ackoff (1970), in defining planning, noted that although planning is a decision-making process, it is a special kind of decision-making process:

> (1) Planning is something we do in advance of taking action—that is, it is anticipatory decision making; (2) planning is required when the future state that we desire involves a set of interdependent decisions—that is, a system of decisions; (3) planning is a process directed toward producing one or more future states that are desired and that are not expected to occur unless something is done. (pp. 2–4)

Strategic Planning Process

A pivotal human resource issue in any school district is the staffing of the organization. Employees are needed to administer the organization, to instruct the students, and to provide necessary support services for students. The numbers and the allocations of employees to each of these functions fall within the realm of strategic planning as related to the human resource function.

Strategic plans must be devised to consider the immediate human resource needs as well as the future human resource needs of the school district. These plans must be tailored to uniqueness of the district, the instructional units, and the classroom settings relative to student needs. Furthermore, these plans must direct the school district toward identified objectives and goals. Different configurations of staffing are needed for special education students, English as a second language students, vocational education students, regular education students, and college preparatory students. Strategic human resource planning must consider these different configurations.

Human resource plans concerning the allocation of employees are governed by many constraints external or internal to the school system. State departments of education have certain minimum requirements concerning the staffing of school districts. In many states, collective bargaining agreements have been negotiated that establish minimum requirements concerning staffing. Beyond these requirements, certain accreditation associations impose restraints on the staffing of a school district. Also, certain local prerogatives come into play.

An effective strategic plan must be tempered, however, by each of the concerns mentioned relative to the staffing of a school district. Failure to do so will render unsuccessful any planning attempts on the part of well-intentioned employees and will also be unproductive in guiding a school district toward maximizing educational opportunities for students. Although any strategic plan must be tailored to a specific school district, there exist certain common elements to any plan. We will present these common elements so that the astute educational planners can interpolate from our presentation to their own school district.

For every school district, strategic plans should set broad directions for guiding the school district in achieving system objectives and goals. Let us look at one kind of planning tool in the family of strategic plans, referred to here as a *process*. Let us also see how this process can be employed in dealing with the complexities of strategic planning as the system is guided from the present into the future. To move from the present state to a desired state requires, in most instances, incremental actions on the part of decision makers within a school district.

Process, as the term is used here, refers to a series of progressive and interdependent steps designed to: (a) enhance actions to bring about positive change in the human resource function, (b) establish a systematic approach for coping with routine and nonroutine human resource problems, and (c) improve human resource problem solving. One example of a planning process for the school system's human resource is illustrated in Figure 2.1. This process includes five different stages or activities on the part of human resource planners.

An examination of the processes illustrated in Figure 2.1 highlights certain aspects to be performed. It should be noted that the processes consist of a series of steps or activities that serve to systematize the manner in which managerial judgments are made relative to people plans and planning. The ultimate ends toward which the overall policy process is directed include: (a) heightening the impact of the human resource function on organizational purpose, (b) contriving ways to bring about desired changes in system performance, (c) orienting the planning process beyond short-term needs, and (d) assessing the internal and external environments likely to influence planning choices.

Stage One: Defining and Clarifying Expectations

This is an age of budget limitations, mandated assessments, an increasingly diverse society, changing social mores, and confusion regarding ends, means, and methods of improving public education in the United States. In light of these constraints, the task of developing strategic plans for an education system appears, initially, to be a rather

Stage	Activity
One	Define, clarify, articulate, and communicate expectations for the system's human resources.
Two	Assess the overall state of the human resource function in the context of the current school system's needs and aspirations.
Three	Develop a strategic plan.
Four	Implement the strategic plan.
Five	Monitor, evaluate, and adjust the strategic plan.

FIGURE 2.1   *Sequential model of the human resource planning process.*

daunting undertaking on the part of those responsible for developing human resource plans. Many of the concerns associated with strategic planning can be overcome by considering planning as a process rather than as an event. As a process, strategic plan for a school system may be described as a planning tool to do the following:

- Move the system from its current state of operation to a desired state of operation
- Establish the basic system purpose, goals to be pursued, and the general means (tactical plan) by which the goals may be accomplished
- Address fundamental questions about the structures needed to develop the system's purpose, direction, and future generations of educational programs and services
- Make planning and tactical decisions within the framework of the system mission, goals, policies, and human resource values of a particular school district
- Provide a point of departure to assess the impact of future environments on strategic plans
- Link functional goals (e.g., educational programs and services, human resources, logistics, and external relations) to the goals of the strategic plan
- Assess social, legal, technological, political, economic, educational, and governmental factors that may create opportunities for or obstructions to strategic plans

Figure 2.2 illustrates the anatomy of the strategic planning process as conceived by the hypothetical Riverpark school system. Through this process, the system intends to address and to explore the range of options, opportunities, and strategies through which it plans to enhance the system's future condition. Perhaps the most appealing aspect of strategic planning is this: It provides a unique opportunity to pull back from the immediate details of everyday school system life—important though they are in their own terms—to examine what is at stake when moving the system from where it is to where it should be.

Contemporary times are full of animation and activity regarding the resolution of problems confronting educational systems in general. Redesign efforts through instructional and organizational reform, restructuring, decentralization, comprehensive care for children from birth to graduation, and site-based management are commonplace within the popular press. The appeal of strategic planning for public school districts is that it serves as a mechanism for weaving the fabric of a school system, through an ongoing process involving position holders working with each other to make school improvement an aggressive movement for dealing with a social failing.

This movement begins with the mission statement developed by a school district. As noted in Figure 2.1, Stage One of the human resource planning model includes definition and articulation of the system's expectations for its human resource functions. The mission statement can be perceived as a frame of reference by which to assess program options, communicate ideas, shape system performance culture, and coordinate system functions such as human resources with system strategic aims.

The future status Riverpark school system desires for its human resources is based upon these common premises for action:

Goals. The primary aim of the system is to achieve teaching and learning outcomes beyond those established by state regulations and those proposed by the federal government.

Planning focus. The underlying intent of the system's strategic planning process is to identify conceivable opportunities, favorable and unfavorable relevant changes, regulatory trends, economic conditions, union initiatives, and sociocultural factors that impact on attainment of our desired future status.

Planning priorities. The following priorities have been identified through systemwide review and given primacy as human resource objectives during the time frame portrayed below:

- Develop and implement a strategic planning model to serve the system's interests effectively and efficiently.
- Take steps to achieve our strategic aims through the collective bargaining process.
- Enhance the recruitment process to attract and retain the quality of personnel needed to improve teaching and learning outcomes.
- Identify anticipated changes in the educational program and their impact on the future workforce.

Time frame. The time frame shown below represents one of the components of the strategic planning process. Current and strategic plans are reviewed, revised, and recast each year and adjusted as necessary.

		Strategic Planning Time Frame				
Current	2	3	4	5		
	Current	2	3	4	5	
		Current	2	3	4	5
			Current	2	3	4	5
				Current	2	3	4	5

Planning involvement. A planning council is established to ensure systemwide participation for developing current and strategic plans. Council members are representative of and accountable to work units (central, teaching, support) for input regarding decisions affecting their work and working conditions. One aim of the planning process is to avoid management exclusivity—unwritten, temporal, and intuitive approaches borne of individual experience rather than of system implications of current developments and trends.

FIGURE 2.2 *Elements of Riverpark school system's strategic planning process for its human resources.*

In establishing school system expectations on the basis of a mission statement, it is important to consider several questions for incorporation into strategic planning for human resources. A mission statement, as well as the entire human resource planning process, involves consideration of the following questions:

- What is the school system *expected to do?*
- What is the system *currently doing or not doing* to achieve its expectations?
- What *should the school system be doing* to achieve its expectations?

The question of what the school system is expected to do provides the source from which the system creates its strategy to carry out the mission. In giving thought to the school system's expectations, examples by Goodlad (1994) as well as examples provided in Chapter 1 are helpful. Expectations that have emerged in the United States may be placed conveniently into four categories: (a) academic—prepare individuals as lifelong learners; (b) vocational—ready individuals for productive work and economic responsibility; (c) social and civic—socialize individuals for participation in a complex society; and (d) personal—provide individuals with personal fulfillment, which is a fairly recent development.

As can be inferred from Goodlad's comments, there are various interests that human resource planning must satisfy, including societal interest (governmental), system interest (strategic aims), functional interest (human resources), and personal interest (economic, social, and psychological objectives of position holders). The scope of the mission statement is to provide a foundation for system-wide planning and to implement plans aimed at achieving primary expectations; to set planning boundaries; to alter, remove, add, or extend existing programs and practices; and to channel available resources into plans to produce intended results. Thus, the human resource planning process, in concert with the system mission, is a tool through which plans are made to accommodate the unique and special characteristics that form the fabric of a particular school system.

Knowledge of the system and of the human resource function is used to engage Stage Two of the human resource planning process (as shown in Figure 2.1). This stage is referred to as the *organizational diagnosis phase* and involves assessing human resource conditions. As detailed in the section that follows, Stage Two involves formation of sources relating to key planning areas in the internal and external environments of a particular school district.

Stage Two: Assessment of the Human Resource Condition

The planning process shown in Figure 2.1 indicates that Stage Two is designed to assess the system and the system's linkage to the human resource function. This step within the human resource planning process is pivotal for creating desired outcomes for the system, its members, and those for whom the system renders service. When executed appropriately, this step increases the likelihood that the system will perform effectively under conditions of continuous change.

Meeting these requirements calls for addressing several questions such as the following:

- How can human resource planning be linked closely to the school system's strategic plan?
- What is the system's current situation regarding attainment of educational expectations?
- Which are the strongest educational programs, and which are the weakest?
- Which informational inputs are needed to develop the strategic plan?
- What will the future external environment likely require in terms of demand for school system services?
- Which priorities should be established for the allocation of anticipated resources? Which current basic priorities should be questioned?
- Which internal or external factors might inhibit attainment of the system's educational aims?

Answers to these questions require information that must be acquired for guiding decision making. In recent years, many school systems have come to realize that information is one of the key assets possessed by the district, along with buildings and equipment, human resources, and fiscal resources. For example, managing the 10 subprocesses of the human resource function effectively and efficiently requires information from both the internal and external environmental forces that influence human resource decisions within the public school setting.

Some of the information needed for human resource planning may be found in established databases that exist within and outside the system. Other information needed for human resource planning may have to be compiled from initial data sources by those responsible for human resource planning.

Among the major classes of information essential to human resource planning are:

- *Purpose information*—The system mission, objectives, goals, strategies, and policies.
- *Program structure information*—Components of the educational program that interact with the human resource function.
- *Pupil information*—Present and future school enrollees for whom the educational program is designed.
- *Position information*—Number, types, and structural location of present and future positions.
- *Organizational structure information*—Assignment of tasks, responsibility, and authority of the human resource function.
- *External environment information*—Economic, governmental, legal, union, and public influences affecting personnel decisions.
- *Internal environment information*—Workforce, negotiated contracts, budgets, audits, structure, technology use, planning efforts, legal compliance, and system culture.

Now let us examine each class of information to illustrate the importance of that informational source in identifying effective programs and practices and for improving those that are less than satisfactory.

Purpose Information

The mission statement establishes the broad parameters for the organization and operation of a public school district. To align the organization and the operation of a public school district with the mission statement, specific objectives are established. Each of these objectives should have identifiable goals that can be measured.

Objectives without measurable outcomes and goals fail the organization and the operation of the school district in several ways. Without objectives and goals, it is difficult, if not impossible, to develop strategies for guiding the school system from where it is currently to where it should be in the future. If the objectives are considered to be a desired state of organization and operation for a school district, then strategies act as a map for guiding the organization toward the desired state of operation.

Human resource planners must rely on purpose information when performing other human resource functions. Purpose information impacts recruitment, selection, development, assessment, and continuity of employment for current as well as future employees. Without purpose information, other human resource functions are less than effective in application and operation.

Program Structure Information

It is reasonable to assume that school officials who make personnel decisions will be better equipped to do so if they are versed fully in the organization of two key aspects of the educational program: *organization of instruction* and *instructional grouping*. Both of these structural characteristics of educational programs have broad implications for the human resource planning process within the public school setting.

Indeed, assumptions are made by policy makers as to the breadth and depth of learning experiences to be included in the curriculum. These assumptions involve where the experiences will be provided, when the experiences will be offered, by whom, in what manner, in what grouping arrangements, and for what purposes. Decisions such as these have considerable influence on the quality and quantity of personnel needed to staff the educational program.

Arriving at such decisions is no easy matter because it involves consideration of conflicting philosophies of education; theories of curriculum development; psychologies of learning; and needs of the individual learner, the local community, the state, the region, and the nation. One of the inferences to be drawn from Table 2.1 is that the choice of alternatives relating to the instructional program affects the number, types, and levels of sophistication of personnel employed by a school system.

Instructional grouping, in contrast to organization of instruction, refers to the organizational unit used for delivering the instructional program. The question of

TABLE 2.1
Illustration of instructional program options that influence human resource plans.

Program Component		Illustration of Alternatives
Program focus	*or*	Central purpose is to develop the intellect. Central purpose is to develop individuals for effective social living.
Program content	*or*	Rigid, grade-sequenced learning experiences. Flexible-sequenced learning experiences determined by learner readiness, interest, and/or needs.
Program breadth and depth	*or*	Program limited to time-tested elements of our social heritage. Program planned to encompass breadth and depth of educational opportunities.
Program location	*or*	Within attendance units of system. Within and outside of system.
Program staff	*or*	Conventional: one instructor per group. Nonconventional: variable staffing at different levels of the system, including volunteers, part-time personnel, aides, and peer instructors.
Program time	*or*	Uniform schedules (day only). Variable schedules (day, evening, summer).
Program flexibility	*or*	Pupil moves through program experiences at a uniform rate (one grade per school term). Pupil moves through system depending on achievement.
Pupil grouping	*or*	Graded (learning groups closed). Nongraded (learning groups open).
Program control	*or*	Program decisions restricted to professionals. Program decisions unrestricted (staff, parents, pupils, and/or community groups involved).
Program instructional methods	*or*	Conventional forms of instruction. Augmented forms of conventional instruction.

how many pupils should be assigned to an instructional group has been and still remains a subject of serious concern to all who are interested in the nation's schools. There are several reasons why so much significance is attached to the question of class size within the human resource context.

One reason is the educator's quest to provide grouping arrangements most conducive to learning and study. Although it is clear that a given class size is no absolute guarantee of the educational progress for all children, many educators are convinced that the grouping plan is an important contributor to educational attainment (National Education Association, n.d.). In fact, most of the recent research indicates that smaller class size is better than larger class size when it comes to instructional groupings of pupils (U.S. Department of Education, n.d.).

Cost is another reason why so much significance is attached to class size within the human resource planning process. The major share of current expenditures in any school budget for a fiscal year is allocated to staffing requirements involving the delivery of instruction. Changes in class size can have a substantial impact on the operating budget of a school district and the ways that funds are allocated within the operating budget.

Despite experimentation with new forms of instructional grouping, educational technology, and staff utilization and deployment, the question of class size cannot be dismissed when developing human resource planning assumptions for a public school district. In making assumptions about instructional groupings, consideration must be given to the purpose for which instructional groups are formed (the type of learning desired), the intellectual and emotional needs of pupils, the skills of the teacher, and the nature of the subject matter. It is equally evident that regardless of the grouping plan used by any particular district, every school system needs a staff that is adequate in size and composition—one that is deployed and balanced properly—to provide all pupils with essential instructional services during their educational encounter.

Pupil Information

For most of the human resource functions, the number and type of students enrolled and projected to enroll has a major implication for planning. To factor into the human resource planning process enrollment trends, enrollment projections are required. Different types of enrollment projection techniques require different types of information that must be compiled by human resource planners (Shaw, Alspough, & Wat-Aksorm, 1997).

Within broad categories there are linear models and nonlinear models for projecting enrollments of students within the public school setting. Linear models work best when school enrollments follow a specific pattern across time. The pattern can be increasing, decreasing, or stable, but the pattern of enrollment must be linear over time.

One of the most common linear models is the survival ratio technique (Tanner & Hackney, in press). This enrollment projection technique requires two sources of pupil information: the live birth rates for the most recent 10-year period and the historical enrollment data for the past 5 years.

When unsystematic events affect the enrollments within a school district, linear models for projecting enrollments are inadequate. Application of a linear model for projecting enrollments to a nonlinear situation will result in either an overprojection or an underprojection. Both types of errors have important implications for human resource planning and staffing.

Nonlinear models for projecting student enrollment are designed to accommodate unsystematic increases or decreases in student enrollment over time. Unsystematic increases or decreases can occur for many reasons that have little to do with either a live birth rate or previous enrollment patterns. School districts can lose substantial enrollments in a single year due to the closing of a major industry within the district, or school districts can also gain substantial enrollments in a single year through the growth of housing developments within a school district.

A nonlinear enrollment project method used by many school districts is the Bayesian estimation technique. This technique utilizes both objective and subjective information, and, by so doing, can account for unsystematic increases in enrollments within a school district. Objective information consists of historic enrollment data, while subjective information consists of variables specific to a school district that impact the enrollments of that particular district.

Without question, accurate enrollment projections are vital to staff planning strategies. Whether enrollments are increasing, decreasing, or remaining stable, this information must be incorporated into the staffing plans. Increasing enrollment can signal additional staff beyond replacements, decreasing enrollments may involve a reduction in force, and stable enrollments imply only replacement hiring within a human resource staffing plan.

Position Information

After the school system's goal structure has been established, the task of categorizing the work evolving from the structure into work units, job categories, jobs, job descriptions, and job specifications can be undertaken. One way to gather information about the work to be undertaken in a school system is shown in Table 2.2. The intent of the display is to characterize the scope of school system work, job clusters evolving from the required work activities, and the structural settings in which the work takes place.

Within Table 2.2, information is presented for types of work, types of positions, structural setting of positions, and percent allocation for system personnel. As indicated in Table 2.2, instructional and related tasks are assigned to attendance units (individual schools), whereas general administrative work is allocated to the administrative unit. Various types of positions are essential both at the central level and in the attendance units for operating a public school district.

Information as contained in Table 2.2 can be expanded and recast into a long-range staffing plan relative to the number of positions to be filled by a school district. Table 2.3 illustrates one of several methods that can be employed to transform planning information into professional position projections that will be required in the future organizational structure of a public school district. Using the projections as set forth, staffing assumptions can be established for a specific time span under a given set of conditions.

The approach shown in Table 2.3 is not difficult to initiate; any school district can use this format to undertake an analysis of staffing objectives and policies needed for their human resource planning. By following this model, many advantages can be derived from this type of personnel projection scheme within the public school setting. These advantages include the following:

- Extending the range of planning activities in a school administrative unit beyond a single year into a multiple-year perspective
- Identifying future trends in enrollment on which to base personnel needs
- Developing an inventory of present personnel components

TABLE 2.2
Nature and scope of school system work, positions, and structural settings.

Types of System Work	Types of Positions	Structural Setting	Hypothetical Proportion of Total System Personnel (%)
Planning, organizing, leading, controlling total system	Professional administrative: superintendent, assistant superintendent, associate superintendent, directors, assistants to higher-level personnel	Central administration	1
Planning, organizing, leading, controlling individual school attendance units	Professional administrative: principals, assistant principals, department heads, team leaders	Individual client service units (schools)	3
Implementing Instructional programs (regular, special)	Professional teaching: classroom teachers Professional specialists: art, health, library, guidance, music, physical education, psychological service, reading, speech correction, home–school visits, audiovisual	Individual client service units (schools)	62
Implementing Instructional support programs: operation, maintenance, food service, transportation, health, security, secretarial, clerical	Classified: skilled, semiskilled,unskilled	Certain personnel work under direction of central administration; others work in attendance units under direction of principal	34

- Projecting the present numerical staff adequacy into the staff size ultimately desired in each of the system's operating units
- Quantifying personnel needs for budgetary purposes
- Translating planning assumptions into a future organizational structure for a particular school district
- Linking personnel planning with other systemwide planning efforts
- Determining the priority order of personnel needs
- Identifying obstacles to realization of the total personnel plan and developing methods for surmounting obstacles

In preparing projections of professional positions, it is important to note that projection results depend on both accuracy of enrollment projections and on the

TABLE 2.3
Projection of professional positions required in the future organization structure of the Cloudcroft School System.

	Base Year	Base Year + 1	Base Year + 2	Base Year + 3	Base Year + 4	Base Year + 5
1. Enrollments						
K–6	6,819	7,153	7,228	7,195	7,083	6,829
7–9	2,583	2,983	3,208	3,457	3,630	3,861
10–12	2,308	2,337	2,449	2,485	2,634	2,839
Total	11,710	12,473	12,885	13,137	13,347	13,529
2. Personnel ratio objectives						
a. Pupil–teaching personnel	28:1	28:1	27:1	26:1	25:1	24:1
b. Pupil–instructional specialist personnel	213:1	211:1	211:1	190:1	178:1	169:1
c. Pupil–administrative personnel	532:1	480:1	460:1	438:1	417:1	423:1
d. Pupil–total professional personnel	24:1	24:1	23:1	22:1	21:1	20:1
e. Professional staff per 1,000 pupils	41	41	42	44	46	48
3. Ratio objectives expressed as staff size						
a. Teaching personnel	420	445	477	505	534	564
b. Instructional specialists	55	59	61	69	75	80
c. Administrative personnel	22	26	28	30	32	32
d. Total professional personnel	497	530	566	604	641	676
4. New positions						
a. Teaching personnel		25	32	28	29	30
b. Instructional specialists		4	2	8	6	5
c. Administrative personnel		4	2	2	2	0
d. Total professional personnel		33	36	38	37	35

Assumptions: Pupil–teacher ratio will be reduced from 28:1 in base year to 24:1 in base year + 5. Professional staff will increase from 41 per 1,000 pupils in base year to 48 per 1,000 pupils in base year + 5. Pupil–instructional specialist ratio and pupil–administrative personnel ratio will increase as shown above.

desired ratios between pupils and professional personnel. If enrollment projections are inaccurate or if ratios are altered, results as found in Table 2.3 will be misleading. To increase the likelihood that enrollment projections will be as accurate as possible, the staffing plan, as found in Table 2.3, must be updated each year.

Failure to update the staffing projections each year has been a major problem for many school districts. All too often, once a long-term staffing projection is compiled, districts fail to revisit the projection for several years. However, the projection should be recalculated each year to incorporate the most recent information.

With respect to the staffing ratios, these indexes reflect a policy decision because a standard ratio applicable to all districts fails to exist. Each district, through careful examination of relevant internal and external variables, must determine the ratio that will work most effectively for that particular system. This involves consideration of the various economic, political, and social concerns that influence such a policy decision.

Once established, this ratio is then used to methodically ascertain professional personnel requirements of the individual system. However, the reader should recognize that the approach suggested in Table 2.3 is not offered as the ultimate solution to long-term human resource forecasting. For example, the technique employed to project professional personnel requirements should be broadened to include data on support personnel to make the planning more comprehensive.

Organizational Structure Information

Compiling the forecast of the long-term human resource requirements for the school system makes it possible to project the organizational structure in detail. Several types of planning tools that can assist school officials in redesigning the organization's structure should be mentioned. These planning tools include the position guide and the organizational chart.

The position guide, an example of which is shown in Figure 2.3, can be used to specify the work or expectations of each position in the organization, relationships of the position to other positions within the organization, and qualifications needed by an incumbent to perform the work allocated to the position. An **organizational chart**, such as the one shown in Figure 2.4, is an extremely useful planning tool for establishing and appraising formal relationships among positions within a school district. The organizational chart helps examine visually the functions, relationships, and levels of various positions in the administrative hierarchy.

Both of these sources of planning information can be used to examine alternative structures for the school district. Sometimes changes in the current structure of a school district can produce positive results relative to goal attainment. More important, planning activities involved in developing the foregoing tools are of considerable importance in that they can help to enhance personnel's role as a viable organizational function, create better role understanding among stakeholders, lead to wiser use of the structural tools, and yield ultimately a more effective and efficient organization than had existed previously.

Goodville School District
Position Guide
Part A: Position Requirements

Position Title: Instructor of Mathematics, Senior High School

Position Code: T68

Primary Function: To participate, as a member of the instructional staff, in directing learning of all students in the area of mathematics. Such participation shall be directed toward attainment of general and specific behavioral objectives of each course, of the school, and of the school district.

Major Classroom Responsibilities: (1) Planning for teaching, (2) motivating pupils, (3) developing classroom climate, (4) managing the classroom, (5) interacting with pupils, (6) evaluating pupils.

Illustration of Key Duties: (1) *Planning for teaching:* within the framework of goals established by the school system, plans the long- and short-range objectives for each assigned course; collects and utilizes a wide variety of information to aid in guiding the growth and development of individual pupils; selects meaningful subject matter and related learning experiences appropriate to various stages of pupil's development; selects and utilizes teaching procedures appropriate to attainment of short- and long-range objectives; selects teaching materials considered to be conducive to attainment of intended goals; (2) *Motivating pupils:* establishes standards for individual pupils in terms of ability level of each; uses a variety of activities to develop pupils' curiosity and discoveries; (3) *Developing a classroom climate:* creates a classroom climate conducive to pupils' intellectual, social, emotional, and moral development; (4) *Managing the classroom:* controls pupils' behavior and activities so that they contribute positively to accomplishment of goals; (5) *Interacting with pupils:* utilizes concept formation, principles, and generalization in helping pupils understand subject matter; (6) *Evaluating pupils:* evaluates pupils' performance continuously to determine nature and extent of direction needed to attain goals.

FIGURE 2.3   *Illustration of position guide for a teaching position.*

External Environment Information

As noted in the previous chapter, human resource planning is influenced greatly by the external environment. Because the number and types of variables in the external environment influencing a school system and the functions of a school system are virtually limitless, one must decide which external factors appear to be critical in planning the system's future. Examples of potentially relevant external variables include the following:

- Extension of regulatory legislation and procedures generated by federal, state, county, and municipal agencies
- School enrollment trends (short- and long-term)

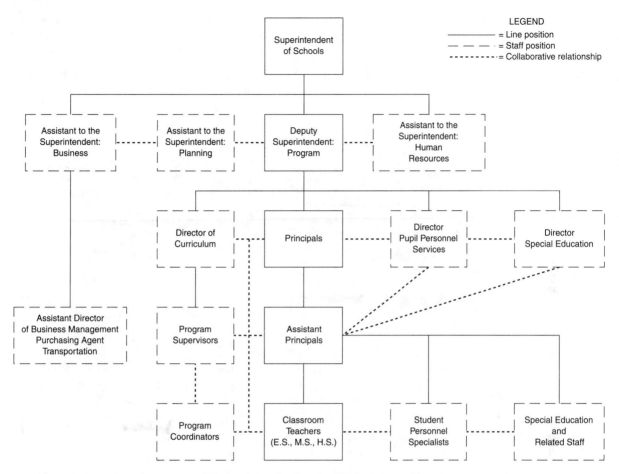

FIGURE 2.4 *System organizational chart of the Cloudcroft School District.*

- Educational reform movements (federal, state, county, and municipal)
- Extension or curtailment of state-mandated educational programs
- Extension or curtailment of financial support for education
- Community pressures for educational change
- Personnel costs under varying economic conditions and contract negotiations
- Personnel composition and skill-level demand under varying employment conditions
- Trends in judicial rulings affecting the human resource function
- Emerging educational technology as a potential for improving teaching and learning
- Emerging technology for improving an organization's information systems as applied to strategic planning within the human resource function

Actual choices among external variables depend on specifics associated with a particular school district. Variables selected for analysis and incorporated within projections should be chosen on the basis of assumed relevance for achieving both system and human resource objectives and goals. The preceding list of variables, as well as emerging issues pertinent to the human resource function, merit continuous monitoring in order to enhance more systematic approaches to strategic decision making as related to human resource planning in the public school setting.

Internal Environment Information

Internal information, as well as external information, has the potential to moderate the design and the implementation of human resource planning within a public school setting. Strategic planning, as related to the human resource function within the public school setting, must consider several sources of internal information. Included among these sources is information pertaining to the labor management climate, to affective reactions of employees, and to conditions anticipated to change in the internal environment.

For some school districts, a major concern for human resource planning is labor–management relationships. Within many school districts, certain aspects of the human resource planning process may be embedded within the existing labor contract as a result of prior negotiations. Issues within the existing labor contract that may have been, at one time, under the complete control of management in the design and execution of human resource plans have been restricted by contact language. Information about these restrictions must be considered by the school district when formulating strategic plans that either directly or indirectly impact the contract contents.

Less tangible than labor contract language are the perceptions of employees as an informational source within the human resource planning process. Employees may have reactions to their job, to their work environment, or to the leadership of the district that influences the development and execution of human resource plans within the public school setting. To assess these types of reactions harbored by employees, information about the internal environment can be assessed through a number of commercial instruments.

Reactions of employees toward their jobs and their job environment can be assessed via job satisfaction instruments. Two commercial instruments used to assess the reactions of educators within the public school setting are the Job Descriptive Index (JDI; **http://www.bgsu.edu/departments/psych/JDI/**) and the Minnesota Satisfaction Questionnaire (MSQ; **http://www.psych.umn.edu/psylabs/vpr/msqinf.htm**). Both instruments provide data that can be compared to national norms.

Similar types of instruments exist for assessing perceptions of employees about school district leadership. One of the popular instruments available to school districts for assessing school leadership is the Leader Behavior Description Questionnaire (LBDQ; **http://www.tc.unl.edu/mbryant/LeaderQuestionnaire.htm**). Results from the LBDQ provide measures of consideration and initiating structure as perceived by followers to be exhibited by leaders.

Strategic plans relating to the human resource function must consider anticipated changes within the internal environment. A demographic analysis of the current workforce can reveal pending retirements and future growth areas. Current labor market conditions concerning shortages (National Teacher Recruitment Clearinghouse, n.d.) and changes in types of applicants seeking positions within public school districts (U.S. Department of Education, n.d.) make this type of information necessary for effective and efficient human resource planning.

Due to the specifics associated with particular school districts, a fixed set of answers fails to exist for the type of internal information that is needed in this stage of the planning process for any particular school district. What does exist for any particular school district are some general questions that can be used to guide the collection of internal information at the local school district level. A list of these questions follows:

- Which organizational characteristics promote or impede the system's ability to increase its responsiveness to current and future demands (policies, programs, processes, procedures, practices, rules, and regulations)?
- What is the quality of leadership within the district as perceived by the system's individuals and groups?
- Is the system's division of labor efficiently structured?
- How satisfactory is the current approach for reward structures within the district?
- Does the present leadership of the school district promote change and innovation?
- What are our strengths and weaknesses in each functional area of the school district (programs, logistics, planning, human resources, and external relations)?
- Are the system's values, expectations, and attitudes being communicated effectively to the membership?
- How effective are the system's efforts to bring about an understanding and appreciation of the values, norms, expected behaviors, abilities, and social knowledge needed to carry out position and performance standards, career development, and interpersonal relationships?

Stage Three: Development of a Strategic Plan

Stages One and Two of the human resource planning process include (a) identification of organizational and human resource objectives and goals and (b) formation of informational sources for use as tools in planning how to achieve future system objectives and goals. Moving from Stages One and Two within the planning process, Stage Three involves drawing inferences, considering planning options, and making planning decisions based on information derived from Stages One and Two. Many factors are involved with decision making for human resource planning at Stage Three of the planning process. Some examples follow:

- What are the planning implications derived from the enrollment forecasts?
- Will there be a shortage or surplus of system personnel to meet future needs as required by the human resource plans?
- To what extent do current job incumbents have the skills, abilities, and attitudes to fill projected positions?

- What assumptions should be made about professional staff size and about support staff size?
- Should staffing ratios be the same in all buildings or at all levels of grades across buildings?
- To what extent should existing jobs be redesigned and new jobs be developed?
- What decisions should be made about various kinds of staff balance (system; work unit; staff category; staff utilization; staff load; staff competency; and racial, ethnic, gender, age, and instructional balance)?
- How can the system redesign the organizational structure to clarify: (a) the location of each position, (b) the functional relationship of positions to other positions, (c) role specifications associated with positions, (d) position level within the organizational structure, (e) interactions among positions, (f) position authority and responsibility, (g) position status and importance, and (h) position expectations and rewards?
- How can the system make more effective and efficient use of its human resources?
- What changes should be made in personnel plans as a result of anticipated developments in the external and internal environments?

In brief, making the transition from an existing organizational state to a more desirable human resource condition requires systematic planning. The planning process described in this chapter should help to chart managerial direction, reduce uncertainty, and minimize random behavior in efforts to achieve the aims of both the school organization and its members. After initial human resource plans have been developed, the next stage of the human resource planning process involves implementation.

Stage Four: Implementation of the Strategic Plan

Introducing changes in the human resource function involves a variety of activities to improve existing arrangements, as well as to develop new approaches and capabilities based on review of external and internal environmental conditions, threats, and opportunities for improving the effective and efficient operation of a public school district. Stage Four of the human resource planning process presumes that there is organizational commitment to implement the design of the strategic development plan. Without commitment on the part of policy makers, administrators, and staff, even the best human resource plans are doomed to fail.

As illustrated in Figure 2.5, implementation strategy takes into account objectives, strategies, programs, projects, timing of activities, delegation of responsibilities, and allocation of resources to undertake specified courses of action. Worth noting is that school systems differ in many ways, including size, location, leadership, resources, quality and quantity of personnel, instructional technology, complexity, stability, and internal and external environments. Each school system must

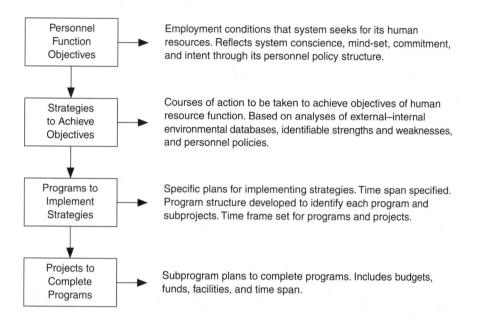

| Personnel Function Objectives | Employment conditions that system seeks for its human resources. Reflects system conscience, mind-set, commitment, and intent through its personnel policy structure. |

| Strategies to Achieve Objectives | Courses of action to be taken to achieve objectives of human resource function. Based on analyses of external–internal environmental databases, identifiable strengths and weaknesses, and personnel policies. |

| Programs to Implement Strategies | Specific plans for implementing strategies. Time span specified. Program structure developed to identify each program and subprojects. Time frame set for programs and projects. |

| Projects to Complete Programs | Subprogram plans to complete programs. Includes budgets, funds, facilities, and time span. |

FIGURE 2.5 *Sequential implementation of change strategies.*

determine how the process can be performed most effectively and efficiently within the constraints of a particular district.

To facilitate the planning process within a particular school district, the planning model shown in Figure 2.1 provides a framework for analyzing problems related to the function and to the steps involved in developing approaches to achieve long-term objectives for the human resource function. More specifically, Table 2.4 illustrates a format employed in the hypothetical Goodville school system to plan, manage, and monitor various activities associated with positions in the organizational structure. Within this format are approaches employed to: (a) govern the creation, specifications, elimination, recruitment, selection, appraisal, forecasts, and relationships relevant to all positions in the budget; (b) allocate authority and responsibility; (c) control guidelines; and (d) provide structural relationships.

Stage Five: Monitoring, Assessing, and Adjusting the Strategic Plan

Within this stage of the human resource planning process, attention must be given to monitoring, assessing, and adjusting the implementation of the plans. Inherent in this stage of the planning process are three closely related steps that must be addressed: (a) reviewing plans (including goals, objectives, programs, and standards), (b) checking results against expectations, and (c) adjusting to correct deviations from plans.

TABLE 2.4
Position planning and control network of the Goodville School System.

Position Network Elements	Professional Administrative Positions	Professional Teaching Positions	Professional Specialist Positions	Instructional Support Positions	Noninstructional Support Positions
Position location	C–A	A	C–A	A	C–A
Position reports to	5	5	5	5	5
New position route	5–3–2–1	5–3–2–1	5–3–2–1	5–3–2–1	5–3–2–1
Position abolition route	3–2–1	3–2–1	3–2–1	3–2–1	3–2–1
Request for new position route	5–3–2–1	5–3–2–1	5–3–2–1	5–3–2–1	5–3–2–1
Temporary replacement route	5–3–4	5–3–4	5–3–4	5–3–4	5–3–4
Permanent replacement route	5–3–4	5–3–4	5–3–4	5–3–4	5–3–4
Transfer route	5–3	5–3	5–3	5–3	5–3–4
Dismissal route	5–3–2–1	5–3–2–1	5–3–2–1	5–3–2–1	5–3–2–1
Position guide route	6–5–3–2–1	6–5–3–2–1	6–5–3–2–1	6–5–3–2–1	6–5–3–2–1
Performance appraisal process	5–R	5–R	5–R	5–R	5–R
Recruitment process	1–3–4–5	1–3–4–5	1–3–4–5	1–3–4–5	1–3–4–5
Internal	4–R	4–R	4–R	4–R	4–R
External	4–R	4–R	4–R	4–R	4–R
Selection process	4–R	4–R	4–R	4–R	4–R
Participation route	7	7	7	7	7
Recommendation route	7–3–2–1	7–3–2–1	7–3–2–1	7–3–2–1	7–3–2–1
Nomination responsibility	3	3	3	3	3
Appointment responsibility	1	1	1	1	1
Rejection resolution route	1–3–1	1–3–1	1–3–1	1–3–1	1–3–1
Position forecasts	6–3–2–1	6–3–2–1	6–3–2–1	6–3–2–1	6–3–2–1
Position relationship within organization structure	6–3–2–1	6–3–2–1	6–3–2–1	6–3–2–1	6–3–2–1

Guidelines elaborating position control concepts:
- Central recruitment, decentralized selection
- Position guides for each position, reviewed annually
- All positions open to internal application
- Unit heads (5) notify Asst. Supt., Human Resources (4) of position vacancy (temporary or permanent)
- Selection committees have joint responsibility of (1) and (2)
- (4) Responsible for forms, documentation, processes in position, control plan
- Positions created or abolished in adoption of annual budgets; interim position replacement route specified above
- Chief Executive makes nomination to Board for each position
- If Board rejects nomination, Chief Executive nominates another candidate

Code
1 = Board as a whole
2 = Personnel committee
3 = Chief Executive
4 = Asst. Supt., Human Resources
5 = Unit head (see administrative almanac)
6 = Planning office
7 = Selection committee
C = Central administration
A = Attendance unit
R = Responsibility for administering

52

Ideally, every human resource plan that a school system places in operation should have *built-in means* for judging the effectiveness of the plan relative to specified objectives and goals. Viewed in this manner, monitoring and evaluating the effectiveness of plans is an omnipresent function of school administration, an aspect of the administrative process designed to keep means and ends in balance. To expect even the best designed human resource plans to flow from initiation through fruition is unrealistic.

Through continuous monitoring on the part of system administration, adjustments can be made within the ongoing implementation process. To help with monitoring, assessing, and adjusting the strategic plan for human resources, specific questions are posed for consideration. Human resources planners need to know the following:

- How feasible are the planning assumptions on which the function is based?
- Is the current organizational structure conducive to system effectiveness?
- Are positions being filled according to position guides?
- Which steps have been taken to implement systemwide development and career paths for personnel?
- Are the numbers and quality of personnel satisfactory?
- Are personnel deployed, balanced, and utilized effectively?
- Which initiatives are needed to adjust differences between actual and expected planning outcomes?

Stage Six: Assessing Effectiveness of Strategic Initiatives

Effectiveness is the ultimate test of any strategic initiative implemented by a school district. Within the human resource context, **effectiveness** is defined broadly as the realization of objectives and goals associated with the planning process. Consequently, district leadership has a strong obligation to define what effectiveness means and how effectiveness should be measured within the school setting.

Exercising this obligation on behalf of district leadership is extremely important for many reasons. Interest groups and constituencies, both internal and external to the school system, have a stake in whether schools are effective or ineffective. Indeed, taxpayers, politicians, government bodies, home buyers, students, other employers, and employees have more than a passing concern about school system quality. All will use this interest to assess effectiveness if district leadership is remiss in their obligation to assess the effectiveness of school district operations relative to human resource plans.

To assist school districts in assessing the human resource plans developed through the strategic planning process, information is presented in Figure 2.6. The figure illustrates a procedure for putting Stage Six into operation. The five strategic initiatives listed at the top of the diagram (A–E) represent criteria for evaluating the effectiveness of the strategic plan.

To evaluate progress relative to the initiatives, a rating scale is provided. This scale has five points ranging from a low of "0" (representing no progress) to a high

The following planning initiatives are intended to
A. Direct all human resource processes of the school system to contribute to raising the student graduation rate from 68% to 90%.
B. Redirect recruitment–selection efforts away from past and present approaches toward realization of future strategic personnel requirements.
C. Develop the performance appraisal process to enhance personnel behavior consistent with meeting strategic personnel goals.
D. Redesign communication channels so that plans, facts, ideas, meanings, information, and understandings are effectively exchanged among system members.
E. Promote continuous improvement in the systematic control of school system records, assisted by information technology during their life span.

Extent and Value of Progress Toward
Realization of Planning Objectives

Initiatives	Weight Assigned	None (0)	Some (1)	Satisfactory (2)	Superior (3)	Maximum (4)	Insert Score
A	5	0	5	10	15	(20)	(100)
B	4	(0)	4	8	12	16	(0)
C	3	0	(3)	6	9	12	(9)
D	2	0	2	4	(6)	8	(12)
E	1	0	1	(2)	3	4	(2)

Total Score   (123)

Note:
   Numbers in the columns under *Extent and Value of Progress* are the product of the value and, for each initiative, the weight selected.

To complete the profile:
•   Under *Extent and Value of Progress* circle for each initiative a number in the column that corresponds to the appropriate descriptor of progress.
•   Then connect the selected numbers to obtain a graphic profile of the performance.
•   The score for each initiative is the number circled as representing the weighted degree of progress.

FIGURE 2.6   *Strategic planning effectiveness rating scale (application of ratings, year 2 of 5).*

of "4" (representing maximum progress) with higher ratings corresponding to a more positive outcome than lower ratings. Each anchor point on the scale is referenced by an adverb.

   Because human resource initiatives as contained in Figure 2.5 may vary in priority, weights are assigned to each initiative. Within this example, the highest weight is assigned to initiative "A," and the lowest weight is assigned to initiative "E." These weights are used for calculating a total score for each initiative.

A total score for each initiative is obtained by multiplying the numerical value of each rating on the scale of 0–4 by the appropriate weight assigned to each initiative (1–5). To assess the overall performance for each initiative, a comparison is made between the calculated score and the maximum obtainable score. Net differences reflect degree of compliance for a public school district relative to a specific initiative.

Performance of a public school district across different initiatives can be measured by comparing the absolute rating assigned to each initiative according to anchor values (see circles). The further the circles are to the left, the poorer the performance of a school district relative to a specific initiative. In most instances, this reflects whether human resource practices reflect preservation of past conceptual underpinnings or whether there is lack of leadership vision, foresight, forethought, and energy devoted to system constituents on system results as suggested by the initiatives.

An inference that can be drawn from Figure 2.6 is that human resource planning in the public school setting is cyclical and will probably fail to reach perfection. Periodic revision of plans and the assumptions on which they are based will always be necessary. Nevertheless, if the planning process is carefully structured, implemented, and controlled, chances are good that the school system will have sufficient high-performing personnel to meet future staffing aims and will not have to endure a constant organizational crisis created by lack of qualified people to perform the variety of tasks essential to its purposes.

Careful consideration of the intent of Figure 2.6 brings into focus several points about defining and measuring strategic initiatives in public school systems. These include the following:

- Variables involved in judging school system progress and its human resource function present complex defining and measuring tasks.
- Quantitative measures of effectiveness are but one of several evaluative approaches. Others include subjective evaluations and judgments, follow-up supervisory information, and periodic checkpoint indicators to determine how well the system is reacting to and coping with internal–external demands.
- Important as the foregoing points are, it should be apparent that leadership is always being judged by the intended future that strategic initiatives represent.

Review and Preview

The purpose of this chapter is to present a human resource planning process—the first of 10 processes that comprise the structure of this text. Six of the planning stages shown in Figure 2.1 include: (a) establishing goals for the system's human resources, (b) assessing the present status of the human resource condition, (c) developing a strategic plan to project what the human resource function aims to accomplish in the long run, (d) stressing the importance of initiating courses of action to implement planning strategies, (e) monitoring and evaluating the strategic plan to check program performance against goals, and (f) assessing the effectiveness of strategic initiatives. Three planning concepts are highlighted as important components of the planning process: (a) viewing human resource planning as a framework for integrating all human resource activities, (b) developing relevant information to facilitate the planning process, and (c) monitoring and assessing the planning process to evaluate progress toward goals, identify performance discrepancies, examine goals, and modify courses of action where assessment indicates justifiable changes.

Chapter 3 is devoted to three components—information, records, and communication—essential to the operation of the planning process and its linkage to internal and external environments.

Discussion Questions

1. What are the *instructional groupings* within your school organization? Which political influences impact the establishment of these groupings? Which social influences impact the establishment of these groupings?

2. How does your school organization gauge its *effectiveness?* Are these indicators developed within the organization, or are they imposed from sources outside the organization?

3. What are the hindrances to effective *strategic planning?* Which internal and external environmental factors impact strategic planning?

4. Consider the statement, "planning is easy; implementation is hard." What are the threats to the implementation of a strategic plan?

5. How can an educational organization assess its *human resource condition?* Which structures should be initiated to support this assessment? Who in the organization should be given the charge for making this assessment, and why?

References

Ackoff, R. (1970). *A concept of planning.* New York: Wiley-Interscience (pp. 2–4).

Goodlad, J. I. (1994). *What schools are for* (p. 44). Bloomington, IN: Phi Delta Kappa Educational Foundation.

Halphin, A. (1957). *Leader behavior description questionnaire.* Retrieved August 29, 2002, from Teachers College University of Nebraska–Lincoln Web site: **http://www.tc.unl.edu/mbryant/ LeaderQuestionnaire.htm**

Haselkorn, D. (1996, August 7). Breaking the glass ceiling. *Education Week on the Web, 15.* Retrieved August 29, 2002, from the *Education Week on the Web* Web site: **http://www.edweek.org/ew/vol-15/41hasel.h15**

JDI Research Group. (1985). *The job description index.* Retrieved August 29, 2002, from Bowling Green State University the Web site: **http://www.bgsu. edu/ departments/psych/JDI/**

Minnesota Vocational Psychology Research. (1977). *Minnesota job satisfaction questionnaire.* Retrieved August 29, 2002, from University of Minnesota Vocational the Psychology Research Web site: **http://www.psych.umn. edu/psylab/vpr/msqinf.htm**

National Education Association. (n.d.). *Reducing class size*. Retrieved August 29, 2002, from the NEA Web Site: **http://www. nea.org/lac/size/**

National School Boards Association. (1976). *Declining school enrollments*. Alexandria, VA: Author.

National Teacher Recruitment Clearinghouse. (n.d.). *Teacher shortage areas*. Retrieved August 29, 2002, from the National Teacher Recruitment Clearinghouse Web site: **http://www. recruitingteachers.org/findjob/ shortage.html**

Phi Delta Kappa. (1989, May). *Enrollment projections*. Bloomington, IN: Phi Delta Kappa.

Shaw, R. C., Alspaugh, J., & Wat-Aksorn, P. (1997, Fall). Accuracy of enrollment forecasting methods. *ERS Spectrum*, 16–19.

Stoops, J. K., & Slaby, R. M. (1981). How many students next year? *Phi Delta Kappan, 62*(9), 658.

Tanner, C. K., & Hackney, J. A. (in press). *Educational architecture: School facilities, planning, construction and management*. Boston: Allyn & Bacon.

U.S. Department of Education. (n.d.). *National reports*. Retrieved August 29, 2002, from the U.S. Department of Education Web site: **http://www.ed.gov/offices/ OESE/ClassSize/reports.html**

Supplementary Reading

Cascio, W. F. (1998). *Applied psychology in personnel management* (5th ed.). Upper Saddle River, NJ: Prentice Hall.

Duke, D. L. (1998, May). Challenges of designing the next generation of America's schools. *Phi Delta Kappan, 80*, 688.

Finn, C. E., Jr., & Walberg, H. J. (1998, June 22). The world's least efficient schools. *Wall Street Journal*, p. A22.

Garfinkel, L., & Campbell, R. D. (1996, June). Strategies for success in measuring performance. *HR Magazine, 41*, 98–104.

Gubman, E. L. (1998). *The talent solution: Aligning strategy and people to achieve extraordinary results*. New York: McGraw-Hill, Inc.

Lapointe, J., & Parker-Matz, J. (1998, September). People make the system go . . . or not. *HR Magazine, 43*, 28–36.

Mornell, P. (1998, June). *45 ways for hiring smart! How to predict winners and losers in the incredibly expensive people reading game*. Berkeley, CA: Ten Speed Press.

Rose, L. C. (1997, September). Connecting with all our publics. *Phi Delta Kappan, 79*, 2.

Starkwether, R. A., & Steinbacher, C. L. (1998, September). Job satisfaction affects the bottom line. *HR Magazine, 43*, 111–112.

3

Information Technology and the Human Resource Function

CHAPTER OBJECTIVES

Furnish an overview of the architecture of the human resource information system.

Introduce the concept of an information system as a plan to acquire, refine, organize, store, maintain, retrieve, and transform knowledge into an organized body of information for the purpose of managing the school system and the human resource function.

Explain the communication process and its potential for integrating the system with its parts and with its internal and external environments.

Examine the relationship between information technology and the human resource function.

CHAPTER CONCEPTS

Archive	Information process
Audit	Information system
Data	Privacy laws
Database	Record
Data processing	Records center
Form information	Report
Information policy	Technology

Information and the Human Resource Function

A school system is composed of a number of functional elements. At minimum, these elements involve a mission, input processes, output processes, a formal organizational structure, and control mechanisms. Collectively, these elements are interrelated and interact with each other to provide direction and motion for a school district.

In addition to the functional elements comprising a school system, a school district is composed of subsystems (individual schools) and homogeneous functions (planning, curricula, logistics, human resources, and external relations). Both the school system at large and each subsystem need certain common information and certain unique information to function effectively and efficiently in an ever-changing environment. Information is intimately and indelibly linked to planning, organizing, directing, and controlling the overall system as well as separate subsystems by which it is comprised.

It is a given that information plays a critical role not only in maintaining the daily life of an organization but also in providing for the organization's survival and development. Figure 3.1 illustrates the concept of unification of subsystems within an organization through information. Five major functions of a school system, shown in Figure 3.1, are linked to each other and to the system as a whole by means of an integrated **information system** (Castetter, 1996).

The concept of information integration may be illustrated by reference to the human resource function and such subfunctions as human resource planning, recruitment, selection, compensation, and appraisal. Human resource planning involves establishing objectives and goals that stem from the basic mission statement

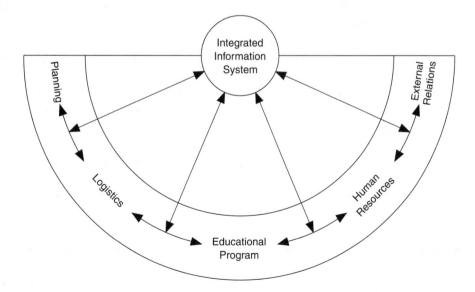

FIGURE 3.1   *Human resource subsystem interactions with other organizational subsystems.*

of a school district. Objectives and goals depend, at least in part, on information about current activities and capabilities of the school system.

Recruitment activities should be related to the objectives and the goals derived from the mission statement of a school district. Information is needed about current staffing capabilities and staffing needs to tailor future recruitment efforts. A non-directed recruitment program serves neither potential applicants nor the system at large, and a directed recruitment program requires information.

Selection involves choosing among applicants generated through a tailored recruitment program designed to attract specific types of job candidates. To select from among those candidates seeking employment with a particular school system or with a specific work site within the school district, a variety of information is needed. Information is needed about applicants as well as about vacant positions.

After selection is completed, information is needed for establishing levels of compensation for newly hired employees. Compensation information is required about the external market and about internal rules and regulations governing compensation processes and practices within a particular school district. As ultimately determined for successful job candidates, compensation reflects both an ability to pay and a willingness to pay, both of which require extensive information.

Once employed, individuals must be appraised in their job performance. Appraisal is not an isolated activity but relies on contextual information. Contextual information is needed about the job and about the candidate for appraisal to be a meaningful activity within the total employment process.

As can be surmised from the foregoing elaboration, recruitment, selection, compensation, and appraisal activities cannot be performed effectively without information pertaining to personnel planning. Hence, there is an interdependence of personnel activities within the human resource function. The need for integration among the major functions shown in Figure 3.1 becomes readily apparent when, for example, newly appointed personnel are to be fully integrated within the ongoing operation of a school system.

A school system, like other organizations, is composed of purposes, people, plans, tasks, technology, and a structure for fitting its parts together. The ability of the system to function effectively and efficiently depends on the bonding of these elements because each element has an impact on other elements and thus on the whole. Interaction of the various parts to achieve broad system purposes is effected through an integrated information system. Information makes it possible to link individualized but coordinated action plans for positions, sections, departments, units, and schools into the overall mission of the system.

Architecture of the Human Resource Information System

Implicit in the administration of any organization is the realization that it is an entity in which people perform tasks in order to achieve established outcomes. School systems fail to be an exception to this generality. The work to be done in school systems is structured into jobs (e.g. instruction); into groups (e.g. elementary schools); and into specialized work such as accounting, clerical, maintenance, operation, and administration.

Each of the previously mentioned structures must be managed. Management has been characterized by Herbert (1981) as being comprised of three categories. These categories involve authority to direct actions, decisions about which actions to follow, and informational needs to direct both authority and decisions. Of these three categories, management relies most heavily on information.

To ensure that school administrators have the quantity and quality of information necessary for overseeing the operation of a school district, an information system is required. Figure 3.2 illustrates common components of an information structure for the human resource function within a school setting. These components include system information, position information, person information, human resource function information, and the information communication network.

These sources of information, when interconnected, provide the framework or structure of an information system. The **database** structure referred to previously is employed through a variety of information channels to enlist member support for making clear ideas about what results are expected and to identify ways and means by which outcomes are to be achieved. Each of the components of a human resource information system, as portrayed in Figure 3.2, is reviewed in the following sections of this chapter.

System Information

The school system acquires, creates, and disseminates information to bring individuals, groups, and the system into congruence with its strategic direction and to enlist

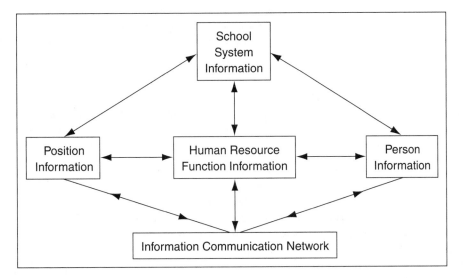

FIGURE 3.2   *Types and interdependence of school system information.*

the support of members to reach higher levels of performance in their assigned job duties. This type of information is used to create an institutional vision of expectations, as well as to establish purposes, structures, plans, policies, programs, and projects for their realization. System information is directed toward shaping specific organizational guides such as codes of ethics, reporting relationships, performance standards, rules, regulations, responsibilities, and controls for internalizing this aspect of system culture and the behavioral boundaries involved.

Position Information

A position is defined as a collection of tasks constituting the total work assignment of a single employee. A position or job description prescribes its purpose and scope, major duties and functions, performance standards, authority, relationship to other positions, terms of employment, and position value (relative monetary worth and authority of the position in the organizational hierarchy). However, positions are governed, to some extent, by applicable legislation and regulations beyond contents contained in a formal position description.

From the standpoint of the human resource function, a collection of job descriptions creates the foundation for virtually all human resource activities. A very useful tool in the human resource function is to create a single source that contains all the position descriptions within a public school district. This source could include a manual or an online listing, but most important is that this source of position information be accessible readily to all employees.

Person Information

Person information is included in a document referred to as a *position specification.* A position specification includes information about the qualifications needed to occupy the position and about factors such as legal requirements (certificate, license, degree), experience, major area of study, health, disability, literacy, citizenship, aptitude, and a variety of additions, including residence within the community. This latter information as contained in a position specification is more detailed than the information found in a position description (both are discussed in more detail in subsequent chapters of this text).

Human Resource Function Information

As can be observed within Figure 3.2, the human resource function occupies a central location. The human resource function receives information from the other informational sources. In return, the human resource function outputs information back to the other informational sources.

Within the input–output process performed by the human resource function, several types of communication are involved. Each type of communication of information travels through a network. We turn our attention to the last box in Figure 3.2—the information communication network.

Information Communication Network

In any organization, information is provided by a communication network. Figure 3.2 emphasizes the principle that a communication network is the tie that binds the organization and operation of a school system. Communication of information allows interaction and interchange among system members and subsystems of a school system. No school system could operate effectively, even for a short period of time, without acquiring and disseminating information about its human resources—those persons who enter, remain in, or leave the school district.

School systems are constantly confronted with information communication problems centering on such matters as keeping abreast of the need for information (both in quantity and in quality), making information accessible to users as needed, and furnishing information to position holders that will help them achieve the position objectives for which they are employed. Isolating key communication system elements enables us to gain a better understanding of the sources of information and the course or flow of its direction. Facets of a communication system that are directly relevant to the school system and its operation are: (a) modes of communication, (b) direction of communication, and (c) formality of communication.

Modes of Communication

Within any school district, several modes of communication exist for delivering and for receiving information. Information can be communicated through an oral mode, written mode, and/or visual mode. Each mode of communication is used extensively by all school systems.

Oral communication is used to transmit and to receive information in every human resource function. For example, oral information is the major mode of communication in all types of interviews (recruitment, selection, appraisal, and exit) and in many strategic planning activities. With the growing popularity of active teleconferencing, oral communication has expanded greatly within the public school setting.

Written sources of communication comprise the majority of the human resource database in a school system. Basic to written sources of information are such elements as personnel handbooks, policy manuals, bulletins, memos, web pages, annual and periodic **reports**, circulars, computer printouts, and personnel forms, which cumulatively represent the written personnel record system. These sources of information provide much of the context for human resource decision making.

Visual information is growing in usage within the human resource domain. Most of this growth can be attributed to advances in video technology. Video conferencing for meetings and instruction is becoming a common human resource tool, while video recording is used for performance evaluation and for performance enhancement of employees.

Direction of Communication

According to Ivancevich and Matteson (1993), the flow of information through communications can be considered in terms of at least three different directions: (a) downward, (b) upward, and (c) horizontal. Direction of communication has an impact on the authority of information. For example, downward communication within the organizational structure includes official statements or plans such as policies, procedures, personnel manuals, memoranda, bulletin boards, and various other types of written information (e.g., a board of education's response to a teacher union contract proposal). Downward communication tends to carry a great deal of authority.

Upward communication within the organizational structure involves message senders rather than message receivers. Its use provides the school administration with information about current problems and issues and encourages personnel participation and involvement (e.g., the teacher union's response to the board of education's proposal for sharing benefit costs). Horizontal communication involves sharing information among peers or other employees occupying the same level within the organizational hierarchy.

Formality of Communication

Within a communication network information can be characterized as either formal or informal. Formal information represents the official stance of a school district relative to particular issues. Examples of formal information found in a communication network include budgets, **audits**, strategic plans, employment contracts, school taxes, and occasional legal issues confronting the system.

Informal communication, sometimes referred to as the *grapevine,* is a means of generating off-the-record information through peer relations. Although this type of information is unofficial, by definition, it can be very influential in the operation and administration of a school district. Indeed, informal information provides opportunities for expressing viewpoints, giving suggestions, challenging improper management actions, and allowing ideas to flow upward to draw official attention.

Despite the array of modern communication technology available for use in school administration, an intractable organization communication problem is unilateral communication, the downward (one-way) transmission of information without benefit of feedback. Experience indicates that both downward and upward flows of communication are essential for an effective information system in today's school system. To complete the information communication network involving upward and downward information cycles, consideration must be given to the demand for and the supply of information available to the human resource function.

Demand for and Supply of Human Resource Information

A distinguishing characteristic of school districts during the 21st century is the demand for information. Information demands exist for large school districts and

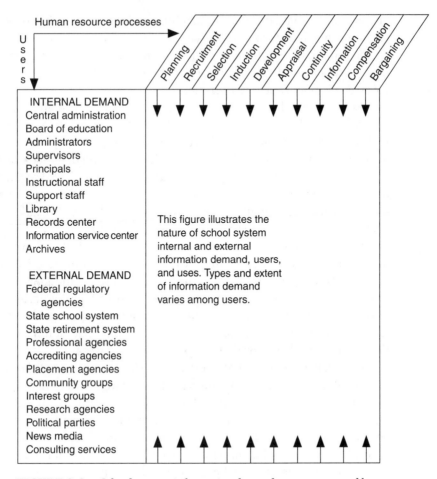

Human resource processes

Users

Planning Recruitment Selection Induction Development Appraisal Continuity Information Compensation Bargaining

INTERNAL DEMAND
Central administration
Board of education
Administrators
Supervisors
Principals
Instructional staff
Support staff
Library
Records center
Information service center
Archives

EXTERNAL DEMAND
Federal regulatory
   agencies
State school system
State retirement system
Professional agencies
Accrediting agencies
Placement agencies
Community groups
Interest groups
Research agencies
Political parties
News media
Consulting services

This figure illustrates the nature of school system internal and external information demand, users, and uses. Types and extent of information demand varies among users.

FIGURE 3.3 *School system information demand, users, uses, and human resource processes.*

small school districts located in urban, suburban, and rural settings. These demands will continue to exist with little foreseeable abatement.

Within the total information demands experienced by public school districts, informational needs of the human resource function occupy a large portion. The nature and variety of information needed to conduct the human resource function can be inferred from the outline of information needs shown in Figure 3.3. More specifically, there is an insatiable demand from within and outside of the system for an extensive array of human resource information to: (a) conduct day-to-day operations, (b) resolve short- and long-term personnel problems, (c) comply with external demands, (d) satisfy system needs for research and planning data, and (e) plan for and implement collective bargaining agreements.

Because school administrative units are becoming more sophisticated during the 21st century, the demand for more and varied types of information has increased. The necessity for creating, collecting, processing, storing, retrieving, disseminating, and integrating data to aid in the administration of an organization is hardly a matter for debate. It is becoming increasingly clear that sole dependence on the time-honored manual system of **data processing** is no longer appropriate to keep a modern educational institution abreast of the informational requirements necessary for an efficient and effective operation.

As more school administrative units become large enough to offer comprehensive educational programs, it is inevitable that improved data processing methods will be employed to integrate information for major areas of the school system—*instruction, funds, facilities,* and *personnel.* The operation of a modern school system, with all the organizational, legal, political, governmental, and social ramifications, has caused the volume of essential records and reports to soar. To cope with problems of record keeping and to make effective use of records that are collected and stored, a new approach to records management is needed.

This need can be met, in part, by making technological improvements in the information system as used by most school districts. Innovation can and should be geared not only to improvement of the human resource function in general, but also to the welfare of each individual employed in the system. Considerable advances have been made in the use of electronic data processing procedures to facilitate collection of data and dissemination of information for decision making that will aid the system as well as improve the work life of employees.

These advancements make possible the storage and retrieval of highly detailed and organized personnel data that are useful as well as necessary in administering the human resource function within the school setting. Although it is true that many personnel decisions cannot be programmed, it is reasonable to assume that personnel decision making can be improved by data that are better organized, more accurate, more complete, and more available. Without reliable and valid data for human resource decision making, much is left to chance.

Surprisingly, it is rare to find a school district that has an information system capable of providing, on demand, information on various personnel and related aspects such as employee data, contractual agreements, regulatory requirements, litigation, disclosure, decision fairness, discrimination, and personnel file access and records. Few systems can readily and fully meet information demands such as those noted, as well as those listed in Figure 3.3. The gap between information supply and demand in many institutions can be due to a variety of problems. Many of these problems can be linked to the absence of reliable records, outdated records, fragmentation of record creation and record keeping, needless files, record duplication, and inattention to transforming quantitative data into qualitative information.

Moreover, and most important, the absence of a centrally directed and appropriately staffed records management program often leads to the inability to resolve satisfactorily questions or disputes about discrimination; personnel performance; salary, wage, and benefit issues; disciplinary actions; and unauthorized disclosure of personnel data. Failure to modernize an information system is an open invitation to a host of human resource problems and charges because of a lack of appropriate information to resolve challenges such as those mentioned. In view of these potential problems, records and records management will be covered in greater detail in the section that follows.

Records and Records Management

The location of records and of the record-keeping function for both the school system and the human resource function is significant. Their importance as components of an information system is linked to meeting legal and contractual requirements, providing data resources, and providing a foundation for carrying out both decision-making and operational activities. An initial understanding of the place of records, records management, and their employment in the human resource function involves an explanation of how certain attributes relating to records are defined.

Any form of recorded information is a **record.** The information may be recorded on paper, microfilm, audiotape, computer generated, or other media. Records are, fundamentally, a means of storing facts or events needed to solve human resource problems. They represent vital activities relative to the human resource function and create essential information material.

Records are stored in a record center. A **records center** is defined as a storage area for records, which can be located on-site within the district or off-site away from the district. Within a records center, records are grouped into files. A *file* is a device (e.g., a folder, case, or cabinet) where papers or publications (records) are arranged or classified in convenient order for storage, retrieval, reference, or preservation purposes.

Every school district must maintain two types of files. One type of file is referred to as an active file, and these files contain information that is necessary to inform ongoing decision making. The other type of file is referred to as an archive and contains information that is seldom used but required to maintain.

Most sources of information needed to construct records for the human resource function are derived from two sources. One source of information involves operational information needed to inform ongoing human resource decision making. The other source of information involves archival data.

Operational information is obtained generally through various data sources within the district. Many of these types of data are obtainable from standardized forms. Examples include forms for employment application, personnel requisition, application identification, employment eligibility, job interest, employment interview, reference check, credit inquiry authorization, applicant flow, job descriptions, performance reports, and signature receipts of handbooks (job description, policy, information, personnel).

Archival data are available through various sources, and an **archive** is a place where public records or historical documents are preserved. In many instances, what was once referred to as operational information becomes archival information. For example, employee application forms serve as operational information during the search process but become archival data after the close of the search process.

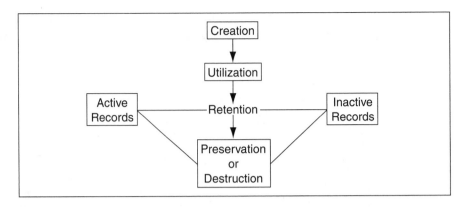

FIGURE 3.4   *Life span attributes of records.*

Figure 3.4 presents the sequence of activities in the life span of records. The sequence begins with records creation. Creation of data, which are later transformed into information, is exemplified by applications for employment, as well as files on current or former employees, medical records files, and computerized personnel files.

Data from the sources noted include facts transformed into information. Decisions on personnel selection, compensation, turnover, performance, termination, promotion, tenure, and benefits are transformed from raw data into information. Active records are those for current employees and applicants, while inactive records are those stored, especially on former employees and applicants, and capable of ready retrieval.

Records are retained or destroyed depending on their legal, administrative, fiscal, historical, or archival significance. Organizational records, such as board of education minutes, contracts, property deeds, leases, and insurance policies, are considered to be vital records and are included in the preservation category (Diamond, 1995). Other records, such as application information and certain budget documents, have a sunset provision that determines the specific period of time this information must be maintained by a school system (time requirements vary by state, reference to state code).

With the emphasis on information and information management, it is ironic that many educational institutions have been criticized for their information systems. Underlying these criticisms are four potential reasons: (a) misunderstanding the importance of comprehensive personnel information for human resource management, (b) proliferation of demand for school system information, (c) failure to capitalize on advances in electronic data processing, and (d) failure to staff the information system properly.

A first step toward rectifying the potential problems is to establish policy guidelines for records management. Policy guidelines should transcend specific technologies and should focus on the purpose of records management. The purpose of records management is to retrieve from the computer or from the file drawer any item needed for operational and human resource function purposes.

Development of policy guidelines or revisiting existing policy for records management provides school districts with the opportunity to address many worthy issues in this general area. Following are some of the issues that must be addressed:

- Possibly appointing professional personnel such as an information systems director and an office service manager, either full or part time, depending on the school system's size, to direct the records management program
- Setting forth policy guidelines for record categories in areas of the human resource function (see Figure 3.5 for an example)
- Appointing record coordinators for work units such as attendance units (individual schools), central administration, and support services
- Developing a system for documenting personnel decisions as a basis for defending charges relating to termination, appraisal, layoff, and employment discrimination
- Meeting statutory requirements for record storage and maintenance
- Utilizing electronic data processing technology when and where appropriate
- Including school system record forms and reports as components of the records program
- Setting aside space to accommodate a records center for storing and retrieving vital, inactive, and archival records
- Issuing a records management manual containing policies, practices, and procedures for directing, controlling, and auditing the system's plan to make the program effective and efficient

In closing this brief discussion of records and records management, it is worth noting that the sophistication of an information system depends on a number of factors affecting its design and operation. There is virtually no limit to the type of information that can be created, stored, used, and employed effectively. In the following section, we explore different types of technology within the information management context.

Information Technology and the Human Resource Function

As noted earlier, **technology** refers to the totality of means employed to achieve the aims of the human resource function as well as the broader mission of the school system. Included within the information technology context are skills, knowledge, tools, mechanisms, techniques, and know-how to carry out the function's objectives. When a broad definition of technology is applied—namely, the application of organized knowledge to inform the **information process** including every form of recorded information, electronic and nonelectronic, programmed and nonprogrammed, computer hardware and software, supported and supporting activities, and information specialists—the meaning of information technology becomes more apparent.

As the term is employed in the discussion that follows, technology refers to a wide range of administrative and instructional devices, including but not limited to

It is the policy of the Riverpark school system to maintain an information system to facilitate the creation, refinement, reporting, utilization, storage, retrieval, and protection of recorded information. Key components include:

- *Purpose.* Establish a course of action to guide and determine present and future decisions concerning all aspects of the human resource information system. Improve individual, unit, and system effectiveness, decision making, and information processing efficiency. Establish paper-based and computer-based records to satisfy both internal and external information requirements.

- *Scope.* Create a uniform filing plan within the central information system to locate and retrieve any record readily, whether the file is centralized or decentralized. Institute guidelines governing the scope and boundaries of administrative decisions pertaining to the collection, storage, retrieval, retention, access, distribution, and disposition of human resources information.

- *Responsibility.* Set forth human resources information guidelines for administrative responsibilities in the central administration, attendance units, and support units relative to the scope of information described above. Place overall operational responsibility in one office, with a systemwide purview, to oversee the progress of human resource information through the several stages of its life cycle (*active, inactive,* and *archival*). A records center and or an information service center becomes the responsibility of the position (supervisor of records). Prepare a system records manual to communicate to employees the manner in which the information system operates at both the central and work unit levels (individual schools, departments, and offices). System members, as part of the information network, are instructed in standard uniform filing procedures.

- *Access.* Identify which classes of information are restricted, how access to restricted categories is granted, who has the authority to grant access or release which categories of information, and what controls will govern photocopying or other means of recorded reproduction.

- *Budget.* Include funding in the annual budget to maintain and improve the effectiveness of the information system.

- *Individual employee file.* The individual employee database consists of three files (*basic file, evaluative file,* and *supervisory file*).

  Basic file: Objective material and no third-party evaluation or personal opinions. Employment profile, payroll, work data, etc.
  Evaluative file: Performance data regarding employment retention tenure, probationary review, and position effectiveness. Destroyed within 5 years after decisions.
  Supervisory file: Confidential property of supervisor. Destroyed after supervisor's death, termination, or retirement.

- *Regulatory.* Adhere to regulatory provisions governing employee records and privacy safeguards.

FIGURE 3.5 *Information policies, practices, and technology of the Riverpark school system.*

computers, networks, videocassette players and tapes, distance learning, cable, radio, microwave transmission, telephones for learning and data transmission, online services, and many combinations of these methods. Part of an information system is a technology plan, especially as it applies to the human resource function. Assessment of the characteristics of existing technology regarding the human resource function includes what technology is currently in operation; how it is being used; what forms are being used in administration, instruction, and support services; how personnel are being trained or retrained; and responsibility for managing information technology.

Human Resource Information and the Computer

It has been said that information technology is the most revolutionary force in modern times. The list of changes being propelled by information technology is striking. In the corporate world, for example, the advent of the facsimile machine made Western Union obsolete in the field of overseas communication.

Similar changes have occurred within the public school setting. Within the public school setting, a cost projection for a salary schedule used to take hours to complete using hand calculators. At present, it takes less than a second to calculate cost projections for a salary schedule using computers.

Likewise, tracking, accumulating, and summarizing employee attendance saves hours of manual labor when using electronic equipment. Applicant tracking, payroll preparation, position control, individual employment files, and résumé scanning can be added to the repertoire of human resource activities for which information can be compiled from various records, analyzed, and presented in a standard format by using modern technology. In fact, all of the human resource functions can be enhanced through application of appropriate technologies.

While the debate in education over school reform, outcome-based education, and site-based decision making goes on, emerging and enhanced technologies and technological opportunities are revolutionizing the world. Education has been slow, however, relative to the business world in adopting new innovations within this area. It is clear that more extensive application of technology to school district information systems and human resource subsystems is needed if educational organizations are to play an essential part in the information revolution, which is bidding to change information creation from a paper to a paperless endeavor.

Computer Availability and Application

For a human resource information system to be effective and efficient, it must be capable of providing the types of information required by those making human resource decisions within a public school district. A human resource system should be designed so that all authorized personnel have available to them information—information of the quality and quantity needed to inform decision making. In addition to the needs regarding the quality and for the quantity of information for human resource decision making, this information must be timely or it may be rendered useless in many instances.

To meet the quality, quantity, and timeliness criteria requires the use of computers for many human resource issues. In order to determine the manner and the extent to which a computer should be linked to an information system, several factors must be considered. Among the more significant factors are: (a) the types of information needed for the human resource function to operate effectively, (b) the strengths and limitations of a computer in providing desired information, (c) the role of a computer in the information system, (d) the people who will select and design software for making the key decisions about processing informational needs, and (e) the procedures and processes employed to optimize computer applications within the educational setting.

The types of information needed for the human resource function to operate effectively depend on the questions being asked by human resource persons. For example, if the question being asked is, what will our enrollment be in 5 years (planning function), then many enrollment projection techniques rely on historical data in the form of enrollment patterns. If the question asked is, what is the average teacher salary (compensation function), then current data and different software are required to calculate this statistic.

It is important to determine what the computer can provide in each of the human resource areas that would be readily attainable through other sources. In some instances, answers to questions may exist without having to rely on an automated system. A key issue to be determined is how the human resource function can take full advantage of computer capabilities for informing decision making.

Strengths as well as limitations of computer applications within the human resource function must be taken into consideration. Computers are readily adaptable to provide selected types of information, save work time, and increase the accuracy of information. A computer can be viewed as a way to extend the human mind, enable it to identify personnel problems, and make wider application of data for informing decision making in a timely fashion.

For example, timely information makes it possible to take corrective action, to initiate investigative action, or to take steps for resolving difficulties before these difficulties escalate into major problems for an organization. In effect, the capabilities of today's computers are numerous and far-reaching insofar as computers enable the system to gather, process, and apply information that in years past was too expensive, too labor intensive, or, in many respects, beyond the power of existing information systems. What in many respects was impossible just a few years ago for school systems to achieve relative to information processing has become routine in many school systems today due to computers and advancement in software applications.

Although the usage of computers has enhanced greatly the information flow and processing within the human resource area, computers are not without limitations when considered as only part of a total information system. Most important, the concept of an information system, as will be noted subsequently, *embraces more than computer application.* Moreover, usefulness of a computer depends on the types of programs and software that have been chosen by decision makers.

Within the public school setting, many of the advances involving artificial intelligence have yet to arrive. As such, computers cannot define personnel system information needs nor can computers make those personnel decisions that are a never-ending organizational responsibility. Nevertheless, computers have become an invaluable tool within the human resource area.

Computerized Human Resource Information Systems

Information derived from both internal and external sources has altered increasingly the decision-making process within the school setting. This alteration is compelling school leadership to upgrade continually the systematization, utilization, and communication of information throughout the school district. Decisions involved in improving an information system within the school setting include two kinds of approaches—strategic and tactical.

The strategic approach involves an information system that supports leadership action to achieve the system's mission, while the tactical approach refers to the technology employed to achieve the system's strategic goals (Meltzer, 1971). Both approaches play an important role in the design and operation of an effective and efficient information system within the school setting. The discussion that follows addresses computer technology as a tactical component of the information system utilized to create, control, and communicate information to support a school system's actions that benefit the system, district personnel, and the children and youth for whom the system is educationally responsible.

As a tactical component of the information system, computer technology has and continues to advance at a rapid pace. Advancements are occurring in the internal hardware of computers. Personal computers, either desktop or laptop, have data processing and data storage capabilities that were associated with only large mainframes just a few years ago. Because of the increased capabilities associated with desktop and laptop computers, information management has been delivered to the fingertips of most school administrators.

Accompanying hardware developments are software developments. Figure 3.6 presents a partial list of the many software programs and areas of the human resource function where these programs are applicable. One impression derived from viewing the software programs listed in this figure is that we have entered a new and entirely unprecedented age of emerging information system technology.

So many technical advances have occurred in computer hardware and software that school administrators, as well as human resource practitioners, are compelled to become computer literate. Literacy about an information system is essential in order to make sound decisions about what information technology is available for a given

Age Discrimination Law	Employee Absenteeism
Applicant Tracking	Employee Accident, Illness
Archival Records	Employee Appraisal
Attendance, Employee	Employee Communication
Benefit Administration	Employee References
Career Development	Human Resource Consulting
Compensation Administration	Human Resource Management
Computer-Based Recruiting	Information Retrieval
Computer-Based Testing	Job Descriptions
Computer-Based Training	Medical Records
Data and Survey Analysis	Personnel Communication
Document Imaging	Position Control
Disabilities Act, American	Position Description

FIGURE 3.6   *Types of computer software applications for the human resource function.*

school system, how the technology should be used, and who will be responsible for its implementation and daily operation. The section that follows provides a structure for considering problems and issues about the extent to which the present information system should be modified or transformed electronically and managed to satisfy human resource needs relating to data gathering and processing, information management, instruction, staff development, communication, and decision support.

The Human Resource Information Process

A general model for analyzing the human resource information process is found in Figure 3.7, and this model can be viewed as an organizational mechanism through which efforts are made to achieve a desired state of operation relative to personnel information in the school setting. Within this model, the human resource information process is characterized as being composed of five separate but interrelated phases. These phases are as follows: (a) diagnosis, (b) preparation, (c) implementation, (d) evaluation, and (e) feedback.

The first phase of the information process model outlined in Figure 3.7 is *diagnosis*. This phase of the model for the information process is designed to assess the extent to which the present information system is providing essential data for achieving the objectives and the goals of the human resource function within the school setting. Diagnostic efforts within this phase of the model should focus on questions relating to what information is now collected, the ability of the system to retrieve information easily and economically, the level of information accuracy and sophistication, the relationship of the information system to the size, structure, goals, and organization style, and the quantity and quality of information needed at the operating and planning levels.

In addition to the specific issues just described, more general issues are broached during this phase of the information processing model for human resource needs. For example, general issues consist of questions such as, is the general system ac-

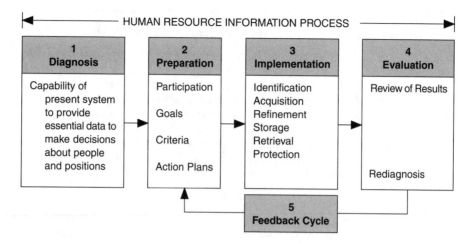

FIGURE 3.7   *Model of the human resource information process.*

ceptable, is the system operating as it should, should the current system be revised, is a new system needed, and should processing be centralized or decentralized? Figure 3.8 illustrates some of the questions involved in determining which aspects of the human resource information system may need improvements.

Information obtained in the diagnosis phase is used in the preparation phase of the human resource information process. The second phase is concerned with translating the diagnoses of phase one (diagnosis) into decisions that lead to a series of action plans to improve the personnel information system. Central to the preparation phase is a set of goals for the human resource information system. The following are examples:

- Improvement and enhancement of the information system for collecting routine data, computerizing these transactions wherever possible
- Elimination of information duplication
- Elimination of useless information
- Standardization, wherever possible, of methods for gathering information
- Justification of information from the standpoints of efficiency and effectiveness
- Improvement in availability, accuracy, flexibility, consistency, accessibility, and utility of information
- Systematization of collection of nonroutine data
- Involvement in the design of the information system of key people who will actually use both routine and nonroutine types of data
- Development of criteria that will govern identification, acquisition, refinement, storage, protection, and retrieval of information (see Figure 3.7)
- Organization and administration of the human resource information system in an effective and efficient manner (The information system should be part of a master plan to use funds, facilities, people, technology, and machines to achieve system objectives. This means appointment of knowledgeable

Human Information Inadequacies

- How adequate are the records in the information system regarding human problems in such areas as recruitment, selection, induction, appraisal, development, justice, compensation, continuity, and union relations?
- To what extent is information accessible regarding grievances, transfers, discharge, discrimination, communications, rewarding, discipline, tenure, promotions, resignations, level of technical competency, medical visits, strikes, alienation, job satisfaction, work stressors?
- Does the information system indicate which of the human resources problems are position related? Nonposition related (personal)?

Nonhuman Information Inadequacies

- *Technology Information Inadequacies*—Which of the following factors are considered to be obstacles to achieving desirable information system standards: money, materials, facilities, personnel, and equipment?
- *Record-Keeping Inadequacies*—To what extent are the following record-keeping facilities adequate: records creation, processing, automation, retention and disposal, security, legal requirements, records management, forms management, records center, and archives?

Organizational Information Inadequacies

- How effective are school system provisions regarding the design, implementation, maintenance, and evaluation of the human resource information system? Regarding interfacing with other system functions?
- To what extent does the system utilize tools of human resource research to gather information about the effectiveness of the information system? (questionnaires, interviews, audits, reports, statistics, critical incidents, comparative studies, historical analyses, and individual and work unit responses to information communication)

Organizational Impact of Information System Inadequacies

- What is the organizational impact of the information inadequacies on the well-being of the human resource function?

Organizational Implications for Action Planning

- What actions should the system take to remove inadequacies in the human resource information system?

FIGURE 3.8 *Probing for inadequacies and issues in the human resource information system.*

personnel with authority to manage the information system, update the plan annually, and focus on specific objectives for hardware, software, personnel, budgets, space, and applications.)

Contained in Figure 3.9 are areas of the human resource function and the applications of these areas to a human resource information system. As can be ob-

Human Resource Areas	Illustrative Applications
• Planning ⟷	Strategic plans, structure projection, employee inventory, employee projections, assessment of impact of internal and external forces.
• Information ⟷	Position control, internal–external communication methods, information manuals (position descriptions, policy, personnel, compensation).
• Recruitment ⟷	Applicant tracking, positions and persons data, technology for assessing potential, recruitment policies, practices, procedures.
• Selection ⟷	Information technology for matching person qualifications and position requirements.
• Induction ⟷	Information, plans to assist inductees in adjusting readily to position, work unit, and system relationships, organizational culture and ethics.
• Development ⟷	Information, plans, and activities designed to enhance or improve employee's current skills and performance; self-awareness and self-development feedback, career movement and counseling.
• Appraisal ⟷	Information technology relating to appraisee–appraiser performance reviews, critical incidents, behavioral checklists, narrative accounts, supervisory reports.
• Compensation ⟷	Information on how compensation is derived and distributed. Rules governing salary, wages, benefits, bonuses, incentives, rewards, position–person worth.
• Continuity ⟷	Information concerning tenure, disability, leaves, health and safety, employee assistance, transfer, reassignment, termination, promotion, demotion, absenteeism, substitution, retirement, death.
• Justice ⟷	Information on employment security, fair treatment, due process, grievances, academic freedom, justice system, ombuds practitioner, legal rights.
• Unionism ⟷	Information relative to bargaining process, scope, contract design, system–union rights and responsibilities, contract administration, arbitration.

FIGURE 3.9   *Areas of the human resource function and their applications.*

served in this figure, each area has multiple applications, and information generated for one human resource function can serve another human resource function. To illustrate, information obtained from performance appraisals can inform human resource decisions relating to development, compensation, and selection.

Within the present context, information may be viewed as either programmed or nonprogrammed depending on the use of this information by other human resource functions. Certain data can be computerized, as illustrated in Table 3.1, but other information of a conceptual, hypothetical, or judgmental nature is not readily amenable to computer programming by today's standards. However, both types of information are shown in Table 3.1, and both types of information are necessary for decision making within the human resource context.

TABLE 3.1
Illustration of programmed and nonprogrammed personnel information.

Programmed Information		Nonprogrammed Information
Payroll	Résumé	Personnel policies and procedures
Benefits	Certification	Performance appraisals
Attendance	Positions	Personnel motivation
Retirement	Master files	Personnel actions
Grievances	Tax reports	Organizational actions
Skills inventory	Turnover	Organizational structure
Personnel budget	Leaves	Personnel planning premises
	Compensation profile	Strategies and supporting plans
	Personnel statistics	

After the school system has defined the objectives of the personnel information system, determined what kind of information is needed, reviewed information sources and acceptance criteria as outlined in Figure 3.3, and allocated responsibilities for administering various activities related to the system, the next phase (implementation) of the personnel information process can be initiated. This third phase, as outlined in Figure 3.7, consists of six key activities: identification, acquisition, refinement, storage, retrieval, and protection. Each of the foregoing activities is important for the design and implementation of a human resource information system and is examined within the context of the human resource information process in the following sections of this chapter.

Identification of Information

The initial activity in the personnel information process, as depicted in Figure 3.9, is identification of information needed by a human resource information system. A primary focus of this activity in phase three of the implementation of the human resource information process is on implementing decisions required by the central administration governing what information is needed to achieve the goals of the system; purposes for which the information is needed; who will use the information; and what means shall be employed to gather, store, retrieve, and communicate information most effectively and efficiently for human resource decision making. Consequently, the initial act in the information process during this phase is the central administration's conceptualization of the type of personnel information system the school system plans to operate to influence personnel behavior in ways conducive to goal attainment.

This perspective, focusing on goal attainment as outlined in Figure 3.7, which construes the purpose of all information, needs to be mission oriented. School administration, as viewed in Figure 3.7, should link information to actions necessary for accomplishing various goals identified previously by the system. Some of the information will indicate what has happened in the past, some of the other information will focus on what is happening at present, and still some of the other information needed should focus on the future. All three types of information, regardless of temporal orientation, should be directed toward influencing the behavior of people for satisfying both individual and system needs.

Acquisition of Information

Information acquisition, as noted in the personnel information process shown in Figure 3.7, follows plans for identification of needed information that is linked to objectives of the system, as well as the objectives of users' needs (including the needs of administrators, staff, board, clients, and the public). Acquisition of information includes identification, selection, development, and, in many instances, purchase of source material. Source material, as noted previously, includes many forms of oral, written, and visual information.

When choosing among source information for inclusion in a human resource information system, acquisition of information should be governed by criteria such as purpose, value, relevance, completeness, cost, validity, reliability, and timeliness. Of these various criteria that can be used to determine what information is acquired for incorporation into the human resource information system for a school district, timeliness is the criterion most often overlooked. Timeliness, or the currency of data, is an important criterion in determining whether information should be acquired.

For example, a personnel roster is of little use to the payroll department if it is not kept current. Information files on recruitable talent, promotable personnel, and position holders who have reached performance plateaus are useless if this information has not been updated. Use of information on collateral benefits for administrative personnel in collective bargaining will be determined, for example, by its timeliness and by the aforementioned criteria.

Up-to-date information is expensive to maintain. Although always desirable, this information must be judged in terms of the cost/benefit concept. Certain kinds of information cost more money to obtain than other kinds of information, and the worth of all information must be judged in terms of benefits to the system within the human resource decision-making context.

Refinement

Most data acquired by the system need to be refined, some to a greater and some to a lesser degree, before data are stored for retrieval and usage. Refinement includes checking data for accuracy. Information on paychecks, retirement contributions, and certification of personnel, for example, must be precise.

Complete and accurate information concerning the skill of every staff member is essential to conduct the human resource planning process efficiently and effectively. On the other hand, any data collected should include only those items the system really needs, inasmuch as the collecting and storing of information is a relatively expensive undertaking within the school setting. Far too often, data are collected by school districts that have little utility for informing decision making within the human resource context.

Other types of data refinement processes include editing all forms of information entering the human resource information system, eliminating redundant information or overlapping information-gathering efforts, and incorporating error checks into the information system in order to call attention to missing or erroneous data. In effect, the purpose of refining information is to ensure that data meet the acceptance criteria mentioned earlier in this chapter. Refinement is conceived as a kind of screen to separate useful from useless information, to code and prepare acceptable information for entrance into the information system, to ensure that the information is valid and reliable, and to bring together one form of data with another form of data, which combined, will create new information and perhaps new perspectives that were not possible before the information was related through a human resource information system.

The concept of information refinement includes many and varied activities aimed at acquiring and storing data in forms that enhance the work of the system. Refinement of data may include editing information inputs (such as payroll verification), combining quarterly performance appraisal reports for a performance profile, employing statistical techniques for meaningful summary descriptions of raw data, and drawing inferences from personnel data under conditions characterized by uncertainty. Information refinement helps to make complex system phenomena more understandable and, in some cases, enables the system to achieve a new level of understanding about managing human resource problems as well as capitalizing on human resource opportunities.

Storage

After information has been identified, acquired, and refined, arrangements must be made to store this information for future usage by the human resource information system and in a manner that informs human resource decision making. As shown in Figure 3.3, information can be stored in manual systems, microform systems, or electronic systems. Manual storage systems include direct files, inverted files, optical coincidence cards, edge-notched cards, and punched cards. Microform storage systems include rolls of film, microfilm jackets, aperture cards, microfiche, and opaque micro-cards.

An electronic storage system is one that processes data by electronic machines quickly, accurately, and automatically. Data processed by a computer are stored on memory devices, such as magnetic tapes, compact discs, Zip discs, hard drives, and floppy discs. These storage mechanisms are not unfaultable and should be backed up in several ways in the event of a system crash or computer virus.

The decision as to which system or combination of systems will be used to store personnel information will depend on a variety of factors, including size of staff, uses to be made of the information, availability of fiscal resources, and whether or not there are competent staff personnel to design and operate the system. Because the primary function of a personnel information system is to provide information when it is needed, where it is needed, and in the form in which it is needed, the storage system should be designed to enhance these objectives. Generally speaking, manual and microfilm storage systems are used to record historical information, and a mechanized storage system is used to address current information needed by the human resource function.

Usage of multiple information storage systems is common practice in school districts because a variety of information is needed to inform human resource decisions. Some of the information needed for human resource decision making is amenable to a mechanized system of storage, while some of the other types of information needed for human resource decision making may not be amenable to a mechanized system of storage. A point to consider is that mechanized storage of certain kinds of information, such as the historical performance profile of an individual staff member, may be prohibitive from a cost standpoint when attempting to codify specific information.

Retrieval

Information retrieval, one of the activities in the implementation of the human resource information process as outlined in Figure 3.8, refers to methods and procedures for recovering specific information from stored data. It goes without saying that information users should be able to retrieve stored information readily and in the form needed for decision making. Sadly, for many school districts, retrieval of information is a difficult process, and, in many instances, information retrieved may be in a form that fails to inform human resource decision making.

Information stored manually, for example, is sometimes irretrievable because the procedures employed in storing this information lacked appropriate organization. Information not properly classified, indexed, and coded will create problems when retrieval queries are posed. Consequently, one of the requirements for operating an effective information storage-retrieval system is training staff personnel in procedures for classifying, indexing, and coding all incoming material.

Retrieval begins with a search strategy or a probe designed to locate information to solve problems posed by the user of a human resource information system. This search strategy includes evaluation of stored information to determine its relevance to such problems. The search is conducted also with consideration for the breadth and depth of information needed.

The foregoing observation indicates that there are various constraints affecting the search for and retrieval of human resource information, including time, funds, and personnel. Because information is the substance that holds an organization together and keeps the organization viable within external and internal markets, designing the storage-retrieval system and training personnel to operate the information system efficiently and effectively are matters of prime importance to the administrative team.

Protection

Any public school district and some private school systems receiving federal funds must be concerned about privacy issues relating to a human resource information system. Information contained within a human resource information system is subject to certain federal and state laws concerning information access. Federal laws applicable to information contained within a human resource information system are the Freedom of Information Act of 1966 (United States Department of Justice, 1966), amended in 1974, and the Privacy Act of 1974 (United States Department of Justice, 1974).

The Freedom of Information Act requires government agencies to make available certain records that are requested by the public, and the Privacy Act is designed to resolve problems relating to disclosure, recording, inspection, and challenges to information maintained by government agencies or political subdivisions. Accompanying these federal acts are state laws addressing accessibility to public information.

Because the Freedom of Information Act applies only to federal agencies, states have developed their individualized set of laws pertaining to public information. These laws have been labeled as "sunshine laws" and address both access to public records and open meeting requirements. Most of the state legislation is modeled after the Freedom of Information Act.

In view of the existing legislation concerning access, school districts should develop policies for protecting the integrity of data contained in a human resource information system. These policies should indicate what records may be disclosed, by whom, and for what purposes; how disclosures are to be recorded; what controls on individual inspection of records; and resolving disagreements about stored information. General guidelines for the policy formation process include the following:

- Set up policies and guidelines to protect information in the organization: types of data to be sought, methods of obtaining the data, retention and dissemination of information, employee or third-party access to information, release of information about former employees, and mishandling of information.
- Inform employees of these information-handling policies.
- Become thoroughly familiar with state and federal laws regarding privacy.
- Establish a policy that states specifically that employees and prospective employees cannot waive their right to privacy.
- Establish the policy that any manager or nonmanager who violates these privacy principles will be subject to discipline or termination.
- Avoid fraudulent, secretive, or unfair means of collecting data. When possible, collect data directly from the individual concerned.
- Do not maintain secret files on individuals. Inform them what information is stored on them, the purpose for which it was collected, how it will be used, and how long it will be kept.
- Collect only job-related information that is relevant for specific decisions.

- Maintain records of individuals or organizations that have regular access to or request information on a need-to-know basis.
- Periodically allow employees to inspect and update information stored on them.
- Gain assurance that any information released to outside parties will be used only for the purposes set forth prior to its release (Cascio, 1998; Cook, 1987).

Evaluation and Feedback

The human resource information process outlined in Figure 3.8 includes *evaluation* and *feedback* as activities essential to its operation and improvement. Every organization should assess how well the system as a whole and each of its subparts are achieving assigned objectives. This is accomplished through assessment procedures by which the outcomes achieved are compared to the outcomes desired.

When meaningful differences are detected between achieved and desired outcomes, remedial action is warranted. Specific information to be gleamed from the assessment process should provide answers to the questions that follow:

- Is the present system operating effectively?
- Do portions of the present system need to be preserved or modified?
- Is the system providing information that enhances the operation of the human resource function?
- How well does the system respond to changes in the environment relative to data collection?
- Do information security tests meet the criteria emphasized in the Privacy Act (see Glossary)?
- Does the human resource information module interface properly with the total organization information system?

Securing answers to these questions involves various types of diagnoses, including determining what the major problems in the information system are, forces causing the problems, nature and timing of the changes needed to resolve the problems, goals to be brought about by the change, and how goal attainment will be measured. Through evaluation and feedback, needed improvements in the information system can be brought about. These improvements will facilitate organizational decisions regarding personnel processes, policies, and the organization's structure.

Review and Preview

This chapter on information technology and the human resource function points out that five major functions of a school system (planning, educational program, logistics, human resources, and external relations) are linked to each other and to the system as a whole by means of an integrated information system.

1. The human resource function, as one of the modules of a total information system, consists of a planned network of forms, files, reports, records, and documents.

2. In order to determine the manner and extent to which the computer should be linked to a personnel information system, factors that bear analysis include the kinds of information needed to effectively contribute to personnel practice, the strengths and limitations of computers in providing essential information, the role of computers in the personnel information system, the people who will create the data designs and make the key decisions about their processing, and the procedures and processes needed to optimize computer applications.

3. The personnel information process, as modeled in this chapter, consists of five phases: diagnosis,

preparation, implementation, evaluation, and feedback.

4. Policy points or protocols for bringing about order, method, and uniformity in the personnel information system include policy purpose, scope, responsibility, access, and active–inactive records.

5. Information technology is viewed not as a cure all for the system's human resource problems, but as an investment in strategic advancement and as an enabling factor in extending the performance capabilities of the position holder, the work unit, and the system at large.

In the next chapter, the processes focus on strategic human resource requirements (numbers, skills, abilities, experience), followed by two stages—screening and selection. Both phases are viewed as being interconnected and interdependent.

Discussion Questions

1. Describe the structure of the human resource information system in your school organization.

2. When is oral communication the preferred method of communication in the organization? When is written communication preferred? When is graphic communication preferred?

3. How can an organization close the gap between information demand and supply? What structures should be initiated to close the gap? How can technology be utilized to close the gap? What is the impact of organizational culture on this gap?

4. Information flow can be considered in terms of four directions: (a) upward, (b) downward, (c) horizontal, and (d) diagonal. Consider the direction of communication you encounter in your work in a school organization. How does the content and tone of communication differ with direction?

5. Has computer technology increased access to the organizational information system, or has it decreased access? Has computer technology increased the efficiency of the organizational information system? Why or why not?

References

Cascio, W. F. (1998). *Managing human resources* (5th ed., pp. 548–549). New York: McGraw-Hill.

Castetter, W. B. (1996). *The human resource function in educational administration* (6th ed., p. 418). Upper Saddle River, NJ: Prentice Hall.

Cook, S. H. (1987). Privacy rights: Whose life is it anyway? *Personnel Administrator, 32*(4), 58–65.

Diamond, S. D. (1995). *Records management* (3rd ed., pp. 2–3). New York: American Management Association.

Herbert, T. T. (1981). *Dimensions of organizational behavior* (2nd ed., p. 38). New York: Macmillan.

Ivancevich, J. M., & Matteson, M. (1993). *Organizational behavior and management* (3rd ed., pp. 638–639). Homewood, IL: Richard D. Irwin.

Meltzer, M. F. (1971). *The information imperative,* (pp. 2–3). New York: American Management Association.

United States Department of Justice. (1966). *The Freedom of Information Act.* Retrieved August 30, 2002, from the U.S. Department of Justice Web site: **http://www.usdoj.gov/04foia/foiastat.htm**

United States Department of Justice. (1974). *The Privacy Act of 1974.* Retrieved August 30, 2002, from the U.S. Department of Justice Web site: **http://www.usdoj.gov/04foia/04_7_1.html**

Supplementary Reading

Galvin, W. (1996, Spring). Communications: The lever of effectiveness and productivity. *Daedalus, 125,* 137–147.

Hurst, B., Wilson, C., & Cramer, G. (1998, April). Professional teaching portfolios: Tools for reflection, growth, and advancement. *Phi Delta Kappan, 79*(8), 578–583.

Lawson, J. W. R., Jr. (1997). *How to develop an employee handbook* (2nd ed.). New York: American Management Association.

Pipho, C. (1998, March). The search for better education information. *Phi Delta Kappan, 80*(3), 422.

Pitone, L. (1994). Employee records. In W. R. Tracey (Ed.), *Human resources management and development handbook* (2nd ed., pp. 467–477). New York: American Management Association.

Roberts, B. (1998, June). Software selection made easier. *HR Magazine, 43*(7), 44–47.

Schuler, R. S. (1998). *Managing human resources* (6th ed., chapt. 3). Cincinnati, OH: South-Western College Publishing.

Spencer, L. M., & Page, R. C. (1994). Management information systems. In W. R. Tracey (Ed.), *Human resources management and development handbook* (2nd ed., pp. 467–477). New York: American Management Association.

PART II

HUMAN RESOURCE PROCESSES: RECRUITMENT, SELECTION, INDUCTION, DEVELOPMENT, PERFORMANCE APPRAISAL, AND COMPENSATION

Part II examines six major human resource processes: recruitment, selection, induction, development, performance appraisal, and compensation. The intent of Part II is to expand our understanding of the key activities that make up organizational staffing. These activities include the following:

- Generating applicant pools
- Matching individual talents with present and future positions
- Adjusting and developing system members
- Assessing the performance of employees
- Establishing and maintaining a compensation system

4

Recruitment and Selection

CHAPTER OBJECTIVES

Develop and describe a model for recruitment of human resources.
Describe the relationship between public and system employment policies.
Provide information about applicant attraction strategies.
Develop an overview of the selection process.
Stress the importance of acquiring knowledge about selection technology.
Demonstrate the linkage between recruitment and selection processes.

School districts must identify, attract, acquire, and retain competent personnel to be effective as an organization in providing education to America's youth. Unfortunately, acquiring and retaining competent personnel necessary for accomplishing the mission of a school district has become more difficult in recent years (Pounder & Merrill, 2001). This seems to be true especially for urban school districts.

"Although teacher shortages affect schools across the country to varying degrees, urban school districts are facing unique challenges, owing to rapidly growing student enrollments, accelerating rates of teacher retirements, class size reduction initiatives, and demanding working conditions" (Fideler, Foster & Schwartz, 2000). As one leading reform group has noted, no longer can school systems count on a captive market of bright, energetic minority members and women. These persons now have attractive alternatives in business, industry, and other professions (Holmes Group, 1995).

Because of changing labor market conditions for many individuals as job candidates, school districts must compete both with other organizations and with other school districts for these applicants. To compete successfully, school districts must become proficient in attracting and selecting only the most capable personnel. Activities associated with attracting and selecting personnel are encapsulated under the human resource tasks of recruitment and selection.

Although recruitment and selection are related human resource tasks, each task serves a distinct purpose and warrants specific differentiation within this text. **Recruitment** concerns those activities associated with generating an applicant pool. **Selection** involves those activities concerned with reducing the pool of applicants and choosing from among the final job candidates.

For both recruitment and selection, attention must be given to diversity and to competency of individuals comprising the applicant pool. Effective recruitment will produce a pool of capable applicants that exceeds in number the vacant positions to be filled, and effective selection will optimize the fit between individuals and jobs. The importance of these tasks is noted by Winter (1997), "If educational leaders are not consistently competent in recruiting and selecting qualified and motivated individuals, efforts to improve the quality of education are bound to fail" (p. 88).

Recruitment

Recruitment involves both short- and long-range planning activities. Short-range activities are needed to meet current demands for personnel that exist in every organization, whereas long-term activities are designed to ensure a future supply of qualified personnel. Both short- and long-term activities are important because an extensive and aggressive program of recruitment is critical to the effectiveness of the organization.

The link between the human resource planning process (discussed in Chapter 2) and satisfaction of the demand for personnel through the implementation of that process is illustrated in Figure 4.1. This figure indicates two key elements in human resource planning: *positions* and *individuals.* Both of these elements are dynamic and vary according to internal and external environments.

Because of changes in positions and in individuals, we shall first discuss coordination of public employment policy, system policy, and recruitment policy. Our purpose is to stress that effective recruitment must be sensitive to changes and must be guided by the intent of policies. It is through the activities of the recruitment process that the system attracts candidates to fill anticipated position vacancies. Each of

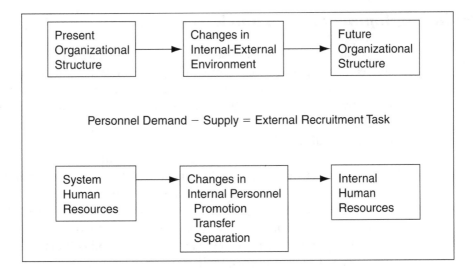

FIGURE 4.1   *Perspective of multiyear human resource planning for an educational system.*

these activities is examined as an interdependent element, along with other components of the planning system. It is important to emphasize that effective recruitment can minimize problems that may follow the *selection* and the *placement* of personnel.

There is a set of internal and external environmental circumstances, facts, and events—the recruitment contexture—that must be considered in developing recruitment strategies and the programs and the processes by which these strategies are implemented. Many of these factors must be determined long before the recruitment process reaches the individual applicant. Some of these factors involve administrative actions on the part of employees; other factors require policy directives by boards of education.

Administrative actions are generally warranted in situations where decision makers require data on specific recruitment alternatives and in situations where procedures are needed to implement certain policies. Data are needed concerning immediate and long-range staffing needs, as illustrated in Chapter 2, and for assessing diversification of the present workforce. Based on the information provided by administrators, school boards should formulate specific recruitment policies and practices.

Most important, recruitment policies are needed in situations where more than one acceptable alternative exists and where each alternative produces a unique outcome. The task of the school board is to evaluate the impact of various recruitment alternatives for the district and to develop recruitment policies and practices for guiding the district. By approving certain recruitment policies and practices, boards of education set both the tone and the direction for recruitment activities.

Public Employment Policy and Recruitment

All public school districts must follow mandated public employment legislation in the recruitment and selection of employees. Failure to do so may bring about judicial sanctions for the district and for those responsible for decision making within the district. As such, those responsible for the recruitment and selection of employees must be knowledgeable about federal and state legislation pertaining to the recruitment and selection processes.

Federal and state legislation pertaining to recruitment and selection is designed to prohibit discrimination, and, in some instances, to correct past discrimination. It does so by identifying certain individuals or groups on the basis of definable characteristics such as gender, race, age, and so on. Individuals or groups possessing at least one of these definable characteristics are afforded protection from discrimination within the employment context, if discrimination within the employment context is related, at least in part, to the defined characteristics.

Individuals covered by these legislative acts are said to have protected class status. The general term **protected class status** replaces the earlier term **minority**

TABLE 4.1
Federal laws influencing selection.

Title VII Civil Rights Act **http://www.eeoc.gov/laws/vii.html**	Americans with Disabilities Act **http://www.usdoj.gov/crt/ada/adahom1.htm**
Age Discrimination in Employment Act **http://www.eeoc.gov/laws/adea.html**	Section 504 of the Rehabilitation Act **http://www.hhs.gov/ocr/504.html**

TABLE 4.2
States with sexual preference clause.

California	Massachusetts	New Jersey
Connecticut	Minnesota	Rhode Island
Hawaii	Nevada	Vermont
Maryland	New Hampshire	Wisconsin

within the general human resource literature due to the categorical inclusion of females as protected class individuals. Because females represent the majority gender and have protected class status as defined by Title VII of the Civil Rights Act, the term *minority,* within the human resource context, is no longer applicable.

Examples of some of the major legislation defining protected class status are found in Table 4.1. This list is by no means exhaustive but it is meant to be illustrative and contains only examples of some federal laws particularly applicable to the recruitment and selection processes in the public school setting. These laws, many of which have been in existence for decades, establish minimum requirements for recruitment and selection within the public sector but have been overlooked by many public school districts in actual practice.

In addition to the requirements as set forth by existing legislation, states and school boards can define additional protected classes as long as these newly defined protected classes do not conflict with those characteristics addressed by existing federal legislation. For example, several states have awarded protected class status on the basis of sexual preference (see Table 4.2). Because federal legislation is silent with respect to sexual preference, these states have expanded the legal obligations for public school districts within the recruitment and selection process.

To guide the recruitment and selection process, school boards must adopt district policies prior to executing any recruitment or selection activities. One important policy concerns whether the school district will be proactive or reactive relative to protected class groups within the recruitment and selection process. That is, a school district can adapt an equal employment opportunity perspective (proactive) or an **affirmative action** perspective (reactive). The difference between these policy perspectives has a profound influence on the actual recruitment and selection practices exercised by a school district.

The equal employment opportunity perspective is proactive. "As applied to staffing, EEO refers to practices that are designated and used in a 'facially neutral' manner, meaning that all applicants and employees are treated similarly without regard to protected class characteristics such as race and sex" (Heneman, Judge, & Heneman, 2000, p. 62). This perspective implies that recruitment and selection practices, procedures, and policies will be based solely on the principle of merit and that recruitment and selection practices will be followed without regard to the protected class status of individuals.

Unlike the equal opportunity perspective that is facially neutral, the affirmative action perspective favors certain protected class groups. Justification for this favoritism is rooted in correcting past injustices incurred by protected class groups. To correct past injustices, a school board can adopt recruitment and selection policies that give preferential treatment to certain protected class groups using an affirmative action policy.

To illustrate the difference between the equal employment opportunity and affirmative action perspectives, consider the following examples. An equal employment opportunity policy would state that "all recruitment and selection decisions will be made without regard to any protected class status." On the other hand, an affirmative action policy would state that "if a protected class individual and a non-protected class individual are deemed to be equally qualified for employment, preference will be given to the protected class individual."

Depending on the school board's choice between the equal employment opportunity perspective or the affirmative action perspective, a specific message is communicated and a specific legal responsibility is established. Problems, including legal difficulties, may occur when the actions and intentions of school boards and system employees are counter to the school board's formal employment policy. For example, if a school board adopts the equal employment opportunity perspective and later gives preferential treatment to individuals on the basis of their protected class status, then a violation has been committed. Likewise, if a school board adopts the affirmative action perspective and later fails to give preferential treatment to an equally qualified protected class person, then a violation has been committed.

System Employment Policy and Recruitment

Recruitment is an essential part of a comprehensive human resource plan. The more today's school administrators consider the educational problems they are expected to solve, the more clearly they realize that they cannot succeed unless the organization is competently staffed. Effective solutions to many recruitment problems depend, to a large extent, on the employment policy of the board of education.

To be meaningful, personnel policies should be written, should inform every individual and agency of system standards, and should minimize uncertainties within the employment process. Without policy guidelines for decisions and actions concerning personnel matters, inconsistencies that develop will cause dissatisfaction and will defeat the aims of the human resource function. Furthermore, policy guidelines provide for the continuity of the personnel process even when administrators and school board members leave the school district.

As noted previously in this chapter, policies related to recruitment and selection should not be formulated in a vacuum. Factors external and internal to the school district must be considered when formulating policy. One external factor that must be considered is the relevant labor market because the relative labor market determines what the composition of a school district should be for different protected class groups.

The relevant labor market is a legal term. It is defined as the distance that an applicant could reasonably be expected to travel for employment consideration when seeking a position. Importantly, distance, as used in defining a relevant labor market, is related only to the consideration of an applicant for employment, not to the daily commute once an individual is employed.

Because different kinds of applicants (clerical versus teachers) could be expected to travel varying distances for employment consideration, the relevant labor market varies by position within a school district. For some positions, the distance may be only a few miles (clerical), while for others it may be several hundred miles (teacher). Consequently, for any particular protected class group, their representation in the composition of a district's workforce varies by occupational grouping rather than being a fixed number for the school district at large.

It is interesting to note, however, that the composition of the educational staff is not directly related to the composition of the student body, at least from a legal perspective. At first glance, this may appear to be detrimental for diversifying school systems. However, to link diversity of staffing to student diversity would be more detrimental because many districts across the nation have few, if any, diverse students.

In addition to the external assessment of relevant labor markets for protected class persons, an internal assessment should be made relative to the distribution of protected class persons employed by a school district. This latter assessment should reflect the number of protected class persons employed by the district and the types of positions held by protected class persons within the district. By obtaining data on the number of persons employed and the types of positions they hold, the school board can assess the organizational distribution of protected class persons within a district and can tailor their recruitment and selection policies accordingly.

Data concerning the relevant labor markets for different positions and for the distribution of protected class persons within a school district are captured by two different statistics: (a) a **stock statistic,** and (b) a **concentration statistic.** Stock statistics provide information about the employment of protected class persons in relation to the relevant labor market for these persons. Concentration statistics provide information about the assignment of protected class persons at various organizational levels within the district hierarchy.

Stock statistics and concentration statistics should be calculated for each group of protected class persons within the relevant labor market. Without this information it

TABLE 4.3
Stock and concentration statistics of a hypothetical school district.

Applicant Stock Statistics			
Current Elementary Teachers		Available Elementary Teachers	
Nonprotected	Protected	Nonprotected	Protected
95%	5%	80%	20%

Applicant Concentration Statistics			
	Job Categories		
	Support	Instructional	Administrative
Females	90%	60%	10%
Males	10%	40%	90%

is unlikely that a school district can formulate adequate recruitment and selection policies necessary for attracting and retaining a diverse group of employees. To illustrate stock and concentration statistics, we have used an aggregated group for all protected classes rather than addressing each specific group of protected class persons separately, as would be done in the field setting (see Table 4.3).

The stock statistics in Table 4.3 indicate a distinct difference in the distribution of protected class persons employed by the school district and available in the relevant labor market. The percentage of protected class persons employed by the school district is only 5% relative to the total workforce, while the percentage of protected class persons relative to nonprotected class persons in the relevant labor market is 20%. This difference between those available and those employed indicates an underutilization of protected class persons relative to their availability.

To illustrate concentration statistics, only three broad categories of positions are used in Table 4.3. In actual practice, concentration statistics should be compiled also in a manner that reflects career progression. This involves dividing broad employee groupings in some meaningful ways.

The administrator group should be divided according to line and staff positions, as well as according to organizational levels of employees. For example, elementary school principals differ from secondary school principals in some very important ways, and concentration statistics should reflect these ways. Elementary school principals tend to earn lower salaries, to be employed for fewer days during the contractual work year, and to have a different career progression (80% of superintendents have a secondary school background).

The concentration statistics in Table 4.3 provide additional insight into the internal staffing patterns of protected class persons employed by the hypothetical school district in question. Protected class persons are reasonably well represented

TABLE 4.4
Policies and procedures related to recruitment and selection.

Nondiscrimination (race, creed, religion, national background, age, gender, disability, etc.)
Fairness in promotions, transfers, and separations
Position postings
Seniority preferences
Correction of staff imbalances within the system
Fairness in recruitment inquiries
Credential requirements
Skill inventories
Special persons (relatives, minors, part-time and temporary personnel, strikers, and rehires)
Position guides
Probationary employees
Proselytizing
Outside employment
Gifts and favors
Candidate information requirements
Testing

---

in support positions but are underrepresented in administrator and teacher positions. Consequently, these data indicate some organizational segregation based on the protected class status of employees.

The data provided by stock and concentration statistics guide boards of education in formulating systemwide policies for recruitment and selection. This information should be used in determining whether the system will be an equal employment opportunity employer or an affirmative action employer. It can also be used to guide the development of other policies and procedures that impact recruitment and selection, such as those listed in Table 4.4.

The Recruitment Process

As Figure 4.1 indicates, action plans and the structure for the recruitment process are derived from the *strategic plan.* In effect, the process model is based on the assumption that decisions have been made through strategic planning concerning the number of positions needed, requirements for the positions, and reallocation of human resources. The *operational plan,* which is derived from the strategic plan, identifies the actions to be taken once the demand for and supply of human resources have been reconciled within the overall strategic plan.

Although the responsibility for several tasks involved in the recruitment process depends in part on the organizational structure of a school district, we can identify two features that characterize most successful recruitment efforts. These features are coordinating recruitment with the human resource plan and formalizing communication between the system and applicants.

Attracting Applicants

Recent research suggests that some school districts may have problems attracting applicants (Winter & Morgenthal, 2002), and these school districts must work particularly hard to attract applicants. As such, many applicants must be induced to change their place or position of employment through an intensive and extensive recruitment system. Clearly, the more intensive and extensive the recruitment system, the higher the cost and, it is hoped, the greater the return on expenditures.

Recruitment policies, established by boards of education with the advice of system employees, provide direction for the actual recruitment efforts of a school district. However, many school districts fail to consider the decisions of applicants, as individuals, when formulating and implementing recruitment policies and practices. This omission on the part of employers can have an adverse impact on the recruitment outcome. If applicants fail to react favorably to recruitment efforts, school systems will have trouble taking advantage of the opportunities afforded by staffing needs and acquiring the best available talent in a competitive labor market.

Research on the reactions of applicants to recruitment efforts is relatively new in the professional literature. This research shows that job candidates make decisions about organizations in much the same manner as organizations make decisions about job candidates. Consequently, if school districts are to be competitive in the labor market, they must consider those factors that influence the decisions of applicants to join an organization.

The decisions of applicants have been found to be influenced by several different recruitment and selection practices. Some of these practices include: (a) the personal orientation of individual applicants, (b) the recruitment message, and (c) the recruiter. Each of these sources of influence can play an important role in shaping successful recruitment practices in the school setting.

Personal Orientation of Applicants

Several different theories exist about the personal orientation of applicants. These theories differ with respect to the basic motivation of applicants and the needs that applicants seek to fulfill when choosing among school districts and jobs as a source of employment. Because of the differences among these theories of personal orientation, each theory has distinct implications for the recruitment and selection processes in a school district.

One personal orientation theory, often referred to as the **objective theory** of job choice, assumes that applicants are economic beings (Behling, Labovitz, & Gainer, 1968). According to this theory, applicants view the job search process as a means of maximizing their economic return. To maximize their economic return, applicants are sensitive to the economic incentives and fringe benefits offered by competing school districts or jobs.

Another personal orientation theory, the **subjective theory** of job choice, views applicants from a psychological perspective. This theory assumes that applicants have certain psychological needs and use the job search process as a means to fulfill these needs. Judge and Bretz (1992) noted that "individuals who match job or organizational values to their own are more satisfied and less likely to leave the organization" (p. 286). From the subjective theory perspective, individuals are sensitive to issues relating to the organizational climate and to the work environment when choosing among competing school districts.

Still another personal orientation theory, different from either the objective or the subjective theory of job choice, is the **work itself theory.** This theory describes individuals as rational beings in the job search process who seek information about the job tasks associated with potential employment opportunities. As such, information about the different job elements, job expectations, and actual tasks becomes important to applicants during the job search process.

Depending on the specific theory or theories of job choice favored by a school system, directions are provided for molding the recruitment process. Each theory provides information for writing recruitment messages and developing a recruitment strategy. The choice of one theory over another depends on its particular advantages for the school system.

Obviously, if a school district is extremely low in economic incentives relative to other districts, it would be unwise to stress economic incentives in either recruitment messages or recruitment literature. In fact, Bretz and Judge (1998) found that "the highest quality applicants may be less willing to pursue jobs for which negative information has been presented" (p. 330). Rather, school districts should trumpet those areas in which the district excels.

Recruitment Message

Attracting applicants to fill positions involves considerable communication between the organization and the candidates. One type of communication directly controlled by the employer is the content of the recruitment message (Rynes & Barber, 1990). Research on this topic has shown that both the content of the recruitment message and the medium used to deliver the recruitment message can have a decisive impact on the job choice of candidates.

The content of a recruitment message can vary in some important ways. "There is a large number of potentially relevant attributes, and the attributes themselves may vary in numerous ways" (Young, Rinehart, & Heneman, 1993). Recruitment messages can be constructed to reflect both positive and negative attributes of the employment opportunity, as suggested by *realistic job preview* (RJP) literature (Wanous, 1992); to reflect either general descriptions of attributes (competitive salary) or specific descriptions of attributes ($50,000 salary), as found in policy research (Rynes & Lawler, 1983); or to reflect homogeneous groupings of attributes, as suggested by different theories of job choice (Young, Place, Rinehart, Jury, & Baits, 1997).

Recruitment messages are communicated to job candidates through several different media. Traditionally, these media have included job advertisements in newspapers and professional trade journals, video presentations at recruitment fairs, and interviews conducted by a system representative. More recently, many school districts have begun to use the Internet to reach potential job candidates.

Although little research exists on the effectiveness of the Internet for reaching job candidates, several studies are available to help school districts shape recruitment messages and determine the medium to be used to communicate messages. Recruitment messages have been systematically manipulated and have been assessed with three types of candidates: (a) inexperienced teachers seeking their first position, (b) experienced teachers considering another position, and (c) potential administrators for public school positions (Pounder & Merrill, 2001). Reactions to recruitment messages have been assessed for position advertisements and for recruitment interviews (Winter & Morganthal, 2002).

It has been stated that "Advertising a vacancy is your first significant opportunity to save time, improve the quality of your applicants, and reduce the cost of your selection process" (Jackson, n.d.). However, certain position postings, such as those used for job announcements, are more effective than others. Effective position announcements identify a specific contact person, address candidates directly ("you should . . ."), and acknowledge applications by a telephone call. Ineffective position announcements identify an office to contact, use impersonal language ("applicant" rather than "you"), and fail to provide a means of acknowledging applications (Winter, 1996).

Like position postings, certain recruitment messages are more effective than others when delivered during an interview by system representatives. Recruitment messages that present information about either the work environment of a school district or the work itself increase applicants' willingness to follow up and accept employment offers. Interestingly, recruitment messages that emphasize economic incentives associated with a school district or a particular job have been found to be particularly ineffective with teachers (Young et al., 1997) but not with school administors (Pounder & Merrill, 2001).

The Individual Recruiter

Regardless of how the recruitment effort is organized, it is likely that several persons will be assigned to make initial contacts and to negotiate with applicants. The significance of the recruiter to the success of the operation is not always understood or appreciated. Consequently, the school system must take several steps in selecting and training recruiters.

At some point in the recruitment process, decisions are made about which personnel will be assigned to represent the school district as recruiters. In larger school districts, this task is usually handled by the director of human resources. In smaller school districts, it is shifted among personnel so as not to overburden any particular individual. However, research on the impact of recruiters in attracting applicants suggests that recruiters should be chosen very carefully.

Well documented in the recruitment literature is the impact of the recruiter/organizational representative on the perceptions of job candidates (Rynes, 1991). In fact, many job candidates have indicated that they chose to join a particular organization because of the person encountered during the recruitment process. Given this finding, research has sought to distinguish between effective and ineffective recruiters.

The most predominant effect found to differentiate between effective and ineffective recruiters is the personality characteristic of personnel warmth (Rynes, 1991). Personal warmth of organizational representatives has been explored by both having applicants rate their perceptions of representatives on a single Likert type scale and by having organizational representatives complete a standardized personality inventory (see Young & Heneman, 1986). In each instance, effective recruiters possessed more personal warmth than ineffective recruiters.

Additional research has shown that recruitment effectiveness can be increased by considering the race and gender of recruiters, as well as the race and gender of applicants, when determining recruiter responsibilities and when writing recruitment messages. One study found that "Black applicants preferred female organizational representatives presenting recruitment messages emphasizing work environment attributes and work itself attributes. White applicants preferred male organizational representatives presenting recruitment messages stressing only work environment attributes" (Young et al., 1997, p. 87). Such recruitment studies provide support for different recruitment strategies for attracting educators.

In summary, every school system must carefully consider the selection and orientation of recruiters who have personal contact with applicants. Moreover, the organization should make sure that the recruiter is fully aware of what is expected. The system should do the following:

- Identify those persons who will be responsible for contacting and discussing with applicants the vacancies to be filled.
- Make every effort to ensure that the recruiters have the knowledge, the interpersonal competence, and the verbal skills essential to the role.
- Standardize the role so that the recruiter will follow definite procedures, such as giving relevant information to each candidate about the organization and about the particular position of interest.

Developing Sources of Applicants

A major objective of personnel recruitment is to improve the quality of the staff. This requires several kinds of analysis to identify imbalances in the makeup of total staff and in the number and types of openings available on both short- and long-term bases. Although the system will probably need to recruit some personnel from outside sources, it is also sound policy to promote and transfer current staff members.

It should be clearly understood that certain types of positions provide no advancement and that certain individuals are satisfied to remain indefinitely in the

TABLE 4.5
Sources for recruiting prospective external candidates.

Professional associations	Placement agencies	Unions
Walk-in candidates	Write-in candidates	Consulting firms
Advertising	Resumes on file	Government agencies
Referrals	High schools	Vocational schools
Technical schools	Conventions	Direct solicitation
Colleges	Specialized career centers	Military services

same position. However, the general policy of promotion from within to better and more attractive positions is to be encouraged. Often overlooked is the fact that "current employees are potential candidates for whom the largest amount of job information is available" (Pounder & Young, 1996).

The manner in which positions are filled from the inside depends on the personnel procedures of the school system. Two methods are generally used: administrative assignment and position posting. Under the first method, personnel within the system capable of advancing to a more desirable and/or higher level position are identified and assigned by management. Under the second method, personnel within the system are encouraged to apply for a more desirable and/or higher level position using their own initiative.

External personnel sources are numerous and varied. The extent to which these sources can be used depends largely on the school system's recruitment policy and plans. If the recruitment effort is to succeed, it must produce a pool of applicants well in excess of the number of openings; otherwise, a selection process exists in name only. Major external sources of supply are listed in Table 4.5; some of them pertain to professional personnel and others to support personnel.

If the system is to attract a pool of qualified candidates from the external sources listed in Table 4.5, a plan for developing each source must be developed. Schools with large numbers of vacancies will utilize different external sources and employ techniques that differ from those preferred by smaller systems. Those employees who operate the recruitment program need to anticipate which sources will provide the greatest number of qualified applicants, how much time and money should be invested, and what methods should be used to attract competent individuals.

Coordinating the Search for Applicants

The recruitment activity moves from the planning stage to the goal realization stage when permission is given to spend recruitment funds. This step begins the applicant search process and necessitates control. This process refers to activities involved in monitoring the progress of each candidate at various steps in the recruitment and selection processes.

Two dimensions of recruitment are essential concerns. The first is *control*, which involves assessing how well the school system's recruitment plans are being achieved and developing courses of action to correct deficiencies. The second dimension is *effectiveness,* which involves checking recruitment performance against standards and linking strategic aims to the recruitment process. Recruitment control primarily involves an internal analysis of the recruitment process; recruitment effectiveness focuses on how well the recruitment process contributes to the strategic aims of the system for its human resources.

Careful accounting of recruitment expenses is essential for preparing the budget and for providing information about costs. In addition to recruitment expenses for personnel (professional and secretarial), there are operational expenses: advertising, communications (writing, telephone calls, and faxes), travel and living expenses, medical fees (physical examinations), printing supplies, and equipment. After the total recruitment costs have been calculated, unit costs, such as cost per applicant employed, cost per applicant by source, cost by recruiter, cost per contact, and cost per professional employee versus cost of support employees hired, are some of the indicators that may be analyzed to get a clear view of the cost of recruitment.

The costs associated with certain activities and certain sources will reveal that some activities and sources are more productive than others. The system is interested in knowing what personnel sources yield the best-quality personnel and at what cost. It is understandable, for example, that the most satisfactory professionals might not be acquired from the nearest teacher education college. It is also conceivable that advertising might provide better secretarial personnel than an employment agency.

The aim of controls is to make certain that recruitment results are in keeping with established goals. If goals are to be met, the collection, analysis, feedback, and use of relevant recruitment information are essential. Evaluation is useful to: (a) extend information about and understanding of issues, problems, obstacles, and opportunities in human resource planning; (b) assess the strengths and weaknesses of the existing strategy; (c) identify new conditions in the internal and external environments and their potential impact on the human resource function; and (d) consider the interrelatedness of strategy, recruitment, work to be done, skilled personnel to do the work, environments, and fiscal resources.

As the process of securing competent personnel moves from recruitment to the selection phase, a number of formidable problems confront the human resource administration:

- Establishing role requirements
- Determining what data are needed to select competent individuals from the pool of applicants
- Deciding what devices and procedures are to be used in gathering the data
- Securing staff participation in appraising the data and applicants
- Relating qualifications of applicants to position requirements
- Screening qualified from unqualified applicants

In brief, one important facet of the human resource function is designing, initiating, and carrying out an effective selection process. Failure to recognize this fact will result in a less than effective recruitment process.

Selection: Purpose, Scope, and Challenges

The purpose of selection is to fill vacancies with personnel who meet the system's qualifications, appear likely to succeed, will remain in the system, will be effective contributors, and will be sufficiently motivated. In addition to these purposes, a properly planned selection process has an additional benefit. This is, the system is able to eliminate candidates who are unlikely to succeed before they become employees.

"Many times, selection is equated with one event, namely, the interview. Nothing could be further from the truth if the best possible person/job match is to be made" (Heneman et al., 2000, p. 368). By definition, selection is a process rather than an event in which one individual is chosen over another individual through a series of decisions. However, before we consider various steps in the selection process, the reader must be cautioned against presuming that selection processes are always perfectly accurate.

Indeed, how to select the best-qualified candidate for an unfilled position is a perennial organizational problem. The selection process is fraught with possibilities for serious errors that can be costly to the school system, the community, the taxpayers, and the pupils. However, many of these potential errors can be minimized or eliminated by developing and applying a selection system based on scientific knowledge.

The Selection Process

Whether a school system is small or large, it is easy to make a compelling case for valid selection procedures because a great deal of time, money, and effort is wasted when people selected for positions fail to meet the organization's expectations. Furthermore, the impact of poor teaching on children is so serious that the selection process in education has been and continues to be a critical issue. By increasing the quality of employees in our nation's schools, it is hoped that tomorrow's youth will be better prepared to function productively in society (Pounder, 1988).

Often overlooked is the fact that a selection process should be tailored to meet the unique characteristics of a school district. What constitutes effective performance in one school district does not always translate to effective performance in another school district. Urban school districts, suburban school districts, and rural school districts vary greatly in demands and needs for educational programs as well as types of students served.

Although the content of a selection process should be varied to meet the special problems, needs, and characteristics of every school system, certain steps within

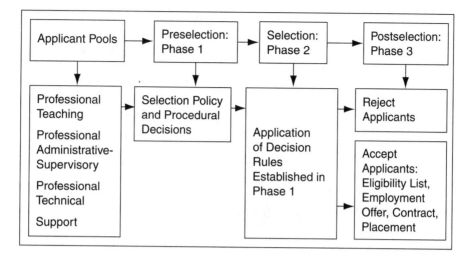

FIGURE 4.2 *Model of the human resource selection process.*

the process are universally applicable. As indicated in Figure 4.2, the first steps in effective personnel selection are the development of employment policies and the recruitment of applicant pools. Because both of these topics are discussed in the section of this chapter on recruitment, here we focus on the other components of the selection process.

Process Model

Most selection processes can be conceptualized as consisting of three components: (a) job content, what is important; (b) job criteria, what are performance indicators, and (c) job predictors, what are measures of performance indicators. These components and the interrelationship among these components are depicted through a Venn diagram in Figure 4.3. This diagram can be used either when developing an initial selection system or when evaluating an existing selection system.

The job content part of the diagram (Set A) consists of those important job tasks performed by position holders. These tasks should reflect behaviors and processes germane to the effective performance of the job or jobs under consideration. To identify the important job tasks associated with a particular position(s), a systematic job analysis (discussed in the following paragraphs) is required.

Job criteria (Set B) are actual performance indicators that employees must possess to perform the job. Performance indicators can reflect either an inferred process or an observed behavior. An inferred process involves a required knowledge base, while an observed behavior involves a specific skill.

Job predictors (Set C) measure those job criteria associated with knowledge and/or specific skills. Predictors may include subjective data, such as performance from an interview, or objective data, such as results from an analysis of transcript

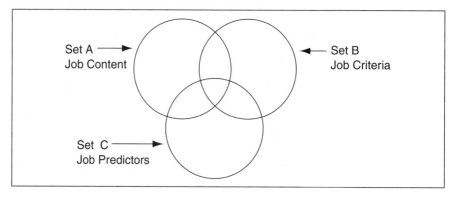

FIGURE 4.3   *Venn diagram for selection components.*

grades. Job predictors are used to assess the preemployment qualifications of candidates relative to the job(s) to be performed.

Each of these separate but related sets helps to establish an effective selection process in the school setting. However, the selection process will be effective only to the extent that the job sets overlap or intersect when applied in the actual field setting. Consequently, the goal of effective selection is to maximize the overlap among the sets involving job content, job criteria, and job predictors.

Procedural Components

Unless there are clear-cut requirements for each position that can be used to assess applicants, it is difficult to select personnel in a systematic fashion. If the selection process is to focus on hiring people who can perform effectively, then work behaviors necessary for effective performance must be identified. The procedure used to identify these essential work behaviors is job analysis.

Job Analysis

It is essential to perform a job analysis before starting a selection process. The information gathered will be used throughout the selection process. In fact, time spent developing a complete list of essential qualifications results in significant time savings throughout the selection process (Jackson, n.d.).

When conducting a job analysis, it is important to note that a job analysis focuses on the tasks comprising the job rather than on the person performing the job. Jobs are controlled by the organization and encapsulate specific tasks, while the person performing the tasks can be effective or ineffective, qualified or unqualified, and can change jobs. More specifically, job analysis should be directed to what tasks should be performed, how these tasks should be performed, and why these tasks are performed.

Job analysis should not be taken lightly or performed unsystematically by those responsible for developing a selection system. Acceptable techniques and standard procedures should be followed because several of the federal acts listed in Table 4.1 consider job analysis to be a crucial process. In fact, the outcome of many legal challenges has been and continues to be decided on the basis of how well the job analysis was performed (HR-Guide, n.d.).

A formal job analysis should be performed before any applicants are interviewed. Written records should be maintained to document the job analysis processes and procedures used by a school system. At a minimum, these records should describe the procedures used to identify job content, the qualifications of persons who conduct the job analysis, and the techniques used to assess the relevance of job content.

Several different procedures are used to identify job content for a job analysis. These include interviewing current employees, observing them performing their duties, reviewing written sources about the job, obtaining information from supervisors, administering job questionnaires, and consulting subject matter experts (HR next, n.d.).

Typically, the more sources used to assess job content, the richer the information yield and the easier the defense of the job analysis when selection decisions are legally challenged.

Job content should be assessed according to two standards of practice: (a) how essential each task is for effective job performance and (b) how frequently each task is performed by the position holder. Answers to these questions have important implications for constructing an effective selection process in the school setting. These answers are used to define job task statements.

In general, the job analysis should yield 15–25 different job task statements for most jobs (Heneman, et al., 2000). Essential job tasks that are frequently performed are retained, while nonessential job tasks are eliminated. More difficult are essential job tasks that are performed infrequently. However, tasks in this category may not be used to exclude job candidates if other staff members can perform them without too much difficulty.

After important job tasks have been identified, the next step is to group different job tasks by common characteristics or dimensions, such as instruction, supervision, communication, and so on. This requires a great deal of theorizing by those who are responsible for developing the selection system. "As a rule, there should be 4–8 dimensions, depending on the number of tasks statements" (Heneman et al., 2000, p. 167).

Job Criteria

Task dimensions are used to define actual job criteria used in the selection process (see Set B in Figure 4.3). These job criteria reflect the knowledge and skills required to perform the tasks associated with particular jobs. Knowledge and skill requirements are defined by the Equal Employment Opportunity Commission (EEOC) guidelines on employee selection. The EEOC defines *knowledge* as "a body of information applied directly to the performance of a function" and *skill* as an "observable compe-tence to perform a learned psychomotor act" (Equal Employment Opportunity Com-mission [EEOC], 1978).

An individual without the knowledge and skill requirements for a particular job would be an ineffective employee. For example, a common task dimension for ele-mentary school principals is instruction, which requires both knowledge and skill. To be effective, elementary school principals need both knowledge of learning theory for early childhood and skill for demonstrating teaching in the classroom setting.

As Figure 4.3 shows, actual job criteria do not completely overlap the required job tasks; instead, the overlap is only partial. This situation is similar to what would be encountered in the field setting. To use the previous example, only part of the knowledge of learning theory for early childhood helps elementary school princi-pals perform effectively in their assigned role.

The overlap between actual job criteria and required job tasks is known as **criterion relevance.** The degree to which actual criteria and job tasks fail to overlap is referred to as **criterion deficiency.** Criterion relevance should be maxi-mized and criterion deficiency should be minimized in an effective selection system.

To assess the relevance of actual criteria for the important tasks comprising the job(s) under consideration, a content validity analysis is required. Content validity, unlike other types of validity to be discussed, is determined analytically through subject matter experts rather than empirically through statistical techniques. For a content validity analysis, subject matter experts with in-depth knowledge about the position(s) under consideration are used to assess the relationship between actual criteria and required job tasks.

Actual criteria, the knowledge and skill required for effective performance, must be developed for each task dimension. The number of actual criteria will vary with the complexity of the task dimension. Some task dimensions may have several dif-ferent knowledge and skill components, and each of these must be identified.

A comprehensive job analysis represents a considerable investment of time and energy. If you fail to complete this essential step, expect delays, increased turnover, and potential problems when trying to defend your selection process from griev-ances or legal actions (Jackson, n.d.).

However, it is a wise investment given the importance of selection for the effec-tive functioning of a school district. All too often, this important step in the selection process is omitted. Unless appropriate job criteria are identified, valid job predictors for an effective selection process are unobtainable, a topic we shall now address.

Job Predictors

After the validities of actual job criteria are established through a content validity analysis, the next step is to identify job predictors that measure these criteria. Job pre-dictors are used to assess the competencies of applicants relative to actual job crite-ria and include "all selection procedures used as a basis for any employment decision" (National Archives and Records Administration, 1978, Section 2B). Examples of some job predictors used frequently by school systems are tests, interviews, references, and related experience.

The actual choice of job predictors is an extremely important decision for school districts and for applicants. Job predictors are used to determine which applicants will be given or denied a job offer. An effective selection process utilizes only those job predictors that are related to actual job criteria.

However, the formal relationship between job predictors and job criteria is seldom assessed by public school districts in the field setting. This omission on the part of public school districts is somewhat surprising because many private sector organizations have been performing such assessments for decades. In actual practice, far too many school systems choose predictors on the basis of untested practices used by other school districts or of promotional literature.

To assess the relationship between job predictors and job criteria, either a content validity analysis or a criterion-related validity analysis is necessary. The choice between these two different types of validity analyses depends on the characteristics of the predictor under consideration. According to federal guidelines, "A selection procedure based upon inferences about mental processes cannot be supported solely or primarily on the basis of content validity. Thus, a content strategy is not appropriate for demonstrating the validity of selection procedures which purport to measure traits or constructs, such as intelligence, aptitude, personality, commonsense, judgment, leadership, and spatial ability" (National Archives and Records Administration, 1978, Section C1).

Because many predictors used by school districts seek to measure certain traits and characteristics of applicants as defined by the federal guidelines, a **criterion-related validity analysis** is required. A criterion-related validity analysis, unlike a content validity analysis, is assessed empirically by statistical techniques, most often a correlation.

A correlation provides a measure of overlap between job predictors and job criteria. This overlap can vary from zero, indicating no overlap, to unity, indicating perfect overlap. In practice, and as depicted in Figure 4.3, the assessed overlap will almost always be far less than unity for any particular predictor of job criteria. According to minimum federal requirements, "A selection procedure is considered related to the criterion, for purposes of these guidelines, when the relationship between performance on the predictor and performance on the criterion measure is statistically significant at the 0.05 level of significance" (EEOC, 1978, Section C5).

Although statistical significance is a minimum requirement for job predictors from a legal perspective, a truly effective selection system must exceed the minimum requirement. Here we can gain additional insight by looking at Figure 4.3. The area where Set B and Set C overlap consists of two separate parts. One part involves only the overlap of job content, job criteria, and job predictors and is defined as predictor relevance. The other part involves only the overlap of job criteria and job predictors and is defined as predictor contamination.

Predictor relevance reflects that portion of the predictor that separates effective from ineffective applicants in terms of future job performance; it represents the practical significance of a predictor. In contrast, predictor contamination reflects that portion of the predictor that hinders effective selection because it contains elements unrelated to potential job performance. An effective selection system is one that uses predictors with high relevance and low contamination.

To obtain predictors with high relevance and low contamination is indeed a challenge for school systems. Unfortunately, most school systems choose predictors on the basis of face validity rather than assessed validity. As a result, many selection systems used by school districts are illegal, counterproductive, and unethical. However, existing selection systems can be improved and effective selection systems can be developed by adhering to this conceptual model, by using current research knowledge about predictors, and by performing additional analyses for predictors.

Actual Job Predictors

Job predictors are proxies used by management to assess the potential job performance of applicants for specific positions. The number and type of job predictors used varies both between and within school districts. Some districts use elaborate selection systems with many job predictors, while others use simple selection systems with few job predictors. Depending on the focal position under consideration, the number and type of job predictors may vary within a particular school system.

In the following section, we focus on those job predictors that can be used by school systems and on those job predictors that can provide insight into current knowledge about these popular predictors. By relying on current knowledge about these popular predictors, school systems can increase the probability of obtaining statistical significance for job predictors, enhance the practical significance of job predictors, and reduce contamination of job predictors. In our discussion, job predictors are classified according to those used to screen applicants and those used to employ applicants.

Screening Applicants

Most school districts delimit the initial applicant pool on the basis of information provided by the applicants themselves (Young & Fox, 2002). Applicants submit information about themselves potentially in several media. In some instances the information is self-reported, while in other instances the information involves external references.

The actual medium used to submit information by applicants for initial consideration is under the control of the school system. School systems can develop policies about application requirements that control the type of information acceptable. Research addressing these different media for applicant information suggests some media are better than other media.

Application Form

Initial information is collected generally through either an application form or a placement file. An application form has several advantages over a placement file. It allows the school system to dictate the type of information sought from applicants, and, unlike placement files from different universities, the application yields comparable information about all applicants. Without comparable information about all applicants, an adequate comparison among applicants is almost impossible.

Although school systems may have separate application forms for classified, certified, and administrative personnel, all application forms should have some common elements. Application forms should provide contact information about the candidate, information on experience relating to position requirements, and disclaimer statements for indemnifying school systems. That is, school systems should be held harmless by applicants for actions related to employment verification, reference checks, and false information provided by applicants.

Items on the application form can be weighted and scored in a way that differentiates between ineffective and effective applicants. Certain items, such as those on related job experience, can be weighted more heavily than other items having less bearing on the positions under consideration (Dessler, 1988). When the items relating to knowledge and skill requirements are weighted more heavily, the predictor relevance of the application form is increased.

Application forms that are scored can be developed. For example, many positions require a knowledge component to communicate clearly, part of which may involve written expression. Applicants' ability to write, as evidenced on these forms, can be scored for grammar, syntax, and clarity based on their responses to open-ended questions on an application form.

In actual practice, many application forms solicit information that is unrelated to job performance, that is a potential contaminant in the selection process, and that is prohibited by federal guidelines. Research has shown that screening decisions of school administrators are often influenced by factors unrelated to job performance, such as the age, the gender, and the disability status of candidates (Young & Prince, 1999). To reduce these contaminants, school systems should carefully analyze all application forms, as well as all other types of information requested from job candidates.

Reference Information

"While it is not very difficult to verify the previous employment of an applicant, it can be rather difficult to verify the quality of his/her previous performance" (Aamodt, Bryan, & Whitcomb, 1993). To assess the work quality of candidates in previous positions, school systems have used a variety of predictors to obtain reference information. The two predictors most frequently used are letters of recommendation and standardized reference forms.

Letters of recommendation can be classified as either personal or professional. Personal letters address the character of the applicant, and professional letters address the competency of the applicant. The former provides little job information and the latter is preferred.

Professional letters of recommendation can be provided by applicants on request, obtained from placement files, or requested by the school district. The information in these letters can be either confidential or nonconfidential, as designated by applicants. Although applicants may waive their right for access to letters of recommendation, it is important to note that employers are not allowed to differentiate among these letters on the basis of confidentiality status.

Research has shown that letters of recommendation influence screening decisions of school administrators. Of particular concern to administrators is the tone of a letter; anything less than a strongly positive letter has a negative effect (Bredeson, 1982). In spite of popular perceptions, the length of letters of recommendation seems to have little influence on the screening decisions of school administrators (Young & McMurray, 1986).

However, research has shown that letters of recommendation often say more about the source (the author) than about the applicant. Interestingly, two letters written by the same author for two different job candidates are more consistent than two letters written by different authors for the same job candidate (Baxter, Brock, Hill, & Rozelle, 1981). Thus, it should not be surprising that letters of recommendation account for less than 2% of the variance associated with job criteria (Reilly & Chao, 1982).

Using a standardized reference form to assess the qualifications of candidates can reduce many of the problems associated with letters of recommendation. A standardized reference form can be tailored to address specific knowledge and skill criteria associated with particular positions. Furthermore, as a predictor of future job performance, the standardized reference form provides comparable information about all candidates.

Employing Applicants

After the initial applicant pool has been delimited on the basis of screening information provided by job candidates, the remaining applicants are subjected to additional job predictors for further assessment. This secondary pool of applicants is formed because these additional job predictors such as interviews and job simulations require a considerable investment of resources. Job interviews and job simulations, when used as predictors of job performance by school systems, are very expensive and time consuming for all involved.

Interviews

By far, the most frequently used job predictor has been and continues to be the selection interview (Arvey & Faley, 1992). However, "what many employers fail to realize is that the interview is classified as a 'test' in the Uniform Guidelines and, as such, is subject to the same scrutiny as traditional pencil-and-paper employment tests" (p. 213). In other words, selection interviews, like other job predictors, should be job related and should be subjected to a validity analysis.

The selection interview provides information about job candidates beyond that obtainable with most other job predictors. However, the format of the interview can vary in several ways. Job interviews can be either unstructured or structured. Unstructured interviews are free-flowing, and topics are explored as they emerge during the interview session. Although unstructured interviews provide interviewers with fewest restrictions and are used frequently as a job predictor, the unstructured interview has been found to be an extremely poor predictor of future job performance because comparable information is not assessed with all applicants during interview sessions (Dipboye, 1992).

A structured interview format eliminates the problem of information incomparability associated with an unstructured interview format. A structured interview format uses a set of prescribed questions, and all candidates are assessed accordingly. These prescribed questions should be constructed to measure the knowledge and skill components associated with the effective job performance of the positions under consideration.

In addition to structure, interviews can be either dyadic or panel in design. In dyadic interviews, only one interviewer assesses all job candidates; in panel interviews, more than one interviewer is involved. Recently, many districts have begun to use panel interviews in schools experimenting with site-based management (Miller-Smith, 2002).

Although the choice between a dyadic and a panel interview is far less important than the choice between a structured and an unstructured interview, decisions made about job candidates have been shown to be a function of interview type. Because fewer candidates are recommended for employment when a dyadic interview is used than when a panel interview is used, selection policy should dictate the use of only one interview type when evaluating job candidates (Young, 1983). Otherwise, evaluation of candidates based on their interview performance may be more a function of the type of interview used than the actual job qualifications of candidates.

Interviews, in general, can improve greatly by following several simple suggestions:

- Aim to allow applicants to demonstrate what they can offer the organization, not to simply confirm expectations or to see how applicants perform under pressure.
- Check on the need for any specific arrangements (e.g., physical access, interpreters, etc.).
- Have questions prepared in advance.
- Ensure consistency and fairness in questioning.
- Focus on the real needs of the job. Don't make assumptions or stereotype individuals.

- The selection committee is entitled to ask applicants whether they can fulfill the requirements of the job (travel, work overtime, perform the physical functions), but such questions must be asked of all applicants.
- It is appropriate to ask people with disabilities whether they require any adjustments to perform the job.
- Allow interviewees time to make their point. Allow silence. Rephrase or clarify if necessary.
- Don't make assumptions about a person's ability to do the job based on physical characteristics.
- Do not ask invasive and irrelevant questions (e.g., Do you intend to have a family?). If necessary, rephrase to gain the essential information you require and ask of all applicants (e.g., Can you commit yourself to the organization for 2 years?).
- Keep records of questions and answers (Payne, n.d.).

Job Simulations

Current research suggests that employee selection can be greatly improved by using predictors based on job simulations. Job simulations involve the use of predictors designed to measure actual job tasks performed by employees. Actual job tasks, when used in the selection process as predictors of future job performance, are referred to as *work samples.*

Work samples can be obtained from the job analysis process used to identify actual job criteria. For a teacher, a work sample might involve teaching a demonstration unit of instruction appropriate for the position; for an administrator, a work sample might involve completing an in-basket exercise. The use of work samples assumes that inferences associated with traditional job predictors are reduced because the selectors focus on the simulated job behaviors of candidates rather than on more distant proxy measures of potential job performance.

Although research on work samples in education is limited, some studies have been done. The validity of certain work samples for school administrators has been examined in assessment centers (Schmitt, Noe, Meritt, & Fitzgerald, 1984). These initial results appear to be promising.

Predictor Assessment

Beyond being related statistically to at least one relevant job performance criterion, each predictor used to select employees should be assessed from at least two other perspectives. One of these perspectives concerns how protected class groups relative to nonprotected class groups perform on the predictor and whether or not the predictor has an adverse impact for protected class groups. A job predictor is determined to have an adverse impact when the selection rate for protected class persons is less than 80% of the selection rate for nonprotected class persons as defined by federal guidelines.

The other perspective concerns the practical significance associated with the predictor. A predictor can be statistically significant but not practically significant. Practical significance concerns the degree to which a job predictor increases the effectiveness of the selection system.

Adverse Impact

To assess the potential adverse impact for a predictor of job performance, flow statistics are calculated. These statistics are based on the number of protected and nonprotected class persons seeking employment, the number of protected and nonprotected class persons obtaining employment, and the selection ratios for these two groups of persons relative to their performance on the job predictor. An example of flow statistics for bus drivers, using gender of applicants as the protected class variable and a selection interview as the job predictor, is presented in Table 4.6. According to these data, the interview used by this system has an adverse impact on female job candidates because the selection rate for females is less than 80% of the selection rate for males.

When flow statistics indicate an adverse impact for protected class persons, school districts have two alternatives under federal guidelines. They can either discontinue using the predictor in the selection of employees or prove that the protected class characteristic, gender in this example, is a **bona fide occupational qualification (BFOQ)** necessary for effective performance. However, within public school systems, few, if any, BFOQ's exist.

In fact, an implied assumption that a BFOQ exists has resulted in many lawsuits related to employment practices of school systems. For example, as shown by past hiring practices of school districts, it was assumed that gender was a BFOQ for a senior high school principal. Based on this assumption, women were excluded almost automatically from consideration for these positions. Although this happens less often today, as seen by the increased number of female senior high principals, all potential predictors of job performance used by school districts should be assessed for an adverse impact with each protected class group as defined by existing legislation (see Table 4.1).

TABLE 4.6
Hypothetical example of applicant flow statistics for school bus drivers.

Classification	Applicant Numbers	Hires	Percentage
Female	100	5	5%
Male	100	30	30%

Practical Significance

Each predictor of job performance used by a school district has a net effect on the effectiveness of a selection system. The net effect of a predictor for a selection system used by a school district concerns the advantage realized by using a particular predictor of job performance as compared to not using that particular predictor. To measure the net effect of each predictor, the job success rates of applicants with and without the use of the predictor must be analyzed.

Success rates of applicants are illustrated in Figure 4.4 by four separate quadrants. These quadrants are determined by establishing the minimum criteria for effective job performance of a position holder (ordinate) and the minimum performance on a predictor required for an employment offer (axis). Because changing the standards of the expected job performance and/or the minimum predictor performance will alter the outcomes, policy makers must consider establishing acceptable levels of performance and cutoff scores.

Each quadrant in Figure 4.4 depicts a specific outcome associated with a particular predictor of job performance: Q1 contains those applicants who were predicted to do well and who did do well; QII contains those applicants who were not predicted to do well but who did do well; QIII contains those applicants who were not predicted to do well and who did not do well; and QIV contains those applicants who were predicted to do well but who failed to do well. Quadrants I and III represent correct outcomes associated with a predictor, while quadrants II and IV represent incorrect outcomes associated with a predictor. Incorrect outcomes are labeled as *false negatives* (quadrant II) or as *false positives* (quadrant IV).

Quadrants I and II are used to calculate a base rate. The base rate indicates the percentage of persons employed by a district who are successful regardless of their

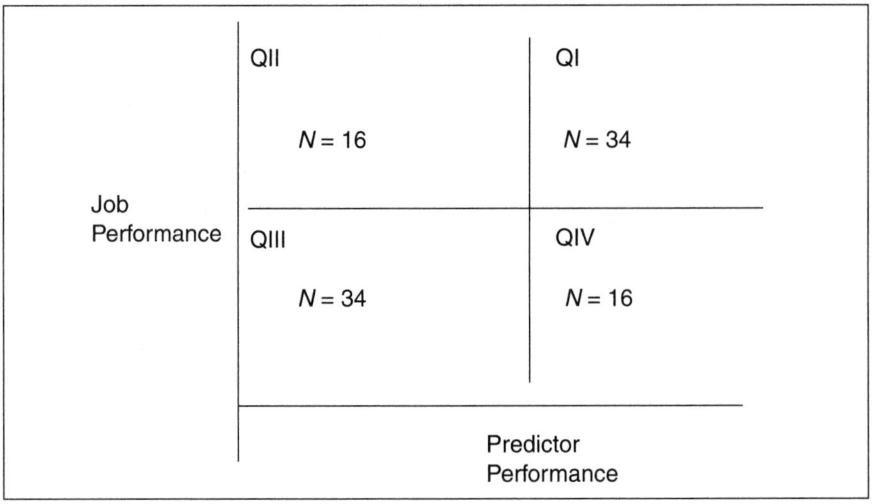

FIGURE 4.4   *Quadrant analysis.*

performance on the predictor. Quadrants I and III indicate the number of correct employment decisions made by using a particular predictor to select employees for placement in vacant positions. By converting these different numbers to a percentage and by comparing these percentages, the practical significance of a predictor is assessed by the net difference. In this example, the school district could realize a net increase in effectiveness of 20% by using this particular predictor of job performance; this net difference provides a measure of practical significance.

The steps in the selection process (Phase 2 in Figure 4.2) examined so far have emphasized the development and assessment of potential predictors of job performance. The next step focuses on the question "How good is the match?" Stated another way, to what extent do the qualifications of applicants meet the requirements for the positions under consideration?

Rejection or acceptance of an applicant is a prediction based on information collected using particular predictors of job performance. The ideal practice is to place a numerical value on information from each of the several predictors in relation to various job criteria identified by the job analysis. Raw scores from predictors can be converted into percentile ranks or standard scores so as to be comparable with normative information. Graphic profiles may be used to portray the results of evaluation. By combining data from application blanks, interview guide sheets, reference and background check forms, tests, and other sources into a profile, the task of relating characteristics of applicants to actual job criteria for vacant positions can be accomplished more effectively.

When all information about a candidate is juxtaposed to the requirements of the position, the selector must compare the two sets of information and predict whether the applicant will perform according to expectations. In various school systems, one employment technique is to place those individuals judged to be qualified for a position on an eligibility list. Before this is done, it is customary to ask each candidate to prove that the certification or license requirements specified by law for a particular position have been met.

Although eligibility is probably defined somewhat differently by various school districts, it generally means that the persons responsible for selecting personnel have designated as suitable for employment applicants who have met established qualifications. The eligibility list should adhere to the employment policy of the board of education (equal opportunity or affirmative action) and should provide a list of applicants, in rank order, who are eligible for appointment as vacancies occur.

In the selection process, it is not unusual to find that some applicants do not meet position requirements. When this happens, several alternatives (which can be explored before deciding to offer employment or deciding to place the individual on the eligibility list) can be considered: (a) delay filling the position, (b) renew the search, (c) provide specific developmental experiences for persons considered to be good risks but who need to improve their skills to fill the position effectively, (d) fill the position temporarily, and (e) employ the applicant, but in a different position.

One difficulty in the selection process is the time factor. Many desirable candidates are lost to competing systems because of the time lag between initial interview and official appointment. Every effort should be made to keep the selection process as brief as possible; in particular, there should be no delay in notifying candidates of their official appointment.

Before the selection process is completed, the applicant and the organization must agree on the terms of employment. It is crucial that both parties completely understand the conditions of employment. Misunderstandings frequently occur about salaries, duties, authority, office or work space, secretarial assistance, collateral benefits, overtime, and extra pay for extra work.

Employment agreements made by telephone should be confirmed in writing. A contractual agreement is essential before hiring is completed. This practice has considerable merit, regardless of how the agreement is made.

Many people develop a negative attitude toward the organization when promises made during the selection period are not kept after the position has been accepted. Therefore, during the final stages of selection, it is good practice to use a checklist containing the terms of employment. This checklist should be designed to ensure that the prospective employee knows the exact nature of the position and its responsibilities, moonlighting policy, compensation structure and its relationship to the applicant's paycheck, terms of the probationary period, collateral benefits, terms of any union or associational contracts in force, and provisions unique to a given position, such as status or status symbols.

Review and Preview

The theme of this chapter is that an extensive and aggressive program of recruitment and selection is necessary for placing and keeping qualified individuals in every position in the system. It was emphasized that recruitment and selection is both an individual and an organizational activity. Individuals must make decisions about organizations, and organizations must make decisions about individuals.

To guide the recruitment and selection processes, certain policies and procedures were discussed. With respect to recruitment, a distinction was made between an equal opportunity employer and an affirmative action employer. Information was provided about orientation of applicants, recruitment messages, and organizational representatives.

A Venn diagram was used to illustrate the interrelationship among the different components and procedures comprising the selection process. Information concerning several types of job predictors was presented. Methodology was discussed for assessing the statistical and practical significance of particular predictors, and attention was directed to assessing the disproportional impact of predictors.

Discussion Questions

1. How does internal recruiting differ from external recruiting? What is the strategic difference between the two methods?

2. What is the relationship between human resource strategy and recruitment?

3. What types of job predictors are used to assess applicants in your school organization? What is your perception of the value of each of these predictors?

4. Your school organization is hiring a new superintendent. 1) What indicators of previous success would you use in assessing the candidates? 2) How would you obtain this information?

5. Identify one classified position, one teaching position, and one administrative position within your school organization. What do you consider the bona fide occupational qualifications (BFOQs) of each of these positions?

References

Aamodt, M. G., Bryan, D. A., & Whitcomb, A. J. (1993). Predicting performance with letters of recommendation. *Public Personnel Management, 22,* 81–91.

Arvey, R. D., & Faley, R. H. (1992). *Fairness in selecting employees* (2nd ed.). Reading, MA: Addison-Wesley.

Baxter, J. C., Brock, B., Hill, P. C., & Rozelle, R. M. (1981). Letters of recommendation: A question of value. *Journal of Applied Psychology, 66,* 296–301.

Behling, O., Labovitz, G., & Gainer, M. (1968). College recruiting: A theoretical base. *Personnel Journal, 47,* 13–19.

Bredeson, P. V. (1982). *The effects of letters of recommendation on the teacher selection process.* Unpublished doctoral dissertation, University of Wisconsin.

Bretz, R. D., & Judge, T. A. (1998). Realistic job previews: A test of the Adverse Self-Selection Hypothesis. *Journal of Applied Psychology, 83,* 330–337.

Dessler, G. (1988). *Personnel management.* Upper Saddle River, NJ: Prentice Hall.

Dipboye, R. I. (1992). *Selection interviews: Process perspectives.* Cincinnati, OH: South-Western College Publishing.

Equal Employment Opportunity Commission. (1978). Guidelines on employee selection procedures. *Federal Register, 35,* 12333–12336.

Fideler, E. F., Foster, E. D., & Schwartz, S. (2000, January). Teacher demand and supply in the Great City Schools. *The urban teacher challenge.* Retrieved from the Recruiting New Teachers, Inc. Web site: **http://www.rnt.org/quick/utc.pdf**

Heneman, H. G., Judge, T. A., & Heneman, R. L. (2000). *Staffing organizations* (3rd ed.). Middleton, WI: Mendota House.

Holmes Group. (1995). *Tomorrow's schools of education.* East Lansing, MI: Author.

HR-Guide. (n.d.). *HR guide to the Internet: Job analysis: Law/legal issues: Court cases.* Retrieved July 29, 2002, from the HR-Guide Web site: **http://www.hr-guide.com/data/G001.htm**

HRnext. (n.d.). *Methods and techniques.* Retrieved July 29, 2002, from the HRnext Web site: **http://www.hrnext.com/content/view.cfm?subs_articles_id=1748**

Jackson, S. (n.d.). *Performance model.* Retrieved July 26, 2002, from the HR Strategy Web site: **http://www.hrstrategy.com/sitemap.htm**

Judge, T. A., & Bretz, R. D. (1992). Effects of work values on job choice decisions.

Journal of Applied Psychology, 77(3), 261–271.

Miller-Smith, K. R. (2002). Effects of organizational representative, school district performance and site based reform status on teacher screening decisions. (Doctoral dissertation, Ohio State University, 2001). *Dissertation Abstracts International, 62*(11), 3645A. (UMI No. AAT 3031231)

National Archives and *Records administration (1978) Federal Register, 35.* Retrieved May 28, 2003, from the National Archives and Administration Web site: **http://archives. gov/federal_register/**

Payne, J. (n.d.). *Information for employers, best practice: recruitment and selection, interviewing.* Retrieved July 29, 2002, from the Australian Human Rights & Equal Opportunity Commission Web site: **http://www.hreoc.gov.au/info_for_ employers/best_practice/recruitment. html**

Pounder, D. G. (1988). Improving the predictive validity of teacher selection decisions: Lessons from teacher appraisal. *Journal of Personnel Evaluation in Education, 2,* 141–150.

Pounder, D. G., & Merrill, R. J. (2001). Job desirability of the high school principalship: A job choice theory perspective. *Educational Administration Quarterly, 37,* 27–57.

Pounder, D. G., & Young, I. P. (1996). Recruitment and selection of educational administrators: Priorities for today's schools. In K. Leithwood (Ed.), *The international handbook for educational leadership and administration* (pp. 279–308). Amsterdam: Kluwer.

Reilly, R. R., & Chao, G. T. (1982). Validity and fairness of some alternative employee selection procedures. *Personnel Psychology, 35,* 1–62.

Rynes, S. L. (1991). Recruitment, job choice, and post-hire consequences: A call for new research directions. In M. Dunnette & L. Hough (Eds.), *Handbook of industrial and organizational psychology* (pp. 399–444). Palo Alto, CA: Consulting Psychologist Press.

Rynes, S. L., & Barber, A. E. (1990). Applicant attraction strategies: An organizational perspective. *Academy of Management, 15,* 286–310.

Rynes, S. L., & Lawler, J. (1983). A policy capturing investigation of the role of expectancies in decisions to pursue job alternatives. *Journal of Applied Psychology, 68*(4), 620–631.

Schmitt, N., Noe, R., Meritt, R., & Fitzgerald, M. (1984). Validity of assessment center ratings for the prediction of performance ratings and school climate of school administrators. *Journal of Applied Psychology, 69*(2), 207–213.

Wanous, J. P. (1992). *Organizational entry* (2nd ed.). Reading, MA: Addison-Wesley.

Winter, P. A. (1996). Applicant evaluations of formal position advertisements: The influence of sex, job message content, and information order. *Journal of Personnel Evaluation in Education, 10,* 105–116.

Winter, P. A. (1997). Education recruitment and selection: A review of recent studies and recommendations for best practice. In L. Wildman (Ed.), *Fifth NCPEA yearbook* (pp. 133–140). Lancaster, PA: Technomic.

Winter, P. A., & Morgenthal, J. R. (2002). Principal recruitment in a reform environment: Effects of school achievement and school level on applicant attraction to the job. *Educational Administration Quarterly, 38,* 319–340.

Young, I. P. (1983). Administrators' perceptions of teacher candidates in dyad and panel interviews. *Educational Administration Quarterly, 13,* 46–63.

Young, I. P., & Fox, J. A. (2002). Asian, Hispanic, and Native American job candidates: Prescreened or screened within the selection process. *Educational Administration Quarterly, 38*(4), 530–545.

Young, I. P., & Heneman, H. G. (1986). Predictors of interviewee reactions to the selection interview. *Journal of Research and Development in Education, 19,* 29–36.

Young, I. P., & McMurray, B. R. (1986). Effects of chronological age, focal position, quality of information and quantity of information on screening decisions for teacher candidates. *Journal of Research and Development in Education, 19*, 1–9.

Young, I. P., Place, A. W., Rinehart, J. S., Jury, J. C., & Baits, D. F. (1997). Teacher recruitment: A test of the Similarity-Attraction Hypothesis for race and sex. *Educational Administration Quarterly, 33*(1), 86–106.

Young, I. P., & Prince, A. L. (1999). Legal implications for teacher selection as defined by the ADA and the ADEA. *Journal of Law & Education, 28*(4), 517–530.

Young, I. P., Rinehart, J. & Heneman, H G. (1993). Effects of job attribute categories applicant job experience, and recruiter sex on applicant job attractiveness ratings. *Journal of Personnel Evaluation in Education, 7*, 55–65.

Supplementary Reading

Barber, A. E. (1998). *Recruiting employees: Individual and organizational perspectives.* Thousand Oaks, CA: Sage.

Eder, R. W., & Harris, M. M. (1999). *The employment interview handbook.* Thousand Oaks, CA: Sage.

Schmitt, N., & Chan, D. (1998). *Personnel selection: A theoretical approach.* Thousand Oaks, CA: Sage.

5 *Induction*

CHAPTER OBJECTIVES

Stress the importance of the induction process to socialization of inductees.
Present a working model of the induction process.
Focus on ways to help inductees achieve the highest level of performance in the shortest period.
Identify adjustments that are essential for inductees to perform effectively.

CHAPTER CONCEPTS

Career planning   Induction

This chapter examines the induction process as a human resource function for as-similating an individual within the position, the school district, and the community at large. Our discussion begins with an examination of induction as it relates to human performance within the position and within the organization. After discussing the behavioral foundations of induction for positions and for public school districts, we present a model of the induction process, examining in detail the activities designed to achieve a long-range induction strategy that is beneficial to all stakeholders.

Induction and Human Performance

Without exception, school districts annually must contend with personnel changes. Every year, school districts must recruit, select, assign, reassign, or transfer personnel to maintain continuity of the educational workforce. Employees leave the organization for various reasons, and new positions are created to address emerging contingencies.

Vacancies created through existing staffing needs provide a window of opportunity for a public school district. Judicious selections and assignments of new employees and of existing employees can provide a public school district with several strategic advantages for achieving system objectives and goals. Individuals with new skills and knowledge can be brought into the system, while existing experiences and abilities of continuing employees can be capitalized on for the benefit of the individuals and of the school system.

For some individuals, these opportunities afforded by vacant positions may represent the initial entrance into the world of work. These individuals could be recent graduates of colleges or high schools seeking their first meaningful professional work experience, or could be older persons deferring entrance into the workforce until later in life. For both groups of newcomers, special induction needs exist.

Personnel new to the system may be apprehensive about many things, such as the community, their coworkers, or their ability to succeed. Generally, these personnel are unaware of "the way we do things here." Most of them know nothing about the organization's objectives, their specific duties and responsibilities, school and community traditions and taboos, and personal and position standards to which members are expected to adhere.

In school systems, many new employees resign voluntarily during their probation period. It has been noted, for example, that the number of first-year teachers who leave the profession is higher than it should be, and that the loss is higher than the profession should sustain. One study indicated that 20% of new teachers left prior to their second year of employment (Chester & Beaudin, 1996), and a recent national report indicated that 22% of all new teachers leave the profession in the first 3 years (U.S. Department of Education, 2000).

Other individuals filling vacancies within the public school district may be seasoned veterans of the workforce. Included in this category are experienced employees new to the public school setting, experienced educators new to the public school district, or experienced employees of the district reassigned to a new position. Again, specific induction needs exist even for the seasoned employees that are different from those induction needs of new entrants to the labor market.

It goes almost without stating that probably at no other time of employment does the newly appointed or newly assigned employee need more consideration, guidance, and understanding than their first few months on a new job. Until these individuals become fully adjusted to the work they must perform, their new work environment, and/or their new colleagues, they cannot be expected to give their best effort. If left unmanaged, the feelings triggered by new work assignments can harm employees as well as the organization.

To avoid many of the problems encountered with new job assignments, an employee induction process is needed. A well-planned **induction** process is a systematic organizational effort for helping personnel to adjust readily and effectively to new work assignments so that they can contribute maximally to organizational goals and objectives through achieving personal and work satisfaction. This definition of an effective induction process, it should be noted, goes beyond the conventional idea that induction is concerned only with personnel new to a public school system.

The induction process, as defined in this chapter, includes all personnel who accept new assignments (see Figure 5.1). This includes personnel new to the profession, new to the system, and new to the position (but not the system). Whether new to the system or new to the assignment, most personnel seek an organizational environment in which they can find a reasonable degree of security and enjoy satisfaction in their work.

Without important knowledge about their new position, the school district, and the community at large, frustrated employees may withdraw from the work environment. This withdrawal takes several different forms including frequent absences from work. This type of withdrawal leads almost always to voluntary resignation by the employee.

Human resource managers know that absenteeism and voluntary turnover of newly assigned employees represent an economic loss to the system. Investment

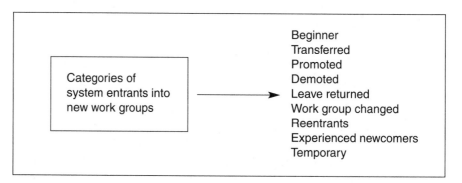

FIGURE 5.1   *Entrants and reentrants included in the induction program.*

costs incurred when recruiting, selecting, inducting, and supervising newly assigned personnel are considered a financial loss when these persons are frequently
absent or resign voluntarily. These costs can range from several hundred dollars for
low-level positions to several thousand dollars for high-level administrative positions (U. S. Department of Education, 2000).

One presumed cause of absenteeism and voluntary turnover is the lack of well-
planned induction practices instituted by the school system. Newly assigned staff
members must make so many adjustments before they are assimilated totally into the
organization that a good induction program is less a luxury than a necessity in modern school systems. An aim of an effective induction program is to minimize the
strain on the school system's financial and human resource allocations by reducing
absenteeism and voluntary turnovers among employees newly assigned to a position.

Indeed, most public school districts have realized the advantages associated
with an effective induction program for newly assigned personnel. To imply that educational systems have not been concerned with the problems of the inductee, either in the past or in the present, would be incorrect. Today, however, many
excellent programs are in operation in a number of school districts (North Carolina
Department of Public Instruction, n.d.).

Some of these induction programs are based on recent educational reform and
restructuring initiatives and include a variety of approaches. Depending on location, size, budgetary constraints, regulatory mandates, leadership, and proactive
and reactive attitudes to institutional change, the activities within these programs
vary. One way to characterize contemporary induction activity is in terms of five
types of programs being used by public school districts to assimilate employees new
to their assignment in a public school system:

- University–school system collaboration
- Consortium programs for area school systems
- Districtwide programs
- School-based programs
- Web-based programs

Due, at least in part, to studies of employees new to their assignment and their
assimilation within the work setting as well as the community at large, induction
has taken more importance in recent times. Reasons for this importance include the
following:

- Individuals change their behaviors when they become members of groups
  (Smithers, 1988).
- Planned induction programs tend to be better than unplanned activities
  (French, 1987).
- Carefully designed induction programs minimize disruptive behavior of new
  employees (French, 1987).

- Induction programs minimize certain inappropriate interpersonal behaviors on the part of employees newly assigned.
- Individuals possessing alternate certification as teachers benefit greatly from induction programs (Shen, 1997).

Behavior and the Induction Process

Existing literature addressing the induction of new employees contains several synonyms for the process of acclimating new employees to their work environment. These synonyms include such terms as *induction, placement, organizational entry, assignment,* and *orientation.* Each of these terms has been used to define the process by which new personnel are assisted in meeting their need for security, belonging, status, information, and direction in both their new position and their new organizational environment.

The induction process begins in the recruitment stage of the human resource model and ends when the newly assigned employees have made the personal, position, organizational, and community adaptations that enable them to function fully and effectively as a member of the school staff. It is not uncommon for the induction program to last the entire first year of employment, especially for persons new to the system (Bergeson, n.d.). For induction programs covering a considerable period, activities encountered involve considerably more than just making new personnel feel at ease in an unfamiliar environment.

Worth noting is that few, if any, employees begin a new job assignment with all the skills necessary to perform every job task with maximum efficiency. Given this limitation, some investigators have categorized the skills of new employees, for both their position and their work environment, into separate behavioral categories. Luthans and Kreitner (1975) developed four categories to classify the behavioral skills of newcomers in relation to their position: (a) desirable performance-related job behavior, (b) potentially disruptive performance-related behavior, (c) behavior unrelated to performance, and (d) performance behavior deficiencies.

Desirable performance job-related behavior defines the core of responsibilities associated with effective job performance. It is those aspects of the job that are germane to organizational goals and the very essence of the focal position for the public school district. Without adequate performance relative to job-related behaviors, individuals are destined to fail in their newly assigned position.

Potentially disruptive performance-related behaviors signal to school administrators important information about individuals in newly assigned positions. These types of behaviors represent acceptable employment practices that have been extravagated by the employee in fulfilling normal job assignments. Examples of potentially disruptive performance-related behaviors may be either a rigid conformance to performance standards of the newly assigned position ("It is not in my job description") or a lack of flexibility in the employee to adjust to the requirements of the newly assigned position.

Behavior unrelated to performance creates the lesser of the problems associated with these behavior indices. Employees new to an assignment may fail to realize all the expectations associated with a position. As such, they may exhibit many behaviors that are unnecessary in the performance of newly assigned duties.

Of major concern are the performance behavior deficiencies by newly assigned personnel. Some of these behavior deficiencies may be attributed to a lack of ability, whereas others may be attributed to a lack of motivation. It behooves the school district to discern this differentiation between ability and motivation because each reason has important implications for an induction program.

By using these behavioral categories to classify the skills of employees newly assigned to positions, certain identified behaviors can be reinforced, modified, or eliminated through what Luthans and Kreitner refer to as a *shaping process*. Shaping is a process by which an employee's behavior is altered through a series of steps involving observation, evaluation, and feedback. For new employees, shaping begins when the system (a) gathers information about newcomers relative to desired behavior in their new position, (b) seeks to positively reinforce acceptable behaviors, (c) uses feedback to correct deficiencies in performance, and (d) helps the individual to become part of the organization through day-to-day supervision.

Scope of the Induction Process

A successful induction process for employees newly assigned stems from a formal plan of action developed and implemented by management. By relying on a formal plan of action for designing, implementing, and managing the induction process, errors of omission are reduced and the induction process will be sequenced. An action plan on the induction process for new employees should begin by exploring answers to the following questions:

- What are the goals of the induction process?
- What types of activities are needed to achieve the goals of the induction process?
- How will induction activities be sequenced within the induction process?
- Who will be responsible for specific activities?
- How will different activities of the induction process be evaluated?
- How will assessment information be used for improving induction?

A conceptual model for an effective induction process can provide guidelines for answering these questions in an orderly manner (see Figure 5.2). This model shows that the steps of the induction process include activities associated normally with most administrative tasks (planning, organizing, leading, and assessing). This should not be surprising because the induction process is one of the components or subsystems of the human resource function that should be executed by a public school district.

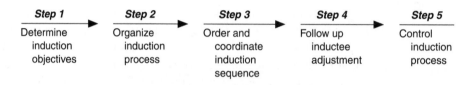

FIGURE 5.2   *Model of the induction process.*

The induction model presented in Figure 5.2 illustrates the kinds of decisions that confront administrators when attempting to assimilate personnel into the system through a formal induction program. By linking specific questions with certain steps comprising the model, the parameters of an induction program can be framed. Within the following sections, we examine how a school system puts into practice the concepts suggested in the questions and steps reflected by this model.

Goals of the Induction Process

The overarching purpose of the induction process is to help newly assigned personnel adjust to their new work environment. However, this purpose will have little significance for those who plan or implement the process unless it is translated into specific goals (the first step in the induction process). Examples of specific goals for an induction process gleaned from the professional literature are presented in Figure 5.3.

In addition to the objectives listed in Figure 5.3, other potential objectives of a successful induction process may be identified by assessing the opinions of knowledgable personnel, reviewing the professional literature, and conducting an electronic search. Interestingly, one single Web site revealed 20 different orientation programs for public school districts that can be used to identify potential objectives for an induction program (North Carolina Department of Public Instruction, n.d.).

When designing an induction program for employees newly assigned to their position, one must keep to a manageable number the specific objectives to be addressed. For any single induction program to accomplish all the objectives found in Figure 5.3 is an unrealistic expectation. In practice, the task for those who develop and implement a successful induction program is to determine the salience of each objective within their own school system.

The identification and selection of objectives to be included within an induction program must be tempered by other aspects of the human resource function. Although induction should begin at the initial start of the employment relationship (Heneman, Judge, & Heneman, 2000), those responsible for recruitment and selection may have omitted important information at this stage of the human resource process. As such, this information must be covered or revisited in the induction program.

- Assist members to appreciate the values, abilities, expected behaviors, and social knowledge essential to undertaking a system role and contributing to its mission.
- Provide inductees with complete and uniform information about the school system's mission, organization, structure, functions, policies, and work requirements.
- Develop loyal, effective, and productive workers.
- Reduce the likelihood of rule violation, discharges, resignations, and grievances.
- Address performance problems before they occur.
- Minimize the gap between employment expectancy and reality.
- Ease the transition from one institutional or work environment to another.
- Promote professional and personal well-being of inductees.
- Satisfy regulatory mandates.
- Develop a basic knowledge of the need for positive adjustment to external, internal, position, cultural, social, and personal aspects of system membership.
- Place inductees in positions so as to balance school system needs with individual competencies and aspirations.
- Reduce inductee anxiety.
- Reduce cost and supervisory time.

FIGURE 5.3 *Induction objectives.*

Fundamental to the entire induction process is the formal commitment of the board of education to the objectives of an induction program. This commitment should be captured in a board policy. Surprisingly, school board policies addressing an induction program for employees are difficult to find in the public school setting.

It is not unusual to find induction policies for school board members in most public school districts, however. Induction programs for school board members exist in almost every school system. These programs address attendance at workshops performed by the state and professional association on entrance to their newly assigned duties as public officials.

If the intent of the school system for induction programs has been formalized in a written document for employees newly assigned to positions within the school system, then the document is found most often in an employee handbook rather than in a school board policy. Because an employee handbook carries less legitimacy than a school board policy, it is recommended that the objectives of an induction program be committed to school board policy. An example of such a policy that can serve as a starting point for public school districts is found in Figure 5.4.

To create a stimulating environment for the investiture of inductees (initial hires, internal transfers, promotees, demotees, and temporaries) the Riverpark school system gives primacy to these courses of action:

- Envision inductee placement in the context of future system positions and human resource strategy.
- Embody state-of-the-art practices in the induction process.
- Establish lines of authority and responsibility for the conduct of the induction process.
- Ensure maintenance of ethical standards and integrity in the conduct of the induction process.
- Deal ethically and professionally with problems posed by special groups (people who are disabled, inexperienced, underprivileged).
- Emphasize variation in work assignments such as team concept, work unit culture, and individual responsibility.
- Give consideration, when there is a diversity of positions available, by comparing an individual's aptitudes, abilities, interests, and temperament with requirements of various openings to determine inductee suitability.
- Design the induction process to enhance the ability of inductees to proceed from "newly appointed" to productive team members without loss or interval of time.
- Form cooperative and interdependent relationships in the system's social, work, and community environments.
- Shape the induction process through policies, programs, purposes, and procedures conducive to performance expectations, position expectations, and retentive power.
- Contribute to assimilation, socialization, security, personal development, and need satisfaction of position entrants.
- Gear the induction process to create a bonding among the three induction phases (preappointment, interim period, and probationary service).
- Update the human resource manual to provide for current information needs of appointees and members of the induction team.
- Utilize, during each of the induction stages, selected induction approaches for systemwide, departmental, work unit, and position application.

FIGURE 5.4   *Form and structure of the Riverpark school system's induction process.*

Organization of the Induction Process

As has been noted throughout this chapter, a major purpose of an induction program is to provide newly assigned employees with information needed to become assimilated into their new work environment as productive contributors to a public school system. When this has been done effectively, many adjustment problems can be prevented. Although the informational needs of newcomers to a focal position can vary, depending on whether they are recent hires or they are reassigned from within the system, certain problem areas common to all new employees have been identified in the literature (LeGore & Parker, 1997):

- Problems in becoming acquainted with the position
- Problems in performing the assignment
- Problems in acquiring knowledge about the system
- Problems in getting to know personnel in the system
- Problems in becoming acquainted with the community
- Problems in adjusting to a new external environment

An examination of these problem areas as noted by recent hires reveals some common themes that should be addressed by an induction program within the public school setting. These themes are concerned with the position, the system, and the community. As such, these themes provide a broad framework for organizing an induction program to aid employees in the assimilation of and acclamation to their new job assignments within a public school district (see Step 2 of Figure 5.2).

To embellish this framework with an effective induction program addressing the concerns of employees newly appointed to their positions, each of these potential problem areas will be discussed in the following sections of this chapter. We begin this discussion at the most immediate level of concern for the employee—the new focal position. Then, we move from the initial level of concern for employees newly assigned through the broader areas of concern for the system and for the community, respectively.

Position Information

For any initial employment relationship between an individual and a public school district, a central point of focus for most new employees is the focal position. Although most focal positions have other responsibilities attached outside of the major job functions, such as organizational responsibilities and community expectations, it is concerns about the primary focal position that dominate the immediate attention of the new job incumbent. Because of the urgency new employees associate with the primary focal position, it is not surprising that the focal position is of major concern to newly assigned employees during the induction period with a public school district.

Many concerns related to the focal position may stem from a lack of sufficient information possessed by the newly assigned employee. For new entrants into the labor market lacking appropriate experiences on which to draw, many voids exist within their work repertory for addressing contingencies associated with a new assignment. Although these persons may have mastered many of the technical skills necessary for effective job performance, they may lack certain knowledge about the informal aspects of organizational life encountered in an actual workplace.

Experienced employees, on the other hand, accepting new assignments may encounter different ways of doing things. Performing the same job in a different system or performing a different job in the same system may require a different set of skills. As such, previous learning can interfere with new learning and can influence negatively the on-job behavior of experienced employees.

The lack of sufficient information about new focal positions and about new responsibilities associated with these positions may be attributed to several causes. Individuals may have been unexposed to the necessary information prior to their initial assignment. Realities of the recruitment and selection processes may have imposed certain time restraints that restrict the information flow between employees and organizational representatives.

It is not unusual for recruitment and selection activities for some employees to take place away from the employing school districts. Many teachers are recruited and selected at job fairs or through college placement office interviews. Recruitment fairs and college placement offices are far removed from the world of work that successful candidates are to encounter within a public school district.

Even when recruitment and selection activities take place within the confines of the school district, these activities may be less than optimal for imparting information about the focal position. It is not unusual for many of the recruitment and selection activities to take place when schools are on summer break. During this period, applicants and new employees have little exposure relative to their new job assignment.

An equally likely explanation for the lack of sufficient information is that employees may have failed to assimilate appropriate job information when exposed initially as applicants during the employment process. With both job fairs and college placement offices, interactions between job candidates and organizational representatives are seldom a singular event. Job candidates as well as organizational representatives encounter multiple exposures within these types of employment contexts.

In fact, research that addresses the recruitment and the selection processes indicates that applicants tend to blur information they encounter within the employment process. For truly competitive organizations encountered during the recruitment process, salient information about districts and job assignments may be very similar across organizations and assignments. Because of this similarity of information across organizations and assignments, individuals, as applicants, may fail to internalize information important for the public school district that they chose to join at the conclusion of the job search process.

To help potential employees differentiate among school districts and job assignments, information about the focal position should be dispensed by a school district early within the employment process. Individuals, as applicants, should receive information about focal positions initially through postings of job openings. Interestingly, some research indicates that individuals choose to pursue certain job opportunities over others on the basis of information provided in position advertisements (Winter, 1997).

Based on this research, public school districts should afford particular attention to the posting of vacant positions. When possible, content of position postings should be specific as opposed to general relative to position characteristics. By providing specific information about focal positions, induction can reinforce position information rather than introducing position information for new job incumbents.

Decisions required by individuals during the recruitment and selection processes can be informed also by using position guides. Position guides are valuable resources in helping new employees become acquainted with their potential job assignments early in the employment process. These position guides should not only prevent applicants from accepting positions for which they are unqualified but also should provide information to those responsible for personnel selection and placement so that candidates and positions can be matched effectively within the public school district.

Individuals have certain skills they bring to the position and have certain needs they seek to fulfill with the position. Skills are abilities and aptitudes related specifically to fulfilling job requirements. Needs may involve a desire for autonomy, affiliation, or achievement.

Likewise, vacant focal positions have certain requirements and have certain benefits associated with the positions. Requirements form the basic necessities for performing successfully in a potential focal position, whereas benefits are derived through such actions on the part of the employee when fulfilling basic job requirements. A match between individual needs and organizational requirements is an integral part of the employment process involving recruitment, selection, and induction.

After the selection process is completed, the new employee is assigned to a work unit within the organization. When selecting and placing individuals in new assignments, certain contextual aspects of the assignment must be considered from a human resource perspective. These contextual aspects include the following:

- How well will the individual fit the leadership style of the work unit?
- How well will the individual fit into the work unit's environment?
- Will the newcomer be accepted by the work group?
- Will the newcomer accept the work group?

If those responsible for selecting and placing individuals in new assignments ignore these questions, then it should be of little surprise that the recently assigned employees have adjustment problems associated with their new positions. These problems arise when the expectations, values, and goals of new employees are inconsistent with the realities of organizational life. Unless the selection and placement decisions are sound, new employees will be unsuccessful in new assignments.

The selection and placement processes overlook frequently these important elements in recruitment, selection, assignment, and induction: (a) leadership styles of the applicant, (b) the persons the applicant will report to, (c) those reporting to the applicant (if the position is administrative), and (d) the structure of the job situation. In the previous discussion of the selection and placement processes, it was emphasized that information is the key to making judgments about placing an individual in a position. Management must learn as much as possible about the applicant, and the applicant must know as much as possible about the position in question if compatibility between applicant and position is to be obtained.

Without such knowledge about the person and about the focal position, adjustment problems of newly assigned employees likely will occur and can spill over into the work unit and cause major disruptions among otherwise satisfactory employees. Widespread dissatisfaction may occur when overqualified or underqualified personnel become part of the work group. No doubt, when members of the work group perceive newcomers as sources of disruption, dissatisfaction becomes widespread in the work setting.

It cannot be emphasized too strongly that improper selection and/or placement can be costly to both the employee and the system. Placing an incompetent individual in any position or a competent individual in the wrong position often leads to years of grief for the administration, low productivity of the employee, and interference with attainment of system goals. Proactive rather than reactive selection and placement decisions are best for everyone involved in the employment process and facilitate the induction of the new employee into a public school system.

System Information

Newly assigned employees seek information about the system as well as about their positions within the system. As noted earlier in this chapter, some of the adjustment problems encountered by new employees are due to lack of information about the system. New employees need to know about the fringe benefits associated with the position, the support services available to the position holder, and the relationship of the position to the organization as a whole.

Recent hires, as well as continuing employees with new assignments, often must make decisions during early periods of employment about certain benefit options provided by the system and unique to their new assignment. Depending on whether the new position is administrative, instructional, or supportive, benefit packages may vary. Examples of benefit options that may vary by job classification include choosing an insurance carrier, selecting a primary physician, opting for a flexible spending account, selecting a retirement plan, and purchasing long-term health care.

The difficulty in choosing among benefit options is compounded for new personnel because these options often have a window of opportunity, which can be either irrevocable or penalty laden. Irrevocable windows require newly assigned employees to choose or to reject the benefit within a specified time, while penalty-laden windows penalize these employees for accepting a benefit at a later date in the employment cycle.

To make an informed choice among benefit options with windows of opportunity is difficult for many newly assigned employees. No doubt, most readers can recall the confusions they encountered in this stage of the employment process. This confusion is heightened by concerns about mastering the skills needed in the new position, understanding the expectations of the new supervisor, and blending with the organization as a whole.

Some of the anxieties in choosing among fringe benefits with windows of opportunity can be reduced by providing appropriate and timely information in the induction process. Providing such information is a major human resource function that must be performed by every school district. However, this information should inform rather than advise; the ultimate responsibility for choice among benefits rests with the employee.

Most, if not all, newly assigned employees in schools have certain support functions provided by the system and designed to help them perform effectively and efficiently. However, knowledge of these support systems is assumed, often at the expense of the individual and the system. Too often within the induction process, information about support services available to a position holder is overlooked.

Many times, newly assigned administrators are confronted with situations involving labor–management relations. In the absence of crystal-clear contract language concerning the specific point of contention, these new administrators may be required to provide an interpretation. Any such interpretation provided by administrators should be tempered by past labor–management practices within the system. Information about these practices is obtainable through the support system provided by the district.

Teachers new to the profession and new to the assignment often are confronted with student-related issues during their induction period. These types of problems and issues surface frequently during this period because students, like teachers, are new to their recent grade-level assignment. With both teachers and students being new to their assignments, adequate induction of the former is germane to an effective classroom setting.

Some of the issues encountered during the induction period are academic, while other issues encountered are nonacademic. In both cases, a satisfactory resolution of the problem may depend on the district's support system. In many instances, teachers serve as a conduit for students with the district's support systems.

Classified employees also encounter problems requiring assistance from support systems in fulfilling position requirements. Equipment for processing information (clerical), preparing food (food service), cleaning buildings (custodians), transporting students (bus drivers), and facilitating instruction (instructional aids) may malfunction in the absence of an immediate supervisor. The support systems available to solve problems caused by malfunctions should be known by all classified personnel to prevent loss of time and effort by new employees.

Although a formal induction program for employees can provide information about available support services, sometimes services and service providers are not linked for newly assigned personnel. And, unless a link is established, new employees may fail to recall what services are available to them when needed. This situation results in underutilization of support systems by new employees.

Seyfarth (1996) suggested that services and providers can be linked by having newly assigned employees interview the service providers. Such interviews, initiated by new employees, open channels of communication and allow the involved parties to establish rapport. Putting a face to a service facilitates the induction process for many employees and reinforces sources of information about support systems available to employees.

In addition to providing information about fringe benefits and support services, every organization should inform members of its purposes, policies, and procedures. Newly appointed staff members want to know, for example, about the operation of the system and about how their position fits into the total picture. They need to know not only the essential components of the system but also how the parts interact and contribute to the success (goal attainment) of the whole—in other words, the culture.

Every school system has a unique culture; that is, a set of interrelated values and priorities, norms and expectations, ideas and beliefs (Comuntzis-Page, 1996). This culture, according to Smithers (1988), serves a variety of useful functions for a system, including (a) establishing standards and shared expectations that provide a range of acceptable behavior for group members, (b) providing guidelines that allow individuals to fit into the group, and (c) setting standards of behavior that facilitate interaction between members and provide a means of identifying with one's peers.

Because each system has a unique culture, inductees often encounter difficulties in the adjustment that takes place between the individual and the organization during initial assignments in a new position. Schools may promote unique beliefs that conflict with those held by new employees (Short & Greer, 1998). Beliefs of new staff members concerning academic freedom, teaching controversial issues, the role of the teacher as a citizen, selection of reading matter, and student behavior, as well as their values, traditions, customs, beliefs, goals, appearance, and student discipline may differ considerably from the system's official values and objectives.

To a certain extent, every system seeks to assimilate new personnel by orienting them to the culture of the system. Whether the new staff members will accept or reject the institution's culture, in whole or in part, is not certain. But awareness of the organizational culture is essential when the inductee is being considered for permanent employment (Winter, Newton, & Kirkpatrick, 1998).

Cultural shaping and reinforcement are important aspects of the induction process for newly assigned personnel. Both at the time when these personnel enter the organization and later on, the system should develop and implement plans for cultural transmission and acquisition by helping inductees understand what the organization expects of its members. Thus, the induction process provides a timely opportunity to translate system philosophy into cultural reality by describing and interpreting the roles, relationships, and behaviors necessary for individual, unit, and organizational effectiveness.

Cultural assimilation is to be achieved most likely in an effective induction process when certain socialization conditions are satisfied. These conditions have been outlined by Wanous (1992) to include the following four-stage framework for the induction of newly assigned personnel:

- Newcomer learns the reality of the work environment.
- Newcomer identifies norms of coworkers and the boss.
- Newcomer makes accommodations between conflicts at the work setting and at home.
- Newcomer accepts norms and realizes that the organization is satisfied with job behavior.

Community Information

The relationship between school systems and communities is complementary. The school system has a vested interest in the community, and the community has a vested interest in the school system. The successes of both the school system and the community are linked closely through common interests.

Although there are exceptions to any generality, there are few exceptions about the relationship between school systems and communities. Seldom does one find an excellent school system in an undesirable community. Likewise, seldom does one find an excellent community with a below-average school system.

Because the success of one entity depends largely on the success of the other, school systems should make every effort to strengthen school–community relations. Research on this issue indicates that effective schools have more contact with parents and the community than less effective schools and that small school districts, like large school districts, must cultivate positive school community relations (Di Benedetto & Wilson, 1982). Positive community relations programs require efforts by all school representatives so that the employing community will be receptive to new employees of the district.

For personnel who are attempting to relocate within the community containing the school district, personal problems may be encountered in this effort that detracts from the on-job performance. Common relocation problems include finding suitable housing; arranging transportation; finding educational, religious, cultural, banking, and recreational facilities; and numerous other issues that must be attended to while adjusting to the new environment. The ability to cope with these problems is important to the administration because complete adjustment to the employee's new role will not occur until the anxieties involved in getting established are relieved.

It is a certainty that newly assigned employees, whether teachers, administrators, or support personnel moving into the community, need various kinds of information. Information on such matters as community geography, economy, government, religious agencies, educational resources, law enforcement agencies, public safety, health conditions, medical resources, recreation facilities, child care, family welfare agencies, and community planning resources is needed to help these beginners better serve the school system, its clients, and the community (White & Wehlage, 1995).

The school system has a responsibility to increase the public understanding of education so that the community will be receptive to recent school employees trying to fit into their new environment. What the school staff contributes to these ends depends to a large extent on the staff's understanding of the community. The induction process gives the administration opportunities to help newcomers adjust to the community, showing them how they can achieve personal objectives and demonstrating how community resources can be used to improve the school system. If the relationship of the community to the school is really as strategic as it is believed to be, then the school system should develop induction programs to help the staff, especially new members, understand the community and its effect on the school system.

Ordering and Coordinating the Induction Sequence

In the previous section, we focused on the information needs of newly assigned employees. For clarity, these needs were classified according to position, organization, and community. Although these sources of information were treated separately, in reality, much overlap exists with respect to the information needs of new personnel.

Because overlap exists among the sources of informational needs, these sources of information should be treated as interrelated components within an induction process. Collectively, information from all sources (position, system, and community) should be integrated and should be ordered in a meaningful sequence for new employees. This process of ordering and sequencing of information within an induction program is noted in Step 3 of Figure 5.2.

Actual content of a particular induction program should be tailored to the specific needs of the program participants. Induction needs vary from one system to another and from one year to another within the same school system. Depending on the characteristics of a particular group of inductees, content and sequence of an induction program may need to be altered.

Even though information needs for new employees may vary among systems and across time, there are certain crucial periods within the employment cycle for all of these employees. We label these periods as the preappointment period, the interim period, and the initial service period for purposes of discussion about the induction process. A brief description of these periods (to be expanded in the following sections), along with some of the key agents for an effective induction process during each period, is presented in Figure 5.5.

Preappointment Period

As has been noted consistently within this chapter, the induction cycle begins before any initial contact is made between the institution and the applicant. Vacant positions to be filled must be identified and authorized, either through a long-range staffing plan, as described in Chapter 2, or by the exit of current personnel. Regardless of whether vacant positions are created newly or established previously, certain

Phases and Activities of the Individual Induction Sequence

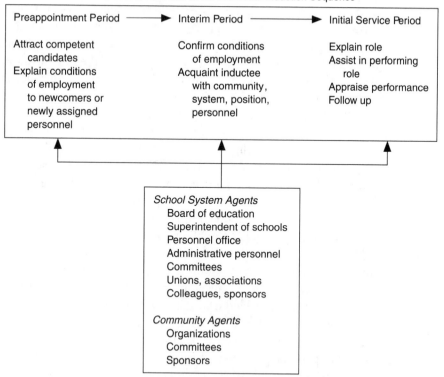

FIGURE 5.5   *Linkage of phases, agents, and activities of the induction sequence.*

types of information must be compiled for every vacant focal position during the preappointment period.

For every vacant focal position, specific information is needed about the position and general information is needed about the school system. Position information may be obtained through several existing sources within the district. Often, school districts used a well-prepared brochure to inform applicants and employment agencies about the characteristics of the system and the community, the application process, and the names of contact persons within the system (Winter, 1997).

Specific information about the position is presented to applicants generally in a position guide. Sometimes a position guide must be developed for new vacant focal positions; in other instances, an existing guide must be revisited and updated for ongoing focal positions. Far too often, however, dated information is provided to applicants and employment agencies during the preappointment period of the induction process. As a result of such information, neither the interests of the system nor those of the applicant are served if the position is described poorly or if the qualifications for the position are misrepresented.

The position guide should contain up-to-date information about the job and the experiential requirements necessary for satisfactory performance of the position. This information is essential to several involved parties during the preappointment phase of the induction process. It gives direction to those responsible for recruitment and selection; makes clear to the applicant the qualifications, duties, and responsibilities of the position; and enables placement agencies and recruiters to locate candidates who meet the requirements.

Recruitment brochures provide information about the system and the community. For the system, information is included about the size of the school district, the number of school buildings, the wealth of the district, and the per-pupil spending. Information about the community includes major industries, median home price, number of residents, and governmental structure of the community.

Sources of information contained in position guides and in recruitment brochures provide topics for exploration within the initial employment interview. Within the initial interview, the organizational representative can give the applicant various types of information likely to be needed in deciding whether to pursue further the employment opportunity. Moreover, during the interview, the applicant is able to ask questions about the position or to get information on a range of relevant issues that may not have been covered by the position guide and the recruitment brochure.

When possible during the preappointment phase of the induction process, initial job interviews should be held at the actual work site for the vacant focal position. By holding initial screening interviews at the actual work site, individuals as applicants can be exposed to important contextual information about the position, the system, and the community. Exposure to this type of information is the primary goal of the preappointment phase of the induction process for public school employees.

Interim Induction Period

Following the preappointment phase of the induction process, job candidates enter the interim induction period (see Figure 5.5). The interim induction period begins by consummating the employment contract. An offer of employment is made by the school system and the offer is accepted by an individual.

After the employment relationship has been solidified, certain induction activities can be accomplished prior to the first day on the job. Although some induction activities must be tailored to individuals and to work groups, other induction activities are somewhat constant across individuals and separate work groups. The following list presents some of the preliminary steps planned and initiated by the human resource function to help all new employees adjust to the position, the system, and the community:

- Letters of welcome are sent by the board of education and the superintendent of schools.
- An experienced employee is assigned to serve as a sponsor for every newly assigned person.

- A brochure is prepared for sponsors that explains the aims of the induction program and the responsibilities of sponsors.
- A preliminary conference is held between sponsors and the immediate supervisor of the new employee.
- A conference between the immediate supervisor and the new appointee is held to discuss the work assignment. The supervisor should avoid giving the new appointee a heavy workload or unusual duties that make it difficult for the beginner to achieve a measure of success in the first year. Whenever possible, assignments should be made on the basis of employee preference and the need to reduce the workload of the employee during the first year of service.
- Copies of handbooks, selected board policies, and relevant labor contacts are given to the new employee.
- Conditions of employment are confirmed. The organization makes certain that the newcomer understands the salary, collateral benefits, extra pay, and other facets of the compensation structure prior to reporting for duty.

By setting in motion during the interim induction period many of the activities described previously, several advantages may be realized. Employees will have more time to devote to the information they receive prior to reporting to work, and the amount of information imparted after reporting to work will be less due to the information received during the interim induction period. As such, some of the anxieties of the employees are reduced, and they are able to cope better on their first official workday.

Within the interim induction period, the immediate supervisor is responsible for helping the employee adjust to the new work assignment. If possible, an initial meeting between the employee and the immediate supervisor should be scheduled prior to beginning work. This meeting should include interpreting plans for the coming year, including those for appraising work performance and evaluating progress; acquainting the inductee with physical facilities, resources, and support services; and explaining the general policies and work routines of the unit.

Prior to beginning the work year, most school districts have an opening day conference for all employees including those new to the assignment and those preparing for another school year. It is usual for many school districts to require new employees to report for a day of orientation before the opening day conference. During the orientation day for new employees, presentations should be made by community representatives, informational sessions about the system should be conducted, and a social reception hosted by the board of education should close the day's activities.

Activities, as just described, are illustrative rather than exhaustive and any given sequence of induction activities will fail to satisfy the needs of all school systems. The wide range of induction problems in different institutions rules out a prescribed program applicable to all school systems. Each system can best achieve the goals of the induction process by developing and assessing the techniques and activities most effective for particular situations and conditions.

Forms found in Figures 5.6 and 5.7 lend specificity to the foregoing suggestions. These forms illustrate a three-part induction plan for the time before the newcomer actually begins work. The following outline is the substance of this plan:

- Sessions 1 and 2 cover central administration responsibilities. The intent is to explain the organization and administration of systemwide personnel policies and procedures applicable to new members.
- Session 3 covers position and unit-oriented responsibilities. The intent is to acquaint individuals with their responsibilities and to introduce them to their new colleagues. This session is handled by the administrator of the new employee's unit.
- Copies of forms are given to inductees to acquaint them with the nature and scope of the conditions of employment, constraints that govern their work, and opportunities that will become available.
- The inductee and the administrator responsible for conducting the session sign the forms; these forms become a component of the new staff member's file.
- Instructional aids available for orientation sessions are virtually limitless, ranging from programmed materials to filmstrips, slides, films, tapes, cassettes, records, charts, transparencies, flip charts, videotapes, brochures, booklets, and Web sites.

Our discussion in this section has addressed certain tasks, procedures, and concerns common to any effective induction process. We have focused primarily on the preappointment period and the interim period of the induction process (Figure 5.5). However, an effective induction process goes beyond these two periods to include the regular work cycle of new personnel throughout their probationary period (see Figures 5.2 and 5.5).

Follow-up of Inductee Adjustment

Induction responsibilities for new personnel continue with the opening of school, as noted in Figure 5.2. Although effective recruitment and selection can improve the quality of applicants and enhance the match between persons, positions, and work environments, both of these human resource functions signal the beginning rather than the end of the induction process (Winter, Keedy, & Newton, 2000). Until the new employee has performed under actual conditions, and until the organization has had an opportunity to appraise the suitability of the newcomer for the position, induction is less than complete.

The need for an induction process to continue after the preopening conference is based on two facts. First, few inductees are ready to perform the new assignment flawlessly, and second, even the best selection process is fallible. For these reasons, a probationary period for all new personnel is becoming increasingly a matter of institutional policy, and effective induction processes cover this period of employment.

Foxcroft School System

Form 100

Induction Checklist for New Personnel
(To Be Processed by Central Administration)

Directions—Form 100 has been designed to facilitate the induction of new staff members to the Foxcroft School System. The content of the three-phase induction program is outlined below, the intent of which is to provide newcomers with an information perspective so that they may readily become informed system members.

Name of new staff member _____ Starting date _____

Unit and position location _____ _____

Session 1: Human Resource Policies and Procedures

　　Date _____ Time _____ Place _____ Responsibility _____

　　a. System mission and administrative structure _____ Policies _____

　　b. Compensation

　　　Salary _____ Collateral benefits _____ Extra pay _____

　　c. Performance appraisal _____ Probationary period _____

　　d. Development _____

　　e. Personnel inventory _____

　　f. Leaves of absence _____ Holidays _____ Vacations _____

　　g. Personnel services _____

　　h. Community relationships _____

　　i. Code of ethics _____

Session 2: Human Resource Policies and Procedures

　　Date _____ Time _____ Place _____ Responsibility _____

　　a. Review and questions on Session 1 _____

　　b. Union relations _____

　　c. Tenure _____ Retirement _____ Social security _____

　　d. Academic freedom and responsibility _____

　　e. Payroll: Deductions __ Issuance __ Adjustments __ Responsibility __

　　f. Transfers _____ Promotions _____

　　g. Grievance procedures _____

All items checked have been discussed with inductee _____

Central administration representative _____ Date _____

Returned to personnel office for individual personnel file _____

Reviewed _____ Filed _____ by personnel office

Signature of inductee _____

FIGURE 5.6 *The three-phase induction plan of the Foxcroft School System (sessions 1 and 2).*

Foxcroft School System

Form 200

Position Orientation Checklist for New Personnel
(To Be Completed by Unit Administrators)

Directions—This checklist has been designed as a part of the induction program of the Foxcroft School System. Its primary intent is to acquaint new staff members with the position to which they have been assigned and the performance requirements that the roles involve. This step of the induction process is one of several planned to enable the individual to adjust quickly to the position, the school, the system, and the community. Directions for processing the checklist are included below.

Name of inductee ______________________________

Session 3: Position and Building Orientation	***Discussion Completed***
1. Welcome and introduction to Foxcroft School System.	________
2. Describe unit organization, objectives, functions, and relationships to system at large.	________
3. Provide copy of position guide to inductee and explain contents.	________
4. Explain the relationship the position inductee will hold to unit and system objectives.	________
5. Explain position performance standards for continuance of employment.	________
6. Explain performance appraisal process and its relationship to continuance of employment and promotion.	________
7. Explain conditions of employment in unit, including:	________

Hours of work	Provisions for lunch
Lunch hours	Parking
Building facilities	Transportation
Supplies and equipment	Services
Behavior	Other

8. Introduce to colleagues within unit and to other contact personnel.

Date ______________

Signature of inductee ______________________________

Signature of unit administrator ______________________________

Returned to personnel office for individual personnel file ________

Reviewed __________ Filed __________ by personnel office ________

FIGURE 5.7 *The three-phase induction of the Foxcroft School System (session 3).*

An effective induction process for employees newly assigned to vacant focal positions requires follow-up (see Step 4 in Figure 5.2). Follow-up on the part of the immediate supervisor is essential for a newly assigned employee during the first few weeks on the job. The timing of such assistance is important because the inductee may have trouble understanding the assignment or may encounter difficulty on the job.

Within the induction sequence of activities, follow-ups should be scheduled. After each follow-up, the administrator should compile a formal report capturing detailing observations and conclusions derived from observations and assessments. Follow-up reports should be submitted by the immediate supervisor to the central administration, which appraises such characteristics as quality of performance, difficulties encountered, and other factors deemed important to the effectiveness of the new employee.

Performance appraisal during the probationary period, as one phase of the total performance appraisal process, is designed not only to assist the competent probationer but also to identify the potentially incompetent, marginal, or undesirable employee as well. Those individuals who fail to perform satisfactorily in one position may be reassigned, given more personal supervision, or provided with intensified training to overcome their deficiencies. Prompt rehabilitation or elimination of unsuitable appointees will save money, time, and effort for the system.

To monitor the job behaviors of newly assigned employees during the probationary period, it is necessary to assess the perceptions of both the employee and the immediate supervisor. Figure 5.8 is an example of a self-appraisal form to be completed by the inductee. It is designed to provide feedback to the immediate supervisor on position problems and on progress toward effective role performance as perceived by the new employee.

Complementing the self-assessment form compiled by the employee is a form to be completed by the immediate supervisor. This form is found in Figure 5.9. The form contains the impressions of both parties and is used to inform the central administration about the progress of employees during the probationary period.

Analysis and synthesis of the information obtained from both forms provides the basis for counseling and coaching during follow-up sessions between the inductee and the immediate supervisor. Formalizing the methods of collecting information about new employees at the probationary stage communicates an important message. That is, the system has a continuing interest in their welfare, their adjustment to the assigned position, and their contribution to the organization.

Managing the Induction Process

Assessments of new personnel are essential to an effective induction program. The financial and human capital investments associated with recruiting, selecting, and inducting new personnel are considerable for most school systems. However, the loss suffered by the system when the inductee's service is terminated or when the inductee leaves the organization voluntarily warrants the attention of management.

Position Design

Do you have a clear understanding of the expectations your immediate supervisor has for you in your present position?

Do you have a clear understanding of the goals of the work unit to which you are assigned?

Does your immediate supervisor give you specific help in improving your position performance?

Do you feel you are well placed in your present assignment?

Performance Appraisal

Does your immediate supervisor give you the necessary information to enable you to know how you are getting on with your role?

How worthwhile was your last performance appraisal in helping you to improve your performance?

Summarize the overall strengths and weaknesses you have demonstrated in performing your present assignment.

Development

How much assistance have you been given by your supervisor in planning your career development?

How do you feel about the progress you have made thus far in performing your role?

How confident are you that your career aspirations can be met by remaining in this organization?

Do you feel you have potential beyond your present assignment?

How have you demonstrated this potential?

Communication

Do you receive sufficient information to perform your role effectively?

Do you receive sufficient information to understand the relationships among your role, the unit to which you are assigned, and the mission of the school system?

Is your supervisor well informed about your requirements for performing the role effectively?

Role Satisfaction

How do you feel about the kind of work you are doing in your present position?

Are there significant observations that you think should be noted about the dimensions of your position that affect your performance and should be brought to the attention of your unit, such as unit objectives, position design, organization structure, supervisory process, and results achieved?

How effectively do you feel you have met the responsibilities of your position?

Signature of inductee _____ Date _____

FIGURE 5.8 *Self-appraisal form for inductees.*

In theory, recruitment, selection, and induction processes should result in the attraction and retention of the number, kinds, and quality of personnel needed by the system for an effective education program. Periodic assessments of the actual outcomes (Step 5 of Figure 5.2) of these three human resource processes should provide information to minimize turnover costs due to faulty recruitment, selection, and placement. If and when these processes do not lead to the desired results, the system can take corrective action.

Assessments of the induction process should focus on several different outcome measures. The most important one is whether the new personnel performed effectively in their assigned position. Because most work assignments have a proficiency curve in which job performance improves over time, the effectiveness of new personnel should be assessed at different times during the probationary period.

It is imperative to determine if the predictions of performance made before selection agree with actual job performance. The ultimate purpose of analyzing the recruitment, selection, and induction processes is to determine how well the system is succeeding in attracting and holding a competent staff. The evaluation should reveal what adjustments must be made to achieve these goals.

Because individuals as well as organizations must commit to the employment process, it is important to give special attention to those employees who performed effectively but resigned during the probationary period. Voluntary resignations of effective probationers may or may not be related to their experiences in the recruitment, selection, assignment, or induction processes. Exit interviews with these employees can be extremely enlightening to those responsible for monitoring the induction process.

Although it is true that much time, money, and talent are invested in recruitment, selection, and induction, it is also true that person–position mismatches are costly, time consuming, and counterproductive. To minimize such potential mismatches, ongoing assessment of the induction process is essential. Without exception, induction processes must be modified each school year.

Induction and Human Resource Strategy

Throughout this book, the various functions of a school system (presented in Figure 1.2) and of the human resource processes (shown in Figure 2.1) have been implicitly viewed as interdependent. For instance, recruitment, selection, appraisal, and development are considered to be intertwined. This interdependence among personnel processes should be taken into account in shaping the overall human resource strategy. Thus viewed, induction, as one of the processes of the personnel function, has considerable potential for achieving the aims of the system, especially the right to be informed, coached, mentored, and assisted in various ways to achieve specific goals.

School systems use many methods to help new employees achieve relative independence as established staff members with personal sets of behavioral determiners.

Name of inductee _____ Organization unit _____ Position _____

Adjustment Progress and Problems	Analysis by Unit Administrator	Analysis by Inductee

What progress has been made by the inductee during the review period in making the following adjustments:
  a. Community adjustment?
  b. Position adjustment?
  c. System adjustment?
  d. Individual and group adjustment?
  e. Personal adjustment?
 	
What are the obstacles to achieving adjustment expectations in the areas listed above?
 	
What comments should be made on the results achieved for each of the adjustments listed above?
 	
In what areas has the inductee made the most progress in adjustment? The least progress?
 	
Do the adjustment expectations need to be revised?
 	
What are the plans and priorities for achieving adjustment expectations?		

Signature of inductee _____

Signature of unit administrator _____

Date of review _____ Next review period _____

FIGURE 5.9 *Form for performance review of new personnel by the unit administrator.*

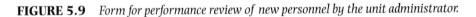

This assistance includes various forms of support designated in the literature by labels such as peer coaching, buddy system, master teacher support, mentor–protégé relationship, and clinical teacher support. The types of staff assistance provided to inductees focus on enhancing their development, depending on the individual's personality and willingness to adjust and adapt to the internal and external aspects of the workplace.

This chapter has emphasized that an effective induction process serves a number of purposes, including socialization, reduction of personnel anxieties, turnover, and supervisory time, helping individuals to understand themselves, and helping the system to understand new employees. Recent educational reform efforts in the United States, however, have caused more and more school systems to reconsider the induction process. Today more than ever, an effective induction process is a necessity for all functional school districts.

Review and Preview

In this chapter, analysis of induction problems suggests that an effective induction process is one way that the system can help new members to assimilate, as well as to enhance their personal development, security, and need satisfaction. A school system can recruit and select personnel, but until new employees become fully aware of and adjusted to the work to be performed, the work environment, and their new colleagues, they cannot be expected to contribute efficiently and effectively to the organization's goals. An induction process is needed to help new personnel resolve community, system, position, and development problems by creating plans to enhance their position knowledge, skills, and behavior. Use of this process indicates a recognition of and an attempt to do something about the fact that human maladjustment is expensive, detrimental to individual and organizational goal achievement, and harmful to the socialization process involving the individual and the system. The induction process also assumes that the main determinant of motivation is the attraction the position holds for the individual, and that induction activities designed to enhance the potential for motivated action will result in better performance on the job.

Chapter 6 is concerned with methods used to achieve individual, unit, and system goals.

Discussion Questions

1. How does your school organization transmit organizational culture to new employees?

2. In school systems, many new employees resign voluntarily during their probationary period. What costs to the school organization are associated with this situation? What can the organization do to reduce the number of new teachers who leave the field after their first year?

3. Who coordinates the induction process for your school organization? Is the induction process centrally coordinated, or is the process devolved onto specific work sites? Identify three strengths and weaknesses of this induction process.

4. Respond to the following statement: "A well-designed, carefully implemented recruitment and selection program eliminates the need for an induction plan."

5. The behavior of a new inductee does not appear to mesh with the school organization culture (e.g., violates dress code, eats lunch alone). What should be done with this employee?

References

Bergeson, T. (n.d.). *Teacher assistance program: A model for a year-long induction program.* Retrieved August 1, 2002, from the Office of Superintendent of Public Instruction Web site: **http://www.k12. wa.us/ProfEd/tap/amodel.asp**

Chester, M. D., & Beaudin, B. Q. (1996, Spring). Efficacy beliefs of newly hired teachers in urban schools. *American Educational Research Journal, 33*(1), 233–257.

Comuntzis-Page, G. (1996). *Critical issue: Creating the school climate and structures to support parent and family involvement.* Retrieved August 1, 2002, from the North Central Regional Educational Laboratory Web site: **http://www.ncrel. org/sdrs/ areas/issues/envrnmnt/famncomm/ pa300.htm**

Di Benedetto, R., & Wilson, A. P. (1982, February). The small school principal and school-community relations. Small schools fact sheet. *ERIC Digests.* Retrieved August 1, 2002, from **http://www. ed.gov/databases/ERIC_Digests/ ed232798 .html**

French, W. L. (1987). *The personnel management process,* (6th ed., p. 297). Boston: Houghton Mifflin.

Heneman, H. G., Judge, T. A., & Heneman, R. L. (2000). *Staffing organizations* (3rd ed.). Middleton, WI: Mendota House.

LeGore, J. A., & Parker, L. (1997). First year principal succession: A study of leadership, role, and change. *Journal of School Leadership, 7*(4), 369–385.

Luthans, F., & Kreitner, R. (1975). *Organizational behavior modification* (p. 97). Glenview, IL: Scott Foresman.

North Carolina Department of Public Instruction. (n.d.). *1997–98 model new teacher orientation program grant recipients.* Retrieved August 1, 2002, from the Department of Public Instruction Website: **http://www. dpi.state.nc.us/mentoring_novice_ teachers/recipnts.htm**

Seyfarth, J. T. (1996). *Personnel management for effective schools.* Needham Heights, MA: Allyn & Bacon.

Shen, J. (1997, Fall). Has the alternative certification policy materialized its promise? A comparison between traditionally and alternatively certified teachers in public schools. *Educational Evaluation and Policy Analysis, 19*(3), 276–283.

Short, P. M., & Greer, J. T. (1998). *Leadership in empowered schools.* Upper Saddle River, NJ: Merrill/Prentice Hall.

Smithers, R. D. (1988). *The psychology of work and human performance* (p. 361). New York: Harper & Row.

U.S. Department of Education. (2000, May). The importance of support. In *Survival guide for new teachers: Message for new teachers.* Retrieved August 1, 2002, from the U.S. Department of Education Web site: **http:// www.ed.gov/pubs/survivalguide/ message.html**

Wanous, J. P. (1992). *Organizational entry* (2nd ed.). Reading, MA: Addison-Wesley.

White, G., & Wehlage, J. (1995). Community collaboration: It is such a good idea, why is it so hard? *Educational Evaluation and Policy Analyses, 17*(4), 23–38.

Winter, P. A. (1997). Educational recruitment and selection: A review of recent studies and recommendations for best practice. In L. Wildman (Ed.), *Fifth NCPEA yearbook* (pp. 133–140). Lancaster, PA: Technomic.

Winter, P. A., Keedy, J. L., & Newton, R. M. (2000). Teacher serving on school decision-making councils: Predictors of teacher attraction to the job. *Journal of School Leadership, 10,* 248–263.

Winter, P. A., Newton, R. M., & Kirkpatrick, R. L. (1998). The Influence of work values on teacher selection decisions: The effects of principal values, teacher values, and principal–teacher value interactions. *Teaching and Teacher Education, 14*(4), 385–400.

Supplementary Reading

Arends, R. I. (1983). Beginning teachers as learners. *Journal of Educational Research, 7*(4), 236–242.

Bradley, L., & Gordon, S. P. (1994, Summer). Comparing the ideal to the real in state-mandated teacher induction programs. *Journal of Staff Development, 15*(3), 44–50.

Brooks, D. M. (1987). *Teacher induction: A new beginning.* Reston, VA: Association of Teacher Education.

Egbert, R. T. (1990). *The employee handbook.* Upper Saddle River, NJ: Prentice Hall.

Evan, W. M. (1963). Peer group interaction and organizational socialization: A study of employee turnover. *American Sociological Review, 28,* 436–440.

Griffin, G. A. (1984). *Crossing the bridge: The first years of teaching.* National Commission on Excellence in Teacher Education: Author.

Haines, R. C., & Mitchell, K. F. (1985, November). Teacher career development in Charlotte-Mecklenburg. *Educational Leadership, 433,* 11–13.

Hartzell, G. (1991). Induction of experienced assistant principals. *NASSP Bulletin, 75*(533), 75–84.

Heckman, P. (1987). Understanding school culture. In J. I. Goodlad (Ed.), *The ecology of school renewal: 86th NSSE yearbook* (Part 1). Chicago: National Society for the Study of Education, University of Chicago Press.

Hoffman, G., & Link S. (1986, January–February). Beginning teacher's perceptions of mentors. *Journal of Teacher Education, 37*(1), 22–25.

Jacoby, D. (1989, December). Rewards make the mentor. *Personnel, 66*(12), 10–14.

Josefowitz, N., & Gordon, H. (1988). *How to get a good start in your new job.* Reading, MA: Addison-Wesley.

Lasley, T. J. (Ed.). (1989) [Special issue]. Teacher induction. *Journal of Teacher Education 37,* 1.

Mardenfeld, S. (1989, November). The best way to get a new employee up to speed. *Working Woman, 4,* 34.

Moran, S. W. (1990, November). Schools and the beginning teacher. *Phi Delta Kappan, 72*(3), 210–214.

Newcombe, E. (Ed.). (1987). *Perspectives on teacher induction: A review of the literature and promising program models.*

Shuman, B. R. (1989). *Classroom encounters, problems, case studies, solutions.* Washington, DC: National Education Association.

Sikula, J. (Ed.). (1987). Teacher induction. [Special Issue] *Action in Teacher Education 8,* 4.

Steffy, B. (1989). *Career stages of classroom teachers.* Lancaster, PA: Technomic.

Veenam, V. S. (1984). Perceived problems of beginning teachers. *Review of Educational Research, 54*(2), 143–178.

Yeager, N. (1988). *Career map: Deciding what you want, getting it, and keeping it.* New York: Wiley.

6
Development

CHAPTER OBJECTIVES

Develop an awareness of the importance and extensive implications of staff development for achieving system goals for human resources.
Consider internal and external conditions that influence staff development programs.
Illuminate key elements in the staff development process.
Stress the importance of organizational development policies and procedures that enhance attainment of individual, unit, and system aims.

CHAPTER CONCEPTS

Career stages
Development process
History
In-service education
Instrumentation
Maturation

Mortality
Regression
Selection
Staff development
Testing

Human resource administration is a function that must be performed day in and day out, year in and year out, if the school system is to work effectively. More specifically, human resource activities do not end when vacancies have been filled; they must be concerned with the destiny, productivity, and need satisfaction of people after they are employed. This involves activities relating to staff development, health, tenure, leaves of absence, substitute service, employee associations, grievances, and retirement. This chapter emphasizes the administrative process by which plans for development of human resources are conceived, implemented, and controlled. A model is used to guide the discussion of the process by which plans for organizational, group, and individual development are planned, implemented, and evaluated.

Staff Development by Design

The previous chapter focused on orientation addressing the development needs for special groups of employees at a particular time of their employment within a public school system. Included among those groups addressed in the previous chapter were those new to the system and those new to the assignment. For both types of employees, the previous chapter focused on facilitating the assimilation of these groups into the community, the system, the work unit, and the position during their probationary period of employment in a newly assigned position.

In this chapter, we consider development activities designed for all employees throughout their professional careers within a public school district. All individuals affiliated with a school district can benefit from a focused program of appropriate development activities for their current role or for an anticipated new role within a public school system. Individuals addressed in this chapter include members of the board of education, school administrators, teachers, and classified staff.

By including all individuals in a formal development program designed to enhance the performance of their current role or their anticipated new role sends a distinct message to employees throughout a public school system. This message is that development is an important organizational activity and that development is expected of all individuals, not just specific groups of employees. Through leading by example in the development process, board members provide one of the most influential means of endorsement for professional development programs in a school system.

During the working careers of individuals within a school district, employees experience many changes that impact the operation of the school system. This is especially true in the 21st century. In fact, for many employees, school reform has been the rule rather than the exception since the 1980s due to the publication of *A Nation at Risk* (U.S. Department of Education's National Commission on Excellence in Education, 1983).

Changes altering the way schools are administered may originate from external sources, internal sources, or some combination of these sources that impact the way business is conducted within the public school setting. External changes impacting the way schools are administered can stem from research findings, international comparisons, federal agendas, state mandates, and community expectations. Internal changes altering school administration can come from priorities of the board of education, desires of the central administration, and needs of individual employees.

Management of change within the school setting to meet emerging needs requires a systematic plan for developing employees and school officials. Development of school employees and school officials should be an ongoing process and should consider immediate as well as advanced career stages and needs of individuals. To maintain the momentum necessary for an effective development process focusing on career stages and needs of individuals, certain tasks must be addressed continuously by those charged with development responsibilities in a public school setting.

Following are some of the more important tasks that must be addressed continuously by administrators of a public school district when attempting to execute an effective and efficient program of staff development:

- Assessing how effective current staff development programs are for improving individual, unit, and system performance of role incumbents
- Highlighting ineffective and inefficient development activities for improvement or elimination in a staff development program
- Designing and shaping development programs to attain strategic human resource goals and objectives as stated in the strategic plan of a school district
- Linking subprocesses of the human resource function such as recruitment, selection, induction, and performance appraisal to the staff development process
- Viewing staff development as an important vehicle for *career development* plans
- Considering the strategic importance of *changes in the internal and the external environments* that impact staff development activities of a public school district
- Establishing a planning agenda that anticipates rather than reacts to the changing development needs of individuals
- Basing the staff development program on the assumption that the needs of a specific school are paramount and critical to any development endeavor, thus, avoiding the temptation to clone other development programs
- Upgrading the investment in staff development activities in areas found to have the *greatest impact on performance improvement* related to the strategic plan of a public school district

Creating a master plan that identifies high-impact development activities, anticipates outcomes, and achieves optimal results is a must for an effective public school system. In fact, many of the goals of effective staff development programs have been identified through extensive research about this topic. These goals are listed here as characteristics of promising professional development programs:

- They focus on teachers as central to student learning, yet include all other members of the school community.

- They focus on individual, collegial, and organizational improvement.
- They respect and nurture the intellectual and leadership capacities of teachers, principals, and others in the school community.
- They reflect the best available research and practice in teaching, learning, and leadership.
- They enable teachers to develop further expertise in subject content, teaching strategies, uses of technologies, and other essential elements in teaching to high standards.
- They promote continuous inquiry and improvement in the daily life of schools.
- They are planned collaboratively by those who will participate in and facilitate the development.
- They require substantial time and other resources.
- They are driven by a coherent and long-term plan.
- They are evaluated ultimately on the basis of their impact on teacher effectiveness and student learning, and this assessment guides subsequent professional development efforts. (U.S. Department of Education, 1998).

Staff Development Problems

Staff development, one of the major processes within the human resource function, has not escaped criticism from several sources. Commission reports, reform initiatives, and the media have criticized staff development efforts in school systems. These criticisms are based on international comparisons, state-mandated proficiency test results, and escalating district operating budgets.

For many school systems, criticisms of staff development efforts have merit. Indeed, staff development efforts in some school systems have been and continue to be a series of haphazard isolated events unrelated to system goals and represent inefficient use of public funds. Some of the most common factors contributing to ineffective staff development efforts by public school districts are listed in Figure 6.1.

Awareness of the most common problems associated with staff development attempts can benefit greatly those responsible for staff development activities within the public school setting. The problems listed in Figure 6.1 can be used to assess the current operation of staff development programs and activities in a school system. Once problems within the staff development program have been identified, corrective measures can be taken to align staff development activities with the strategic plans of a particular public school district.

Underlying many of the problems, as listed in Figure 6.1, is the absence of any systematic attempt to link staff development efforts to the strategic plans of the school system. This problem can be attributed, at least in part, to the tendency to view staff development as a series of isolated events rather than as a continuous

- Allocating staff development resources without knowing what, if anything, has been derived from the expenditure.
- Spurning the concept of staff development as a tool for leveraging human resource strategy.
- Viewing staff development as an end in itself rather than as a means to an end.
- Initiating unguided and unorganized staff development programs.
- Disregarding the need for professionalization of internal change agents.
- Giving individual development precedence instead of linking individual, group, and system development.
- Taking for granted that there is a close fit between programs and individual and group needs.
- Failing to apply recruiting, selection, and induction strategies to find, attract, and retain the right candidates.
- Minimizing the importance of validating job-relatedness of staff development programs.
- Offering tuition reimbursement programs without linkage to position requirements.
- Disregarding needs assessment when granting funds for self-nomination development plans.
- Assuming that correcting staff development problems will solve major organizational problems.
- Lacking models to analyze whether programs produce changes; whether they were desired ones; and whether changes in performance met targeted need.
- Viewing staff development conventions as vacation time, as rest and recreation, as a position perquisite, as a hiatus in position demands.
- Failing to aim the staff development process at specific behavioral objectives in advance of program initiation.
- Emphasizing program activities rather than facilitation of learning and resultant behaviors.
- Extending benefit provisions of system–union negotiated contracts without serious review of objectives, costs, outcomes, or linkage to aims of strategic human resource planning.
- Precluding greater centralized control over the cost effectiveness of staff development programs.

FIGURE 6.1   *Illustration of contemporary staff development problems.*

program of development. Using a systems approach to staff development can solve many of the problems that are found in Figure 6.1.

A systems approach for linking staff development efforts to the strategic plans of the district has been suggested by Asayesh (1993). Asayesh's approach uses the

- Each individual is a part of a whole—every individual action has consequences for the system as a whole.
- To change the outcomes of an organization, one must change the system—not just its parts.
- Organizations must focus on the root causes of problems and long-term goals and consequences, not the symptoms.
- Effective change occurs by understanding the system and its behaviors, and working with the flow of the system, not against it.

Effective staff development for a systems approach includes:

- Training in the concepts, values, and specific tools of systems thinking.
- Ongoing processes that involve all segments of the organization in a dialogue so that there is collective rather than individual staff development.
- A focus on the application of the beliefs and tools of the system in the context of day-to-day workings of schools and the school system.
- Questioning and examining underlying assumptions and beliefs.

FIGURE 6.2   *Key principles of systems thinking.*

Source: Adapted from "Using Systems Thinking to Change Systems," by G. Asayesh, 1993, *Journal of Staff Development* 14(4), 8–140.

concept of system's thinking (see Figure 6.2). System's thinking is a planning tool for dealing with various organizational problems that are difficult to resolve by the temporary application of isolated practices.

A major benefit of applying a systems approach to staff development is that this methodology enables planners to consider both the internal and the external dimensions of organizational behavior in the design and the execution of staff development programs in a public school district. School systems acquire substantial resources from external sources, are regulated externally, must satisfy a host of external interests, and are subject to various forces over which they have little control. Thus, systems theory embraces the view that organizational effectiveness depends on the ability to adapt to the demands of the external environment and to shape the culture of the internal environment to meet external demands in an efficient and effective manner.

Staff Development Domain

Providing systematic means for the continuous development of skills, knowledge, problem-solving abilities, and attitudes of system personnel has been a cardinal professional tenet of all organizations for centuries. Education has been no exception to this tenet. Considerable efforts and numerous resources have been and continue to be directed toward the improvement of educators as professional employees within the public school setting.

For example, many states have passed laws requiring staff development activities for certificated personnel. Some states require these individuals to obtain a master's degree within a specified time period following initial certification by the state department of education, and other states have required individuals to complete an approved plan for staff development as a condition of continuing employment. Failure to satisfy these regulatory requirements often renders an individual ineligible for future certification in these states.

Almost without exception, states have codified **in-service education** expectations for employees by designating a minimum number of days that must be devoted to in-service activities each year. Initially, in-service education was restricted to teachers and other certificated personnel; later on, it was expanded to cover all employees in the school system. According to most state codes, failure to perform in-service activities is grounds for employee termination.

Accompanying state-mandated requirements for development activities have been certain historical trends. Political action in the late 1970s resulted in the creation of federally supported teacher centers as a means of upgrading staff development programs (DeLuca, 1991). In the 1980s, state legislators and local school administrators viewed staff development as a key aspect of school improvement efforts. Most recently, this trend has been reinforced by President Bush's initiative of "No Child Left Behind" (U.S. Department of Education, 1998).

When staff development for educational organizations is viewed as an integrated activity from a systems perspective, staff development can be linked to those processes designed by the system to attract, retain, and improve the quality and quantity of staff members needed to achieve desired goals. Staff development is vitally linked to human resource planning because, as the reader may recall from the previous chapter, a sound human resource plan calls for:

- Improving the job performance of all employees
- Developing key skills of selected personnel to fill anticipated vacancies
- Promoting the self-development of all employees to facilitate need satisfaction
- Identifying and developing individuals in each employee group who have the potential to be promoted

Staff development, as considered within this chapter, includes both informal and formal approaches to the improvement of effectiveness on the part of individuals in their assigned positions. As illustrated in Figure 6.3, this involves both short- and long-range activities; each activity has different objectives, involves different levels of personnel, and addresses a variety of ways for conceptualizing and organizing the staff improvement function. In effect, staff development is the process of staff improvement through approaches that emphasize self-realization, self-growth, and self-development.

Development includes those activities aimed at the improvement and growth of abilities, attitudes, skills, and knowledge of system members for both current and anticipated assignments. Figure 6.3 indicates that staff development includes various situations in every work organization and calls for some form of individual or group development. The following statements are illustrative:

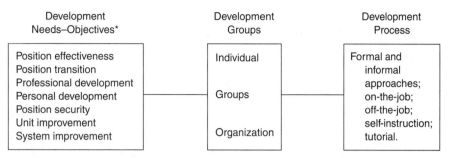

Development Needs–Objectives*	Development Groups	Development Process
Position effectiveness Position transition Professional development Personal development Position security Unit improvement System improvement	Individual Groups Organization	Formal and informal approaches; on-the-job; off-the-job; self-instruction; tutorial.

* A need is defined as a discrepancy between an actual and desired state. Objectives are the counterpart of needs and are employed to translate problems into programs.

FIGURE 6.3   *A typology of personnel development.*

- Development requires interrelationships among system, unit, and individual goals and has implications for the design and implementation of development programs.
- Development includes all school personnel within the public school system.
- Development entails meeting two kinds of expectations: (a) the contribution of the individual to the school system and (b) the rewards anticipated by the individual in return.
- Development involves all activities designed to increase an individual's ability to work effectively in an assigned or anticipated role.
- Development is focused on two kinds of activities: (a) those specifically planned and administered by the school system (formal approaches) and (b) those initiated by personnel (informal approaches).
- Development is concerned with values, norms, and behaviors of individuals and groups.
- Development is designed to serve the following purposes: personal growth, professional development, problem solving, remedial action, motivation, upward mobility, and member security.
- Development programs initiated by the system are aimed at educating individuals above and beyond the immediate technical requirements of their position.
- Development programs sanction activities related to practical and position-oriented needs, as well as to longer-range purposes focused on full development of the individual.
- Development encourages career-long staff development for all personnel as an organizational necessity.
- Development activity has been evaluated judgmentally rather than empirically in the past.
- Development has failed to capitalize fully on existing knowledge and theory regarding staff development.

- Development programs have been subjected to an array of fads and fashions that have not been based on a sound process development model (such as human resource objectives) or carefully designed, administered, and tested experiences.
- Development is a powerful tool for effecting individual, unit, and system change.

Improvement of employee performance calls for a variety of approaches to modify and enhance the behavior patterns of individuals and groups to maximize organizational effectiveness. A framework by which efforts are systematized to deal with the many development problems arising continually in school systems, both individual and group, is referred to as a process model. The section that follows presents a comprehensive development process model consisting of sequential and interrelated phases for an effective and efficient staff development process.

Staff Development Process

Staff development activities in educational organizations have changed substantially over the last two decades. Beginning as a group of unconnected, isolated events, staff development has become one of the key human resource functions in a school system. Some of the changes in staff development that have evolved over time are presented in Figure 6.4.

Many of these changes associated with staff development stem from certain inferences about labor markets and certain views about **career stages** for individuals as employees. From a labor market perspective, boards of education are beginning to view staff development as an ongoing process rather than as a periodic event and have taken note of the emerging reality for human resource planning. This emerging reality reflects a dramatic shift taking place in the workforce of this country—a shift that affects every employer in America, not just educational systems.

No longer are traditional labor pools available for recruitment and selection (see Young, Jury, & Reis, 1999). Growth of the pool of workers is slowing, and the workforce is diversifying. Because of these changes, recruiting and retaining knowledgeable personnel have become extremely difficult for all organizations.

Recent research addressing the recruitment and selection of employees indicates that this problem is likely to continue in the near future for educational organizations (Prince, 2002). What was once a captive pool of potential educational employees fails to exist. Many of those who once would have chosen education as a career have other viable options in more lucrative labor markets.

One way of identifying and maximizing the talents of existing labor pools is by viewing development activities from a career perspective within the educational setting and using this view as a means for enticing applicants to consider a public school district as a career option. In the professional literature and in the work

Away from . . .	Toward . . .
Top-down approach	Bottom-up approach
Narrow approach to staff development	Comprehensive approach to staff development
Isolated projects	Interactive and interdependent programs
Control	Empowerment
Off-the-shelf projects	Customized programs
System-initiated changes	System and staff initiated changes
Inattention to school culture	Collaboration to change school culture
Centralized plans	Site-based plans
Solving problems for staff members	Building staff capacity to solve own problems
Individual emphasis	Individual and team emphasis
Preparation and experience emphasis	Performance emphasis
Indifference to development outcomes	Emphasis on staff development outcomes
Development of teaching staff	Development of all classes of personnel
Sole emphasis on self-fulfillment	Individual, unit, and system goals
Development as an event	Development as a continuous process
Sporadic and disorganized programs	Systematic strategies and well-defined objectives
Limited financial support	Local, state, and federal support
Focus on remediation	Focus on remediation and growth
Administrative initiative	Administration–individual initiatives
Formal approaches	Formal and informal approaches
Programs preplanned	Staff participates in planning
Reliance on external agents/agencies	Inside or outside support as appropriate
Assuming positive program impact	Evaluating actual impact
Intuition and prior experience	Theoretical exploration
Role development	Role and career development
Random-based planning	Systems-based planning
System evaluation	System and self-evaluation
Uncoordinated, ad hoc, and fragmented projects	Staff development models
Limited use of electronic technology	Emerging emphasis on use of electronic technology
Limited methods and types of delivery	Unlimited methods and types of delivery
Lack of application of systems thinking	Using systems thinking to change systems

FIGURE 6.4 *Value trends in staff development.*

• Early Stage
  Tenured Stage
  Retirement Stage
  All Stages[a]
	• Pre-work Stage
	  Initial Work Stage
	  Stable Work Stage
	  Retirement Stage[b]
		• Establishment Stage
		  (early adulthood)
		  Advancement Stage
		  (mature adulthood)
		  Maintenance Stage
		  (midlife)
		  Withdrawal (old age)[c]

FIGURE 6.5 *Three descriptions of career stages.*

Sources: [a] *Almanac Supplement* by the University of Pennsylvania, February 28, 1989, IX-XII.
[b] *Foundations of Personnel/Human Resource Management,* (3rd ed., p. 523), by J. M. Ivancevich and
W. F. Glueck, 1983, Plano, TX: Business Publications, Inc. [c]"Career Dynamics: Managing the
Superior-Subordinate Relationship," by L. Baird and K. Kram, 1983, *Organizational Dynamics, 11,*
pp. 209–216.

world, increasing attention is being devoted to the relationship between career
stages and staff development programs. Three descriptions of career stages for employees of a public school district are presented in Figure 6.5.

It is important to stress that staff development occurs over time, goes through
several stages, cuts across a wide range of development issues, and includes changing positions and personal needs of employees. Traditionally, some organizations
have viewed these career stages only from a vertical perspective. From this perspective, individuals enter the organization and move up the hierarchy through a series
of promotions during their term of employment.

However, career stages involving only vertical movement may have little appeal today for many employees in school systems. For some positions requiring certification (e.g., teacher, psychologist, librarian), incumbents have invested several
years in specialized training and have established an identity with a professional
group. To move vertically within the school system would require further study in
a different subject matter area and professional affiliation with a different group.

For example, unions representing certain employees have made substantial
economic gains through collective bargaining with boards of education. These economic gains have often exceeded those of entry-level management and supervisory
personnel. For midcareer employees to use vertical movement for career progression would often result in less economic benefits than those enjoyed by employees at
the top of the career ladder in their current bargaining unit position.

Management and supervisory personnel have career needs, as do all employees of
a public school district. Although some of these individuals occupying managerial and
supervisory positions may have cleared successfully some of the hurdles associated
with vertical movement confronting their subordinates, other supervisory and managerial employees may be relegated to the same position or to the same level within the
organization for many years. These employees, like all others, have career plateaus and
career needs that must be addressed through a staff development program.

Overlooked by many is that the single largest employer in most communities is the school system. School systems are, however, pyramidal in structure, and the number of opportunities near the top of an educational organization is small relative to the number of employees that may seek higher-level positions through promotional opportunities. Therefore, even if most employees sought vertical movement as a means of career progression, only a few of these employees could be accommodated within their current school system.

To protect their initial investments in recruitment and selection, as well as to keep effective employees in their current position or in similar positions at the same organizational level, innovative school systems have changed their ideas about career stages within the staff development process. These farsighted school systems now view career stages from a horizontal as well as from a vertical perspective. Effective staff development programs include ways to enrich and revitalize the work life of all employees, including those seeking vertical as well as horizontal advancement.

Research and practice addressing career stages from both vertical and horizontal perspectives suggests many implications and raises several considerations, including the following:

• When staff development becomes a policy commitment, this commitment signals that the system is willing to provide continuing improvement opportunities for personnel. These opportunities may relate to career goals, career counseling, and career paths; information about position openings; and various forms of development programs, some of which address special needs such as problems relating to outplacement, retirement and preretirement, induction, and choices confronting midcareer staff members and those who have developed physical disabilities.

• Many types of opportunities exist for enhancing career development. The development process model should include decisions to develop programs most suited to specific work group needs.

• Recognizing that the pool of talent is decreasing, organizations throughout the nation are broadening their roles regarding staff development and retention. (This is especially true in the cases of women and minorities.)

• Emerging questions relating to the design of career development programs include the following: What are the system's ambitions for the career stages of its employees? Does the system have sufficient mechanisms in place to support career development? In an era of increased competition for personnel, what career plans are best calculated to retain and improve current and future staff members?

• Opportunities may exist to include particular development incentives such as sabbaticals, tuition grants, research accounts, or flexible teaching loads that have the potential to enhance the pursuit of careers within the system.

A process model provides a framework to facilitate the systemization of development activities and to resolve some of the issues concerning staff development activities. An example of a process model for development activities that could be

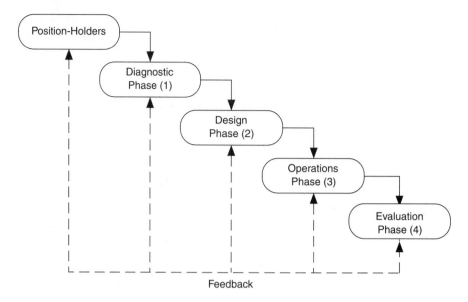

Feedback

FIGURE 6.6   *Model of the personnel development process.*

used by school systems is presented in Figure 6.6. This model contains four phases, each of which requires certain decisions and actions by those responsible for establishing and implementing development activities at the local level.

Phase 1: Diagnosing Development Needs

The initial step in the process model (see Figure 6.6) is diagnosing development needs. Development needs are defined as a discrepancy between the actual level of functioning and the desired level of functioning. The purpose of a staff development process is to reduce the discrepancy between actual and desired levels of performance.

Development needs vary according to source, and sources include the individual, the group, and the organization. McGehee and Thayer (1961) identified these potential sources of development needs over 40 years ago. Since that time, according to Scarpello, Ledvinka, and Bergman (1995), these sources of development needs have become an accepted standard for most development processes and models used today by the majority of public and private organizations.

Development needs of the individual focus on the person as an employee. These needs may be attributed to skill deficiency, skill obsolescence, and/or motivation to perform. Skill deficiencies occur when individuals lack knowledge or the basic skills necessary to work in a satisfactory manner. Without knowledge and skills, these individuals fail to know how to achieve satisfactory performance.

Skill obsolescence occurs when the individual's skills and knowledge become outdated. New developments may alter the way work should be performed. Persons experiencing skill obsolescence know what work to perform but lack skills or knowledge to perform the work according to best practices.

In some cases, the individual may know what to do, as well as the best way to do it, yet may still fail to perform at an optimal level, as defined by organizational standards. In this situation, the employee may have a motivational deficiency (Farber & Ascher, 1991) rather than a skill or knowledge deficiency. A major cause of motivational problems in employees who fail to perform optimally is believed to be burnout (Mondy & Noe, 1996).

In addition to variation in sources of development needs (individual, group, and organization), development needs vary by content. Seyfarth (1996) identified two content areas for development needs: technological and structural. However, this classification of content omitted consideration of the affective needs of employees in educational organizations, and in many instances, affective development needs are the most important within the public school setting.

Technological needs stem from technological advances that can enhance the way work is performed. Today, more than ever, technological advances have changed the way educational organizations conduct business (National Center for Educational Statistics, (National Center for Education Statistics, 2000). Efficient school systems have incorporated many of these technical advances into their operation, and the incorporation requires extensive development activity on the part of an organization to change the attitudes and skills of employees.

Structural needs address the manner in which the work is performed. Many school districts have begun to experiment with alternative management strategies involving decentralized decision making such as site-based management (Miller-Smith, 2001). These strategies alter substantially the way work is performed and may require considerable development efforts on the part of employees if success is to be attained.

Affective needs pertain to employees' attitudes toward and perceptions about the work and the workplace. Often overlooked as appropriate content for a development program by school districts, affective needs have long attracted the interest of the private sector. Many times, affective needs of individuals are the cause of dysfunctional behaviors such as absenteeism, tardiness, and grievances (Markley, 2001). Development efforts have focused erroneously only on the symptoms of dysfunctional behavior rather than on its causes.

In keeping with the systems view of development, potential needs diagnosed in this phase of the development model may have internal or external origins. Internal development needs may be due to program initiatives, performance assessments, or opinion polls. External causes may include current events, government agencies, and research and development outcomes.

Development needs (technological, structural, or affective) may surface at various levels (organization, unit, or individual), at different times, and for various reasons (internal or external). Personnel shortages may occur, legislation may be passed requiring new programs, or information may be compiled that indicates certain types of skill deficiencies. Consequently, every development need is likely to be subjected to some form of priority analysis to determine if it should be included in the staff development plan currently in operation.

Before development needs are translated into program designs, several questions pertaining to planning need to be examined. Among these are the following:

- Is there a consensus that a need exists?
- How important is the need in terms of system priorities and resources?
- Can the need be met through system action?
- What is the probability that satisfaction of the need will be cost effective?

Underlying this discussion is the premise that ongoing diagnosis of system development is an essential management task. These diagnoses identify which needs are important to individual, group, and organizational effectiveness, and which ones are faddish and unnecessary. Also, these diagnoses pinpoint the content area of development needs as technological, structural, and/or affective.

Phase 2: Designing Development Plans

In the design phase of the planning process, considerable effort is devoted to issues related to the format of a staff development program in a public school district. Format within the design phase of staff development refers to the way program elements are translated into program specifics for execution. Format components of a development program are content, methods, location, participants, implementation, and assessment.

These format components are incorporated into a structural model contained within Figure 6.7. Each of the elements contained within the structural model has several subsets. Following is a discussion of each component of the structural model that must be addressed in the design phase of a development program for employees.

Program Content

Within the design phase of a development program two types of learning must be considered when identifying program content for staff development (see Block 1 in Figure 6.7). One type of learning that must be considered pertains to theories, concepts, and principles, and the other type of learning that must be considered relates to the application of theories, concepts, and principles. Both types of learning are necessary for content of a development program to transfer from the program setting to the job environment of participants.

Firestone and Pennell (1997) suggested that these types of learning involve acquiring both procedural knowledge and conceptual knowledge about program content delivered through a staff development program. According to these investigators, procedural knowledge is acquired by mastering the content of a development program. Content acquisition of procedural knowledge is, however, only part of the learning process that employees need for application of program content within the job setting.

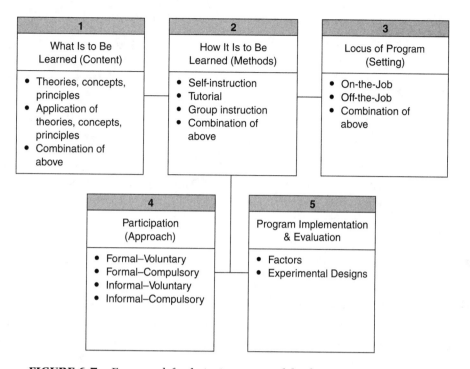

FIGURE 6.7   *Framework for designing personnel development program formats.*

On-the-job application of the content of a development program requires conceptual as well as procedural knowledge. Conceptual knowledge represents a higher level of learning than procedural knowledge. To acquire conceptual knowledge, individuals must be able to internalize the information presented in a development program and to apply this information in the work setting.

Far too often, development programs and activities in public school systems have focused on procedural knowledge and have neglected conceptual knowledge in the design phase of staff development. This neglect occurs when participants are treated as passive learners and are given content but little contextual information about applying program content within the job setting. Because conceptual knowledge is often ignored in the design phase of the development program, the most common criticism offered by program participants is that the content of staff development programs is not relevant to their actual job setting.

Although procedural knowledge may be all that is necessary for certain development activities or certain elements within a development activity, most development efforts require both types of knowledge for an effective development program. The key task of program designers, at this phase of a staff development program, is to decide which type of knowledge is needed to achieve the particular program objective and how all elements of a planned development activity can best be learned by participants. This decision has important implications for other components of the framework in Figure 6.7.

Program Methods

Block 2 in Figure 6.7 addresses the method used to present the content of development activities to participants. The method to be used in a particular program format or in a particular element of a program will depend on a number of factors. These factors include the objectives of the program, number of personnel involved, cost per participant, availability of personnel to conduct the program, availability of learning aids, and learning ability of program participants.

All potential methods for delivering a staff development program can be effective in certain situations. Effectiveness of any particular staff development program will depend on the learning conditions, including what is to be learned and the type of knowledge to be acquired. Especially important within this phase of program design, according to research, is the relevance of a particular method for attaining a specific organizational goal as noted within the strategic plans of a school district.

Many teaching methods can be used when designing development programs and activities for public school employees. The most effective methods rely on a variety of procedures and processes. Some of these procedures and processes for effective staff development are passive, while other methods are active.

Passive teaching methods rely heavily on individuals as self-directed learners. Within this method the content of development programs and activities is communicated largely by a single method. Passive learning techniques commonly used by school systems include conferences, academic classes, and independent study.

Conferences have been and continue to be a mainstay for development programs and activities involving personnel at all levels of the school system. Most conferences focus on a single topic and are of short duration. In communicating the content of development programs and activities, conferences are particularly effective in increasing the employee's procedural knowledge about certain topics or issues but are less effective in communicating conceptual knowledge to participants.

With the recent emphasis on distance learning in colleges and universities, academic classes are becoming a viable development option for many school districts when relying on passive methods to present contents of a staff development program. Academic classes can cover a broad range of topics and can take many weeks to complete. Class assignments can be designed to enhance both the procedural and the conceptual knowledge that employees need to transfer the content of development programs and activities to the work setting.

Independent study, as a passive teaching technique, has an advantage over conferences and classes. The content can be tailored to the specific needs of the individual and of the work assignment. Selected readings and programmed instruction can often reduce the difference between actual and desired levels of performance as assessed earlier within the development process.

In contrast to passive techniques, active delivery methods for development programs and activities require behavioral as well as cognitive responses from participants. With active methods of delivery for staff development, participants are given opportunities to apply the skills, knowledge, and/or behaviors they have been exposed to during the staff development process. Common examples of active methods for delivering development programs and activities with public school employees are role playing, simulation, and coaching.

Role playing allows individuals to act out certain skills or behaviors in a protective environment away from the actual work setting. Using this method for presenting staff development content, program participants often act out the counterpart to their role in the organization. By assuming the role of their counterpart, individuals may gain a better understanding of their own organizational role by viewing it from the perspective of the other person rather than from a self-perspective.

Simulations, like role playing, are removed from the actual job setting of an employee. With this development technique for delivering staff development content, employees are required to perform or to exhibit the actual skills and behaviors required by their current position or by an anticipated position. This technique gives them an opportunity to develop and refine certain job skills and behaviors in a protective setting where errors and omissions are permissible.

Coaching involves acquiring and developing job skills and behaviors in an actual job situation. With this technique, individuals practice the skills and behaviors under the tutelage of an accomplished mentor in the work setting. Mentors provide modeling behavior, performance assessments, and critical feedback designed to promote the development of employees in their current or anticipated position (Middle Web, 2002).

As previously noted, the choice between a passive or active method for delivering content in development programs or activities depends on many contextual variables. One method of presentation is not necessarily superior to other methods of presentation, and each method of presentation must be evaluated within the constraints of the development program at a particular school district. Again, it must be emphasized that effective development programs and activities utilize more than one of these techniques for enhancing the job skills of employees within a particular school system.

Location of the Program

The program setting for staff development, as indicated in Block 3 of Figure 6.7, can be located on-the-job, off-the-job, or some combination of these locations. The choice among these options for location of staff development depends largely on the resources of the school system. Resources that may impact the delivery of development programs within a particular school system include instructors, facilities, funds, time, and materials.

One key question incurred during the planning phase of staff development is where can the most competent instructor be found? The search for a competent instructor to lead staff development efforts may extend to colleges or universities, regional education agencies, commercial enterprises, private consultants, and/or personnel within the system. Because the school system's funds and facilities are usually limited, some organizations share instructors, facilities, and materials in the staff development process as a means for controlling costs associated with this important human resource function.

Another problem associated with development programs is the need to free personnel from their assigned organizational duties to participate in development programs and activities. The organization must subsidize the time of these personnel in the form of paid leaves of absence, time off with pay, or time off during the school day without extra pay. Lack of funding for release time has been and continues to be a major deterrent to the improvement of development programs for employees at all levels within the school system.

Still another issue associated with the location of staff development activities involves the administration of development programs and activities. Each program format, if it is to succeed, involves an administrative process that includes planning, organizing, directing, coordinating, and controlling. These processes call for a combination of data, competence, and participation, which must be provided by the system to ensure an effective and efficient program for staff development.

Answers to many of the format issues require alternative ways of viewing development programs and activities that involve a combination of locations. This suggests that staff development programs and activities must be diversified. Diversification can provide new and exciting alternatives to traditional staff development activities for all educational employees.

One relatively new method for diversifying traditional locations and for delivering staff development activities within the public school setting involves using computers to establish professional networks. Professional networks connect a number of individuals, both inside and outside the school system, who have a common interest and a common identity. Professional networks focus on a single topic (reform movement, subject area, etc.), support a number of activities (workshops, conferences, etc.), provide ongoing discussion, and give participants opportunities to lead in the staff development process (Lieberman & McLaughlin, 1992).

Another relatively new method for diversifying traditional locations of staff development programs involves collaboration between school systems and outside agencies (Holmes Partnership, 1987–1997). Partnerships are formed in which development activities and resources are shared by the organizations. Initially conceived as university–school agreements focusing on instructional issues involving teachers, collaborative efforts have been expanded to include other types of organizations and all categories of personnel.

Participation

Approaches to staff development programs and activities are listed in Block 4 of Figure 6.7 and are classified as either voluntary or compulsory. Both types of participation may be either formal or informal, depending on the staff development's objectives. Examples for each type of participation and each type of program follow:

- Formal-voluntary system: conducts an informational seminar for technology users.
- Informal-voluntary system: awards a budgetary allowance to teachers for personal and professional development.
- Formal-compulsory system: conducts a seminar about new state mandates for public school districts.
- Informal-compulsory system: establishes a deadline for personnel to meet certification requirements. Individuals are free to choose among various approaches to meet the requirements.

Depending on whether a staff development program is formal or informal as well as whether a staff development program is voluntary or compulsory has implications for participation of public school employees. Public school employees have both professional demands and personal demands that must be managed in their everyday lives. Today, more than ever, public school employees must contend with dual family careers and single-parent responsibilities, both of which can influence participation in staff development activities.

Formal staff development programs tend to have a fixed schedule of events. Informal staff development programs tend to have a flexible set of activities. The choice between these two types of programs must be afforded employees of a public school district if the ultimate goals of staff development are to be realized.

Voluntary staff development programs may require public employees to preregister and be subject to enrollment caps imposed by physical limitations. Compulsory staff development programs are more restrictive than voluntary staff development programs and may be disruptive to the work setting or the personal life of employees. Although the latter type of staff development program may be a necessity in some instances, these instances can cause undue hardship for certain public school employees.

Examination of these forms of participation leads to two inferences about approaches to personnel participation in staff development activities offered by a public school district. The first inference is that uniformity in the design of development programs and activities is neither feasible nor desirable for most public school districts. A second inference is that program format planning calls for great flexibility in meeting the development needs of various types of personnel through providing a variety of locations for staff development activities.

Program Evaluation

The last step in the design phase of staff development involves specifying means for evaluating the staff development program outcomes (see Block 5 in Figure 6.7).

Program evaluation has been overlooked within the staff development process by many school districts. In the past, the emphasis for most school districts in staff development has been placed on processes and procedures for administering the staff development activities rather than on assessing outcomes.

Far too often, little thought is devoted within the development phase of staff development to evaluation. Without adequate evaluation of staff development activities, it is impossible to determine if these efforts are fulfilling the goals of a strategic plan as set forth by a public school district. In the absence of a formal evaluation, the outcomes of development efforts may be difficult, if not impossible, to evaluate precisely.

It is not only likely, but quite probable, that outcomes from many staff development activities may be due, at least in part, to factors other than those associated with the staff development activities. Many of the factors that can influence potentially the outcomes of a staff development program have been identified by Campbell and Stanley (1963). Because these factors have important implications for assessment of development programs and activities in the work setting, each factor should be considered when designing an assessment process of a staff development program.

By considering the factors, as described by Campbell and Stanley, when designing the evaluation component of a staff development program or activity, important planning information can be realized by a public school system. Although these factors will be treated independently in this discussion, in practice, these factors may interact and may have a combined influence on the assessment of outcomes associated with development programs or activities. These factors include history, maturation, testing, instrumentation, regression, selection, and mortality.

History includes external events or factors outside of the staff development activity that influence the desired knowledge, skills, and/or attitudes of participants beyond the content of the program. This factor is of particular concern when development activities address topical issues such as substance abuse or violence control, which are often covered in the popular press. Because this coverage is outside the development program, the effects attributed to the program may be overestimated by ignoring this external influence when assessing the impact of a specific development program or activity.

Maturation concerns developmental changes experienced by employees due to the normal developmental process. Employees new to the organization or new to their assignment will become somewhat acclimated over time, regardless of any development programs or activities. Programs and activities designed to acclimate new employees may appear to be effective when, in fact, a certain level of adjustment should be expected to occur normally without the benefit of staff development activities.

Testing involves the preassessment of the knowledge, skills, and/or attitudes of participants in regard to development activities before actually involving them in development programs or activities by using a pretest. Initial deficiencies in content knowledge, as detected by pretesting, may sensitize participants to certain content areas that might go unnoticed during a training program in the absence of pretesting. Because of information gaps detected by pretesting, certain content areas may become important for employees taking part in development programs or activities due to pretesting exposure of voids.

Instrumentation pertains to changes in the measuring instrument during the development process. For many staff development activities, the measuring instrument is the immediate supervisor. If the proficiency of this supervisor improves through practice during the staff development process, changes in employee performance may be attributable to the improvement in the supervisor rather than to the content of the development activity.

Regression occurs when employees are selected for development programs or activities because of their extremely poor performance on certain measures (job performance, absenteeism, etc.). Because their current performance is well below average, it can only improve (rise toward the mean) if they are to remain employed by a public school district. As a result of regression, remedial programs often appear to be effective when effectiveness is due the regression phenomenon.

Selection relates to the choice of participants and to the motivation of these employees. Participation in development programs and activities can be either voluntary or compulsory (see Block 4 of Figure 6.7). Development programs and activities that appear to be highly successful with voluntary participants may be disastrous with compulsory participants even when the content and methods of these programs and activities are the same for both groups of employees.

Mortality focuses on the number of individuals who complete development programs and activities. Some of these programs and activities require a great deal of time and effort on the part of participants. If participants are allowed to drop out, an assessment of the knowledge, skills, and attitudes of only those who remain in the program may provide a distorted view of the program's effectiveness. Assessments should include both those who drop out and those who complete the program.

These factors may influence assessments of development programs and activities and may provide misleading information to those responsible for developing, implementing, and evaluating these programs and activities within the public school setting. Although not all of these factors may be pertinent to all development programs and activities, some of the factors can influence every staff development program and activity within the public school setting. To control for or to assess the impact of the factors mentioned, consideration must be given to these factors in the design phases of staff development processes as these processes are addressed in the evaluation phase of the staff development process.

Before we discuss Phase 3, as found in Figure 6.6, which involves implementing development programs and activities in a school environment, certain issues should be recapitulated. The specifics of each program format for staff development, as discussed in Phase 2, need to be summarized and disseminated for review, formalization, and implementation. A form for linking program formats to development objectives is shown in Figure 6.8.

This form, as found in Figure 6.8, emphasizes, prior to implementation of staff development activities, that each development program should be reviewed for links

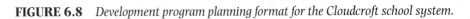

Form D-10

DEVELOPMENT PROGRAM PLANNING FORMAT

1. Title of program: _____

2. Program purpose:

   ___ Personal development   ___ Professional development

   ___ Position effectiveness   ___ Position transition ___ Position security

   ___ School unit improvement   ___ School system improvement

3. Specific program objective:

   ___ Dissemination of knowledge   ___ Developing skills

   ___ Acquisition of knowledge   ___ Creating organizational climate

   ___ Interpersonal skills   ___ Changing attitudes

   ___ Problem-solving skills   ___ General development of personnel

4. Organized for: ___ Administrative and Supervisory Personnel

   ___ Instructional Personnel   ___ Support Personnel

5. System level: ___ Elementary ___ Intermediate ___ Other

6. Level of learning: ___ Simple   ___ Complex   ___ Highly complex

7. Content: Theories, concepts, and principles: application of theories and concepts

8. Program scope: ___ Systemwide   ___ Building   ___ Individual

9. Duration: _____ to _____

10. Number of participants: _____

11. Funds allocated: ___ Amount   Source of funds: ___ Internal ___ External

12. Program/methods: ___ Self-instruction ___ Tutorial ___ Group instruction

13. Program setting: ___ On the job   ___ Off the job

14. Participation: ___ Voluntary   ___ Compulsory

15. Linked to performance appraisal: ___ Yes   ___ No

16. Program resources needed:

   ___ Funds   ___ Facilities   ___ Materials   ___ Personnel

   ___ Management   ___ Information

17. Program leadership: _____

18. Program evaluation responsibility: _____

19. Evaluation criteria: ___ Participant reaction   ___ Learning behavior

   ___ Results

20. Outcome intent: In what way will system, unit, or individual change as a result of the program?

FIGURE 6.8 *Development program planning format for the Cloudcroft school system.*

between program format, program objectives, and strategic goals of the organization. By analyzing the items contained in the form, human resource planners can determine whether development objectives have been translated into specific operations and whether the program format is capable of achieving the objectives of the program and the strategic goals of the system. The analysis should reveal gaps to be filled and revisions needed before development plans are implemented in the work setting.

Phase 3: Implementing Development Programs

Reexamination of the model in Figure 6.6 indicates that completion of Phase 2 (program design) leads to Phase 3 (implementation of development activities). Phase 3 occurs when the design of the program is shaped into an operational structure and when the planning activities are put into operation. At this time, Phases 1 and 2 are meshed to link together individual, unit, and organizational goals as contained within the strategic plans of a school district.

In the implementation phase of the development process, several types of human resource decisions are required. The persons responsible for developing and implementing the process must determine the timing and sequencing of development activities and events within the staff development process. These decisions are incorporated into an operational structure known as the experimental design.

The experimental design of development programs or activities determines the protocol for program administration. The experimental design dictates which employees will be exposed to certain program components and activities, as well as when these program components and activities are to be administered. The answers to these questions have profound implications for Phase 4 (evaluation) of the development process.

Experimental Design

The experimental design provides the framework within which development programs and activities are carried out by a public school system. Public school systems use several types of experimental designs. These designs vary both in complexity and sensitivity to those factors that can potentially confound the assessment of development programs and activities (history, maturation, testing, etc.). Choosing among experimental designs is a major human resource task in Phase 3 of the implementation process (see Figure 6.6).

Three of the experimental designs used most frequently for staff development programs and activities in public school districts are shown in Figure 6.9 (see Campbell & Stanley, 1963). In these designs employed by public school districts for assessing the effects of staff development programs and activities, two symbols are used to denote the implementation and assessment of program activities. "X" represents the actual staff development program or activity, as executed in the work setting, and "O" represents an outcome assessment associated with that particular program or activity following the presentation.

Design A	Design B	Design C
$X\ O$	$O\ X\ O$	$X\ O_1$
		O_2
One Shot	Pre-Post	Post-Control
Note: X denotes training: O denotes assessment.		

FIGURE 6.9   *Experimental designs.*

Design A, as found in Figure 6.9, is used most frequently by public school districts for assessing staff development activities in the educational setting. This design is labeled as a *one-shot case study.* In a one-shot case study, participants take part in a staff development program or activity as denoted by "X." After taking part in the staff development activities, the program or activity is assessed with the participants as noted by "O."

Although educational organizations use often the one-shot case study to evaluate staff development activities, this design is an extremely poor choice for the implementation phase of the staff development process. With a one-shot case study, it is impossible to determine what effects are attributable to the development program or to the staff development activity and what effects are attributable to outside factors (history, maturation, testing, etc.) rather than to program content. Even when participants perform exceptionally well on the assessment following presentation of staff development content, their assessments may reflect a prior level of performance rather than an actual performance level enhanced by the development efforts afforded through the public school district.

To provide information about the prior level of performance of participants in development programs or activities, design B is used often when implementing staff development activities. This design is labeled as a pre-posttest design. With the pre-posttest design, participants are assessed prior to the staff development program or activity and are assessed, again, immediately after they complete the staff development program or activity. When the two assessments are compared, a measure of program or activity effectiveness is obtained through a discrepancy analysis involving pre- and posttest comparisons of assessments.

The pre-posttest design is slightly superior to the one-shot case study because the pre-posttest design provides baseline data on participants taking part in the staff development activities. However, the pre-posttest design may sometimes pose a problem because of pretesting as previously noted. Also, the pre-posttest design has some of the same problems as the one-shot case study design with respect to controlling for history, maturation, testing, regression, instrumentation, and mortality associated with staff development activities in the public school setting.

Substantial improvements over the one-shot case study and the pre-posttest design can be achieved by using design C in Figure 6.9 when implementing and when evaluating staff development activities in the public school setting. Design C, as found in Figure 6.9, is a posttest control group design. In this last design, as found in Figure 6.9, some participants receive the development program or activity and others do not (at least not at the time of assessment). Both groups are assessed at the same time at the conclusion of the staff development activities.

A posttest control group design, when properly constructed, provides an extremely effective framework for implementing and evaluating staff development programs and activities in the public school setting. By using a proper control group for comparison, many potential factors other than those attributable to the development effort can be addressed is this type of design. Specifically, the posttest control group design either assesses or controls for such factors as testing, selection, regression, history, instrumentation, and mortality.

Those designs presented in Figure 6.9 are only some of the designs used frequently to implement and assess a staff development program in the public school setting. Other designs and other options exist, and those responsible for implementing development efforts must make an informed choice based on the potential factors in a given situation. The design chosen specifically for staff evaluation influences the implementation phase of the development process as well as the evaluation phase of staff development.

Phase 4: Evaluating Staff Development Programs

Development efforts of public school districts have been criticized often for failing to focus on significant individual or organizational needs, attacking the wrong problems, or attempting to solve the right problems with inappropriate staff development techniques. It should be noted that: (a) in some school systems, evaluation fails to take place at all, and (b) that evaluation occurs frequently to human resource planners as an afterthought within the staff development process. The development process introduced in Figure 6.6 includes Phase 4 (evaluation) as the last step in the development model for a public school district.

If the evaluation phase of a staff development process is omitted, then feedback is lacking to identify and correct program defects, information is unavailable to enhance decision making, and a sound foundation is lacking for improving the total staff development effort within a public school district. There are many constraints and many obstacles to overcome in evaluating staff development programs. In addition, there are varying viewpoints regarding the necessity for, approaches to, effects of, and values derived from evaluation of school district efforts.

Nevertheless, it is generally held that staff development requires a sound evaluation based on appropriate data. There is, also, considerable agreement that awareness of important factors in the evaluation phase makes it possible to avoid useless evaluations and to derive information that will be helpful in directing development planning. In this connection, key considerations in the evaluation of staff development programs are outlined in Figure 6.10.

It is worth emphasizing that program content (what to deliver) and program methods (how it should be delivered) are critical decisions in the design and evaluation

Factors	Illustrative Questions
Purposes of evaluation	What is to be evaluated? (Program objectives? Methods? Program? People? Processes? Products?)
Principles of evaluation	Will the evaluation be based on principles? (Systematic? Objectivity? Relevance? Verification of results? Quantification? Feasibility? Specificity? Cost effectiveness?)
Types of evaluation	Evaluation of a specific program? Specific technique? Total program effort? (Formative? Summative?)
Criteria	Reaction criteria? Learning criteria? Behavioral criteria? Results criteria? Combinations of the above?
Criterion measures	What criterion measures will be employed? (Observational techniques? Tests? Ratings? System performance records? Interviews?)
Evaluation data	How will the data be recorded? Analyzed? Interpreted? Valued?
Outcomes	What types of outcomes will be evaluated? (Professional competence? Learner gain? Program involvement? Training validity? Performance validity? Intraorganizational validity? Interorganizational validity?)

FIGURE 6.10   *Major considerations in the evaluation of staff development programs.*

of staff development programs in the public school setting. The learning process by which new behaviors (skills, knowledge, abilities, and attitudes) are acquired involves practicing those behaviors so that those behaviors result in relatively permanent change and enhance the performance of public school employees. The types of questions used to determine whether a development project has succeeded include the following:

- *Participant impact:* What has the project done to change the behavior of the participant?
- *Position impact:* Did the participant's performance in the work setting improve?
- *Organizational impact:* In what ways and to what extent did the development efforts contribute to attainment of organizational goals?

These questions bring into focus the need to specify carefully the objectives of a staff development program and to identify criteria by which to measure the objectives sought by a public school system. If the objectives are unclear, it will be difficult to choose or to develop appropriate measuring techniques and to judge whether the intended results were achieved by the school district's efforts.

Rational decisions can be made with greater conviction when there is some basis for determining whether improvement programs have been or will be effective and efficient means for improving the skills and knowledge of public school employees. There are many questions relating to the extent to which knowledge, skills, attitudes, work behavior, and organizational impact have changed. In addition, some persons want to know whether changes in these variables are due to the staff development program or to some of the extraneous factors previously discussed.

Analysis of Figure 6.10 leads to these observations:

- The evaluation process is complex and extensive. Sophisticated knowledge is needed to initiate, implement, and coordinate all of its facets.
- The evaluation phase requires knowledge, skills, attitudes, and position behaviors to improve the system's evaluation capabilities.
- The purposes of evaluation constitute the "engine" that pulls the evaluation train. Evaluation methods, criteria, criterion measures, and collection and refinement of data derived from evaluation inform future development efforts.

We summarize this section on the evaluation phase of staff development by suggesting that nurturing an organization's human resources is a primary leadership responsibility. This requires an organizational investment of considerable time, money, and talent to solve major evaluation problems. These problems—either by design or by default—have been seriously neglected and will become even more critical in light of social change, technological development, and public concern about the quality and effectiveness of the nation's schools.

Review and Preview

This chapter has stated that the school system that embraces the policy of continual development has important strategic advantages. Key ideas of this thesis include the following:

- School improvement through personnel development is best accomplished within individual schools and school systems. Traditional practices do not generate effective staff development programs.
- The staff development process includes identifying needs, establishing program objectives, creating plans to achieve the objectives (including teaching methods), and evaluating program outcomes.
- Staff development includes individual, group, system, and board member development.
- Major factors to be considered in the assessment of personnel needs are the external and internal environments,

the school system, positions, position holders, position–person matches, position context, and work groups.

- Cues for designing programs can be derived from system policy, research and practice, value trends, career stages, and the external environment.
- Formal development program design includes program content, methods, setting, participation, and resources.
- Criteria for evaluating staff development programs include the participant, position, work group, and organizational impact.

In Chapter 7, appraisal will be treated as a process that is closely intertwined with the staff development process, and one that can provide meaningful information to help decision makers answer questions about the selection, implementation, and evaluation of development methods and the entire development effort.

Discussion Questions

1. You have been given oversight of the development program for a small school district. What information will guide your decisions on the content of the staff development activities that you will implement?

2. What is the relationship between staff development and strategic planning?

3. What external factors influence the direction of staff development in your school organization? What inner factors influence that direction?

4. You oversee employee development for a school organization. What are the implications of career stages on the staff development program you implement?

5. Consider the in-service education that you have undertaken in your career to date. What have been the strengths of this activity? The weaknesses?

6. Development activities can be targeted at the individual, the group, or the organization. Give three examples of activities at each of these levels.

7. What are the advantages of voluntary development? The disadvantages?

References

Asayesh, G. (1993, Fall). Using systems thinking to change systems. *Journal of Staff Development, 14*(4), 8–140.

Campbell, D. T., & Stanley, J. C. (1963). *Experimental and quasi-experimental designs.* Chicago: Rand McNally.

DeLuca, J. R. (1991, Summer). The evolution of staff development for teachers. *Journal of Staff Development, 12*(3), 45.

Farber, B., & Ascher, C. (1991, July). Urban school restructuring and teacher burnout. *ERIC Clearinghouse on Urban Education, 75.* Retrieved August 14, 2002, from the Eric Clearinghouse Web site: **http://ericweb.tc.columbia.edu/digests/dig75.aspcoran**

Firestone, W. A., & Pennell, J. R. (1997). Designing state-sponsored networks: A comparison of two cases. *American Educational Research Journal, 34*(2), 237–266.

Holmes Partnership. (1987–1997). *Origins of the Holmes Partnership.* Retrieved August 14, 2002, from the Holmes Partnership Web site: **http://www.holmespartnership.org/origins.html**

Lieberman, A., & McLaughlin, M. W. (1992). Network for educational change: Powerful and problematic. *Phi Delta Kappan, 73,* 673–677.

Markley, M. (2001, August 15). Districts taking new steps to stem teacher turnover. *Houston Chronicle.* Retrieved August 14, 2002, from the *Houston Chronicle* Web site: **http://www.chron.com/cs/CDA/story.hts/topstory/1006096**

McGehee, W., & Thayer, P. (1961). *Training in business and industry.* New York: Wiley.

Middle Web (2002). *Some teacher mentoring resources.* Retrieved May 23, 2002 from the Middle Web: **http://middleweb.com/mentoring.html**

Miller-Smith, K. R. (2001). *An investigation of factors in resumes that influence the selection of teachers.* Unpublished doctoral dissertation, Ohio State University, Columbus.

Mondy, R. W., & Noe, R. M. (1996). *Human resource management.* Upper Saddle River, NJ: Prentice Hall.

Prince, C. D. (2002, January). *The challenge of attracting good teachers and principals to struggling schools.* Retrieved August 13, 2002, from the American Association of School Administrators Web site:

http://www.aasa.org/issues_and_insights/issues_dept/challenges_teachers_principals.pdf

Rowand, C. (n.d.). Teacher use of computers and the Internet in public schools. *Education Statistics Quarterly, Elementary and Secondary Education*. Retrieved August 14, 2002, from the National Center for Education Statistics Web site: **http://nces. ed.gov/pubs2000/quarterly/summer/ 3elem/q3-2.html**

Scarpello, V. G., Ledvinka, J., & Bergman, T. J. (1995). *Human resource management: Environments and functions*. Cincinnati, OH: South-Western College Publishing.

Seyfarth, J. T. (1996). *Personnel management for effective schools*. Boston: Allyn & Bacon.

U.S. Department of Education. (1998, September). Improving professional development practices. In *Promising practices: New ways to improve teacher quality*. Retrieved August 13, 2002, from the U.S. Department of Education Web site: **http://www.ed.gov/pubs/PromPractice/chapter6.html**

U.S. Department of Education's National Commission on Excellence in Education. (1983). *A nation at risk*. Retrieved August 13, 2002, from the North Central Regional Educational Laboratory Web site: **http://www.ncrel.org/sdrs/areas/issues/content/cntareas/science/sc3 risk.htm**

Young, I. P., Jury, J. C., & Reis S. B. (1999). Holmes versus traditional candidates: Labor market receptivity. *Journal of School Leadership, 7*(4), 330–344.

Supplementary Reading

Andreson, K. M., & Durant. O. (1991, Winter). Training managers of classified personnel. *Journal of Staff Development, 12*(1), 56–60.

Barnett, B., & Ginsberg, R. (1990, April). Creating lead teachers: From policy to implementation. *Phi Delta Kappan, 71*(8), 616–662.

Bird, T., & Little, J. W. (1985). *From teacher to leader: Training and support for instructional leadership by teachers*. San Francisco: Far West Research Laboratory for Educational Research and Development.

Brown, B. (1992, Spring). Designing staff/curriculum content for cultural diversity: The staff developer's role. *Journal of Staff Development, 13*(2), 16–22.

Caldwell, S. (Ed.). (1989). *Staff development: A handbook of effective practices*. Oxford, OH: National Staff Development Council.

Christensen, J. C., McDonnell, J. H., & Price, J. R. (1988). *Personalizing Staff Development: The Career Lattice Model*. Bloomington, IN: Phi Delta Kappa.

DeMoulin, D. F. (1988). Staff development and teacher effectiveness: Administrative concerns. *Focus*, 81.

DeMoulin, D. F., & Guyton, J. W. (1990–1991). An analysis of career development to enhance individualized staff development. *National Forum of Educational Administration and Supervision Journal, 7*(3), 3011.

Fitch, M. E., & Kopp, O. W. (1990). *Staff development: A practical guide for the practitioner*. Springfield, IL: Charles C. Thomas.

Gilley, J. W., & Eggland, S. A. (1989). *Principles of human resource development*. Reading, MA: Addison-Wesley.

Gross, J. A. (1988). *Teachers on trial: Values, standards, and equity in judging conduct and competency*. Ithaca, NY: ILR Press.

Houston, R. W. (Ed.). (1990). *Handbook of research on teacher education*. New York: Macmillan.

Jandura, R. M., & Burke, P. J. (1989). *Differentiated career opportunities for teachers*. Bloomington, IN: Phi Delta Kappa.

Joyce, B., & Showers, B. (1988). *Student achievement through staff development*. New York: Longman.

Katzenmeyer, M. H., & Reid, G. A., Jr. (1991, Summer). Compelling views of staff development for the 1990s. *Journal of Staff Development, 12*(3), 30–34.

Lambert, L. (1988, May). Staff development redesigned. *Phi Delta Kappan, 69*(9), 665–669.

McKay, I. (1989). *Thirty-five checklists for human resource development.* Brookfield, VT: Gower.

Mecklenburger, J. A. (1988, September). *What the ostrich sees: Technology and the mission of American education. Phi Delta Kappan, 70*(1), 18–20.

MiddleWeb. (n.d.). *Some teacher mentoring resources.* Retrieved August 14, 2002, from the MiddleWeb Web site: **http:// www. middleweb.com/mentoring.html**

National Staff Development Council. (1991, Winter). Nine perspectives on the future of staff development. *Journal of Staff Development, 12*(1), 2–12.

Neubert, G. A. (1988). *Improving teaching through coaching.* Bloomington, IN: Phi Delta Kappa.

Owen, J. M. (1991, Summer). Three roles of staff development in restructuring schools. *Journal of Staff Development, 12*(3), 10–16.

Perelman, L. J. (1987). *Technology and transformation of schools.* Alexandria, VA: National School Boards Association.

Quinn, M. J. (1990, March). Staff Development: A process of growth. *The Education Digest LV, 7,* 43–47.

Showers, B., Joyce, B., & Bennett, B. (1987). Synthesis of research on staff development. *Educational Leadership, 45*(3), 77–87.

Sousa, D. A. (1992). Ten questions for rating your staff development program. *Journal of Staff Development, 13*(2), 34–38.

Thompson, J. C., & Cooley, V. E. (1986). National study of outstanding staff development programs. *Educational Horizons, 86*(1), 94.

West Loogootee Elementary. (n.d.) *Educational chat rooms.* Retrieved August 14, 2002, from the West Loogootee Elementary Web site: **http://www.siec.k12. in.us/~west/edu/chat.htm**

Wood, F. H., & Caldwell, S. D. (1991, Summer). Planning and training to implement site-based management. *Journal of Staff Development, 12*(3), 25–30.

Wood, F. H., & Thompson, S. R. (1993, Fall). Assumptions about staff development based on research and best practice. *National Staff Development Council, 14*(4), 58–63.

7
Performance Appraisal

CHAPTER OBJECTIVES

Understand what performance appraisal is expected to accomplish.
Describe the organizational context of performance appraisal.
Identify the purposes of performance appraisal.
Develop a model of the performance appraisal process.
Discuss the ethical aspects of performance appraisal.
Examine the interaction between the performance appraisal process and the human resource function.

CHAPTER CONCEPTS

Alternative ranking
Checklist
Compensatory model
Criterion-referenced
Eclectic model

Forced distribution
Graphic rating
Individual portfolios
Multiple-cutoff model
Narrative system

Norm-referenced	Reliability
Paired comparison	Self-referenced
Portfolios	Simple ranking
Ranking system	Validity
Rating system	Work diaries

This chapter draws together several streams of thought about performance appraisal in the educational setting. Most notably, performance appraisals are not based on one approach considered to be successful in all situations and under all circumstances. Instead, several approaches of performance appraisal exist. Their success depends on the purpose for which they are used and on certain operative decisions made about the components of the appraisal system.

Performance Appraisal

Within this chapter we address one of the most important functions of the different human resource tasks associated with the operation and administration of a public school district. The human resource task addressed in this chapter is the assessment of an employee's ability to perform assigned job duties within the organizational setting. To address this task, we examine several different models and separate techniques that have been evoked by public school districts in the quest to evaluate the job performance of employees when executing their assigned duties.

Fundamental to this perspective for evaluating employees is the notion that a single approach to this important administrative task fails to exist in practice. Rather, any effective performance appraisal system for employees requires certain types of *a priori* decisions on the part of those endorsing and those administering an employee appraisal system. Some of these decisions are policy decisions required of those endorsing an employee appraisal system, while other decisions are administrative decisions required of those administering an employee appraisal system.

The Context of Performance Appraisal

Appraisal of performance, in general, has never been more popular and has never received more attention in the popular press than it has in recent times. Almost without exception, most states mandate the assessment of school districts/and buildings and of school children through report cards for organizations and through proficiency tests for students. Indeed, few public school districts and few children have escaped performance assessments in this new millennium that has placed an emphasis on accountability.

Because the level of performance exhibited by public school districts as organizations and by public school students as individuals depends, to a large extent, on the performance of employees, the focus on performance appraisal for individuals, as employees, has been rekindled. People no longer expect some means of performance appraisal be performed for employees but demand that the assessment of all educational employees be performed on a continuing basis. This demand is both warranted and expected if the United States is to maintain its global position in the world economy.

Different, however, from the appraisal expectations associated with school districts as organizations and with students as individuals are certain requirements for performance appraisals of employees. Unlike districts as organizations and students as individuals, employees enjoy certain types of legislative protection within the performance appraisal process. These different types of legislative protection come into play depending on the purpose of and outcomes for an employee appraisal system.

Purposes of Performance Appraisal Systems

A performance appraisal system for employees should accomplish specific purposes as designated by boards of education. Historically, the purposes of a performance appraisal system for educational employees have been categorized grossly as being either *formative* or *summative* (Harris & Monk, 1992). This nomenclature has been found to be too restrictive in actual practice.

For example, a formative performance appraisal system is purported to be process oriented and is designed primarily for the professional development of individuals as employees. In contrast, a summative performance appraisal system is purported to be outcome oriented and is designed primarily for decision making about continuation of employment for individuals. Because these two systems fail to be mutually exclusive in practice as well as in reality, these classifications have done more to confuse than to enhance the evaluation of employees.

Indeed, the problems associated with developing and administering formative or summative performance appraisal processes are well documented in the professional literature. These terms are not only confusing to policy makers (boards of education) responsible for approving performance appraisal systems but also restrictive for administrators responsible for executing performance appraisal systems. The following are some of the more common problems associated with these classifications that have been a deterrent to the school district and a source of alienation for the employees:

- Appraisals focus on an individual's personality.
- Appraisal tools lack reliability.
- Appraisal tools lack validity.
- Raters display biases.
- Ratings and raters are subject to influence by the organization.
- The appraisal system does not apply to all personnel.

- Results of appraisal are not used to promote individual development.
- Appraisal devices do not provide administrators with effective counseling tools.
- Most plans fail to establish organizational expectations for individuals.
- Appraisals used for discipline, salary, promotion, or dismissal are arbitrary.
- Personnel do not understand the criteria on which performance is appraised.
- Performance is unrelated to the goals of the organization.
- Appraisal procedures hamper communication between appraiser and appraisee.
- Appraisal methods fail to change individual behavior.
- Appraisal methods do not encourage the satisfaction of higher-level needs.
- Appraisal models do not complement appraisal purposes.

In lieu of using technical categorizations such as formative and summative for describing performance appraisal systems, significant stakeholders are served better by using normal descriptive terms for describing the purposes of a performance appraisal system than by using traditional nomenclature as used in the past. In fact, most performance appraisal systems in education can be defined by one of the following purposes: compensation, employment continuation, and development. Each of these broad purposes has meaningful subdivisions affecting policy and practice in the execution of an effective performance appraisal system within the public school setting.

Differences within as well as between each of these categories are nontrivial with respect to the performance appraisal process. These differences are nontrivial for a performance appraisal process in the sense that separate purposes require different decisional criteria, different evaluation systems, and different models for combining information in a meaningful fashion. Before we address the requirements for each category, an elaboration of the separate purposes is in order.

Compensation

In some public school districts, outcomes from the performance appraisal process are used to make decisions about an employee's level of compensation (Kelley, Heneman, & Milanowski, 2002). From an individual perspective, compensation decisions resulting from performance appraisal outcomes should be differentiated. One type of compensation decision concerns merit, while another type of compensation decision concerns an award.

Merit decisions and award decisions differ in some very important ways within the performance appraisal context. With respect to decisions about merit increases, all employees are eligible that exhibit the prerequisite level of job performance necessary to qualify for a merit increase. In fact, the goal of a performance appraisal process focusing on merit is to increase the job performance of all employees and to motivate all employees toward merit increases.

Unlike the unrestricted opportunities associated with merit programs, eligibility is restricted generally in award programs. It is not unusual for award programs to limit the number of awards available for employees, and this number is often considerably less than that which is available in a merit program. Also, monies allocated in a merit program are incorporated into the base pay of employees, while monies allocated as awards are a one-time benefit and fail to be incorporated into the base salary of an employee that has exhibited outstanding performance.

Employment Continuation

Another purpose for a performance appraisal system beyond compensation considerations is to provide information for employment continuation decisions about employees. At least two types of employment continuation decisions exist in most public school districts. One type of employment continuation decision concerns probationary employees, while the other type of employment continuation decision concerns employees with a continuing contract.

With respect to the former group, probationary employees may or may not be new to the school district. What distinguishes probationary employees from nonprobationary employees is that the former have been assigned newly to positions with temporal performance contingencies attached to the assignments. For some positions (civil service) the probationary period may be several months; for other positions (teachers) it may span several years.

Having satisfied the probationary contingencies required by a newly assigned position, employees are considered continuing employees with either implied property rights limited by contractual terms or specified property rights prescribed by legislative enactments. The existence of property rights for employees places a higher burden on the performance appraisal process than those associated with probationary employees because employment discontinuation decisions must be based on just cause when property rights are involved. However, the mere existence of property rights for continuing employees does not shelter an employee from the scrutiny of the employer and the use of a performance appraisal process for decisions relating to the continuation of employment.

Development

Still another purpose of a performance appraisal system is to enhance the job performance of employees independent either of compensation rewards or of employment contingencies. This purpose is, by far, reported as the most common reason by school board members and by educational employees when polled relative to the purposes of the performance appraisal system used by their school district. Underlying this approach involving development of an employee's skill as a purpose for performance appraisal is the general assumption that most employees can improve their on-the-job performance.

To improve the performance of individuals as employees, performance appraisal systems can be designed either to identify weaknesses or to pinpoint strengths on the part of an employee. Even though the identification of both weaknesses and strengths focuses on the single continuum involving development, the focus of each approach is on opposite ends of the same continuum. As such, different standards of comparisons and different appraisal techniques are required to maximize the particular opportunity for development, depending on the purpose of the performance appraisal system.

Standards of Comparisons for Performance Appraisals

Within the context of performance appraisal in general, a standard of comparison is the referent source(s) against which the observed or inferred job performance of an employee is compared. Depending on the purpose(s) of a performance appraisal system, different standards of comparison are required to accomplish expeditiously the designated purpose of a performance appraisal system. A particular standard of comparison may be norm-referenced, criterion-referenced, or self-referenced.

In a **norm-referenced** system for performance appraisal, the standard of comparison for the observed or inferred job performance of an employee is the job performance of other employees. By comparing the job performance of one employee to the job performance of other employees, a relative measure of job performance is obtained. The measure of performance is relative in that the job performance of any employee can be categorized as either less than or greater than the job performance of other employees used as a reference standard.

Norm-referenced performance appraisal systems are useful particularly in certain situations. For example, if the purpose of a performance appraisal process is to determine eligibility for an award, then a norm-referenced system will identify the highest performers within a particular work group. Likewise, if the purpose of a performance appraisal system is to identify particular employees to meet reduction in force mandates, then a norm-referenced system will identify the lowest performers within a particular work group.

The major weakness of a norm-referenced performance appraisal system is the inability of this type of system to establish absolute levels of job performance that may be necessary for certain types of managerial decisions. A norm-referenced system allows administrators to determine if one employee's performance is better or worse than another employee's performance, but norm-referenced systems fail to provide adequate insight relative to whether the actual job performance of any employee is satisfactory or unsatisfactory. Such a distinction between satisfactory or unsatisfactory job performance may not be important if only a few awards exist for a particular group of employees or if only a few persons must be released to meet reduction in force mandates.

To assess the absolute level of job performance for employees, a standard of comparison other than norm-referenced must be employed. The absolute level of job performance for employees may be assessed by using a **criterion-referenced** standard of comparison. A criterion-referenced performance appraisal system designed to assess absolute levels of job performance compares the observed or the inferred performance of an employee against some preestablished standards external to any particular work group.

Preestablished standards are determined by policy rather than by group performance within a criterion-referenced system. The preestablished standards could be a minimum level of acceptable job performance or could be some meritorious level of exceptional job performance. Criterion-referenced systems are particularly advantageous for making continuation of employment decisions and for making merit pay decisions, but entirely ineffective for making either reduction in force decisions or for making award decisions.

More recently, many school districts have been employing **self-referenced** standards of comparison for performance assessments of employees. Rather than relying on the performance of others (norm-referenced) or some preestablished standards (criterion-referenced) for assessing job performance of an employee, a self-referenced performance appraisal system focuses on the job behavior of an individual employee. By focusing on the relative performance of an individual employee across different dimensions of job performance, the relative strengths and the relative weakness of an employee can be identified.

Self-referenced systems for performance appraisal are well suited for individual development of job skills. Based on an employee's job performance, goals or benchmarks can be established for an individual employee. In some instances, the goals or benchmarks may be remedial addressing a particular deficiency, while in other instances, the goals or benchmarks may be enhancing by building on the specific strengths of an employee.

Because most self-referenced systems are unique to an individual, these types of systems fare poorly when used for allocating awards, for reducing the workforce, or for promoting individuals. To accomplish some of these last concerns both different standards of comparison and different evaluation systems are needed. It is the latter that we address next—evaluation systems.

Evaluation Systems

A review of the professional and popular literature will reveal many different performance appraisal systems used by organizations to evaluate the job performance of employees (Heneman & Ledford, 1998). Both the number and types of performance appraisal systems continue to increase each year. However, at the very basic level, most, if not all, of the performance appraisal systems can be classified into one of three basic categories.

The basic categories are as follows: (a) ranking systems, (b) rating systems, and (c) narrative systems. Differences across these systems have important implications both for evaluation purposes and for choice of evaluation standards. It is not surprising that, within each of these basic systems, a number of procedural variations exist.

Ranking Systems

As a means for performance appraisal, ranking systems are among the oldest and the simplest used by organizations to differentiate among employees on the basis of assessed job performance. Within the performance appraisal context, all ranking systems involve comparing the overall job performance of one employee with the overall job performance of other employees. Because of this type of comparison, ranking systems are very effective procedures when the purpose (or purposes) of the performance evaluation demands evaluators distinguish among employees on the basis of their relative job performance.

Examples where the purpose of the performance appraisal process must distinguish among employees on the basis of their relative job performance are compensation awards, reduction in force, or promotion from within the school district, to mention a few. When applied to these decisional situations, ranking systems are excellent choices for educational organizations because these different decisional outcomes require a norm-referenced standard. A norm-referenced standard, however, can be utilized by several different ranking techniques.

One type of ranking technique using a norm-referenced standard is the **forced distribution** method. This technique has been described as somewhat analogous to grading on a curve (Dressler, 1988). Preestablished categories (e.g., exceptional, above average, average) varying in performance levels like academic grades (A, B, C, etc.) are used to group employees on the basis of relative performance. Within a single grouping, employees are presumed to have equivalent levels of job performance, and between separate groupings, individuals are presumed to have differing levels of job performance.

A major advantage of the forced distribution technique is that the performance appraisal system can be tailored to the specific decisional context of a school district. For example, if the purpose of a performance appraisal is to identify the upper 2% of the workforce for economic awards, then the forced distribution method may contain only two categories with the percentage allocations assigned to the categories matching the decisional demands of the organization. By using only two categories rather than an expanded range of categories, political issues associated with the lowest performers and the intermediate performers can be avoided.

By far the most frequently used ranking technique is referred to as the **simple ranking** method. This technique is norm-referenced and focuses on the criterion of overall job performance. For a particular group of employees, the individuals are ranked according to their overall job performance from the highest performer to the lowest performer within a target group of employees.

When using the simple ranking technique, performance assessments are accomplished generally by having the evaluator or evaluators sort 4 × 6 index cards, with each card listing the name of a sole employee. In some instances, evaluators may have difficulty with ranking employees from highest to lowest relative to their job performance and may render this technique as ineffective. To overcome this problem involving ranking from highest to lowest on the basis of job performance, other ranking strategies have emerged within the professional literature.

Rather than rank employees from highest to lowest on the basis of their relative job performance, another strategy is labeled as the **alternate ranking** technique. The alternate ranking technique consists of identifying first the employee with the highest level of job performance, and then identifying second the employee with the lowest level of job performance. Following the identification of the highest and lowest performers, evaluators select the next highest performer and the next lowest performer from the remaining pool of employees being evaluated.

The process of choosing the next highest and the next lowest among employees proceeds until the entire pool of employees have been ranked on their relative performance. By choosing extremes from the distribution of remaining employees each time, maximum differentiation is achieved for each comparison. However, problems with the alternate ranking techniques are to occur likely in the middle of the distribution where little variability may exist with respect to relative job performance of the remaining employees.

Problems with the middle-ranked groups may not necessarily be an issue for certain decisional situations being faced by an educational organization. If the purpose of the rankings is to identify employees for awards, determine which employees are promoted, or select employees for reduction in force, then middle-rank groups of employees are of little concern in these different decisional situations because middle ranks fail to enter within the decisional context. When even finer differentiation is needed than afforded by the alternate ranking technique, the **paired comparison** technique can be used.

With the paired comparison technique, the job performance of each employee is contrasted to the job performance of all other employees on an individual basis. For every dyadic comparison between the employees, the evaluator must determine if the target employee's job performance is higher or lower than the comparison other (ties are not permitted). According to the paired comparison technique, an employee's overall job performance is determined by summing the number of times that an employee's job performance was perceived to be higher than all comparison others' job performance.

Although the paired comparison technique provides the maximum amount of information for a norm-referenced system, this system can be taxing with large work groups. The formula for calculating the number of individual comparisons among employees is found in Table 7.1. As can be observed, when the work group doubles in size, the number of comparisons increases exponentially.

TABLE 7.1
Formula for calculating the number of comparisons relative to the number of positions.

# of Comparisons = $N(N - 1)/N$
N = Number of positions being compared

Rating Systems

By far, **rating systems** are used most frequently as a means of performance appraisal within the organizational setting (Arvey & Murphy, 1998). In contrast to ranking systems relying on a norm-referenced criterion, rating systems are criterion-referenced. Because criterion-referenced systems rely on an external standard, these types of systems provide information about an absolute level of job performance defined by an external standard.

Several different types of rating techniques exist. These techniques vary in form and in focus. Most popular among the rating techniques are the critical incident checklist, graphic rating scale, and the behavioral anchored rating scale.

Underlying the critical incident technique is that certain job behaviors are critical to the performance of a focal position. Some of the critical behaviors are important for effective job performance. Likewise, some of the critical behaviors are major contributors for ineffective job performance.

Effective behaviors as well as ineffective behaviors critical to the performance of an employee are gleaned generally through interviews with job incumbents. Job incumbents are asked to provide examples of incidents for job behaviors that are particularly potent for effective or ineffective job performance. These critical incidents are used to develop a **checklist** that is used subsequently for the assessment of employee performance.

To assess an employee's level of job performance using the critical incidents checklist, the supervisor marks those behaviors that are characteristic of an employee's performance. In most instances, some of the behaviors marked will be positive and some of the behaviors will be negative. An employee's level of job performance is determined by the net difference between the two types of attributes.

In contrast to indicating whether a specific job behavior is either present or absent via a checklist, **graphic rating** scales attempt to measure the degree by which an employee exhibits certain behaviors or traits within the job setting. For a graphic rating scale, the behaviors or traits are distributed along a bipolar continuum. Within the confines of each continuum are varying degrees of each behavior or trait reflecting an absolute level of job performance.

Graphic rating scales are anchored directionally either by numerals (e.g., 1–7) or by adverbs. Numerals begin with the number "1" and continue consequently until the maximum interval is reached. In contrast to numerals, adverbs, when used as anchor points, begin typically with "never" and end with "always" or begin with "unsatisfactory" and end with "exceptional."

Because the immediate values associated with graphic rating scales may cause problems of interpretation in practice, more descriptive rating scales have been developed. Foremost among these later rating scales are the behavioral anchored rating scales (BARS). BARS are considered by most authorities to be among the best for assessing the actual job performance of employees. Rather than relying on numerals or adverbs as anchor points, BARS use actual job behaviors as descriptors for anchor points throughout the scale range.

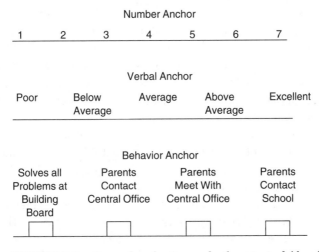

FIGURE 7.1 *Examples of rating scales for principals' handling of parent concerns.*

Included in Figure 7.1 are examples of each type of rating scale. Each of these different rating scales purports to measure a principal's ability to address student discipline at the building level. Although each scale addresses the full gamut of behavior along a single continuum, each scale provides both the person performing the evaluation and the person being observed with varying levels of definition relative to specific criteria or job behaviors.

When constructing rating scales, several issues emerge concerning the structural characteristics of these instruments. Common concerns are the number of points for each scale, polarity for ordering scales, and dimensionality of scales. Fortunately, considerable research exists about each of these concerns, and this information can be used to guide practice in the field setting.

With respect to the number of points for each scale, the research indicates that each scale should range between 4 and 11 anchor points and that an odd number or an even number of anchor points for each scale is of little importance in the field of practice. Polarity (direction, positive to negative, or negative to positive) for scales should be consistent throughout the appraisal instrument and should not be reversed or alternated even though this practice of alternation of scale polarity has been endorsed in the survey literature. Finally, each scale should measure a single concept and should be unidimensional.

Narrative Systems

Recently, considerable interest has been directed toward narrative systems as a means for assessing the job performance of employees in the educational setting (Peterson, Stevens, & Mack, 2001). Unlike either norm-referenced systems using other employees as a standard or criterion-referenced systems relying on external standards, **narrative systems** are self-referenced. Narrative systems are self-referenced in that the focus of the later systems is on the individual as an employee.

Narrative systems of employee appraisal are tailored to meet typically either an individual objective or an organizational need. As such, narrative systems of performance appraisal provide little insight both about the relative level of job performance as compared to other employees and about the absolute level of job performance as compared to an external standard. Most common among the narrative systems for performance assessments with public school districts are work diaries, goal-setting techniques, and individual portfolios.

Work diaries are compiled in narrative format at scheduled times during the work cycle to provide adequate job sampling of actual tasks performed by a position holder. Specific incidents of on-job behavior are cataloged, enriched with contextual information, and analyzed by an employee in a reflective summary. Information encapsulated within the diary is shared with an appraiser, and a plan of action for the employee is developed based on the narrative information provided by the employee.

Goal-setting techniques (management by objectives [MBO], administration by objectives [ABO], education by objectives [EBO], etc.) are future oriented and rely on preestablished objectives through mutual agreement between the employee and the appraiser (Heneman, 1998). Ideally, the employee and the appraiser develop independently a set of objectives for the employee, and these objectives are commingled and negotiated. Once agreed upon by the appraiser and the employee, fulfillment of the objectives serves as the vehicle for evaluation.

Individual portfolios are, perhaps, the most recent appraisal technique to emerge in the public school setting (Painter, 2001). Compiled by the employee, individual portfolios contain samples of the work performed, supporting materials for the work performed, and outcomes attributed to the work performed. Portfolio assessment involves a content analysis of the integration of means, methods, and outcomes used by and produced by the employee when fulfilling assigned work duties.

Evaluation Models

The literature on performance evaluation indicates that all jobs have many different dimensions necessary for effective performance. For example, in most school systems, three broad dimensions of job performance are student concerns, district responsibilities, and community relations. These dimensions pertain to all employees, from custodians to administrators, and are necessary to describe how an individual performs assigned duties.

Regardless of the purpose to be served by a performance appraisal system, any adequate performance appraisal system must capture these different job dimensions. To do so, the appraisal system must measure each dimension of job performance. The method used to combine these different job dimensions for managerial decision making in an appraisal system will vary depending on the purpose of the system.

At least three different models have been used to combine job dimensions for assessment by a multidimensional performance appraisal system: the multiple-cutoff model, the compensatory model, and the eclectic model. Each of these models has a different implication for the performance appraisal system adopted by a school system.

In the **multiple-cutoff model,** job performance on each dimension is examined separately for every employee. That is, for every employee, performance on each dimension is viewed in either a relative or an absolute sense. This method is particularly appropriate when specific diagnostic information about employees is needed.

With a **compensatory model,** information about an employee's performance on all job dimensions is combined to form a composite measure of job performance. Low performance on one dimension can be balanced by high performance on another dimension. However, when job performances across all dimensions are combined, certain strengths and weaknesses on individual performance dimensions may be masked through the use of a composite score to define overall job performance.

The **eclectic model,** as the name implies, combines certain processes of the multiple-cutoff and the compensatory model. In the eclectic model, an initial level of minimum competence is required on each dimension of a multidimensional performance appraisal system. After a minimum level of performance has been achieved by the employee on each dimension of job performance, appraisal efforts focus on the employee's performance across all dimensions, rather than on performance on each dimension.

Alignment of Performance Appraisal Decisions

Previous sections of this chapter address important decisions that must be made with regard to a performance appraisal process in the public school setting. Some of these decisions are policy decisions, whereas others are administrative decisions. Policy decisions are needed that specify the purpose or purposes that a performance appraisal must serve.

Once the policy issues have been resolved relative to the purpose(s) of the performance appraisal, several administrative decisions are required. Administrative decisions are needed about the standard of comparison, the method of performance appraisal, and the model for combining information. These later decisions should complement the policy decisions to most expediently accomplish the purpose of the performance appraisal process.

Contained in Figure 7.2 is a decisional matrix that can be used to guide the decision-making process when designing a performance appraisal process for a public school district. For example, if the purpose of the performance appraisal process is to determine merit (AI), then the standard of comparison should be BII and the evaluation system should be CII. However, if the purpose of the performance appraisal system is to allocate awards, the standard of comparison should be BI and the evaluation system should be CI.

Some reflection on Figure 7.2 indicates that a variety of decisions must be made when developing and implementing a performance appraisal process. Research and practice indicate that there are limitations associated with any of

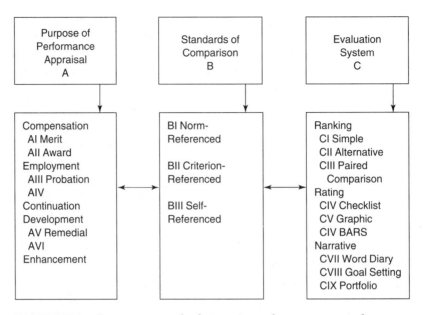

FIGURE 7.2   *Decision matrix for designing a performance appraisal process.*

these decisions. There are problems, situations, and conditions in every school system that may limit or enhance the use and effectiveness of certain appraisal methods.

By following the decisional stream as outlined in Figure 7.2, policy makers and administrators will gain a broad repertory about some of the salient issues involved with performance appraisal. An understanding for and an appreciation of these different issues will explain, at least in part, why performance appraisals may have been less than satisfactory in many instances. However, the solution for better performance appraisal is not to eliminate it altogether but to make it more efficient and effective through use of current knowledge and continuous experimentation on this very important topic.

Interestingly, most public school districts do little in the way of assessment concerning a performance appraisal process. Although performance appraisal processes and procedures represent measurement and are amenable to measurement assessment techniques, these issues are seldom broached in the field setting. As a result of this void, we will touch on these important issues in the following section.

Psychometric Properties of Performance Appraisal Systems

Almost without exception, most textbooks addressing human resources in education state that performance appraisal methods and techniques should be reliable and valid. However, other than this passing recommendation as reflected in published educational textbooks, little other attention is afforded to the issues relating to reliability and to validity as applied within the performance appraisal context. Because of this void, we will address some of the important decisional issues associated with reliability and validity within the performance appraisal context.

An in-depth discussion of each of these important psychometric concepts for reliability and validity is well beyond the scope of this text. What we will provide is a conceptual overview of some of the techniques used most commonly within the performance appraisal context. First, we address reliability and then turn to validity.

Many different types of **reliability** exist and many different procedures of assessing reliability can be found within the psychometric literature. Depending on the purpose of the measuring instrument, some types of reliability are more appropriate than others. Within the performance assessment context, reliability is defined most often by either a coefficient of stability or a coefficient of consistency.

A coefficient of stability assesses how reproducible results from a performance appraisal are across time. To assess a coefficient of stability, results from a performance appraisal process at time one are correlated with results of a performance appraisal process at time two. This reliability technique requires that the performance appraisal process be administered two different times for each appraisee by the same appraiser.

Critical to this technique for assessing reliability is the time period between appraisal one and appraisal two. The period should be long enough so that the appraiser fails to rely on results from the first evaluation when performing the second evaluation, and this period should be short enough that the actual job performance of the appraisee does not change between time one and time two. Some authorities estimate that this time period should be 4–6 weeks between the first and second appraisal.

If the time constraints are met between the first and second evaluation, then the coefficient of stability provides valuable insight about the performance appraisal process. A high coefficient of stability indicates that those aspects of performance being assessed are likely to be enduring and unlikely to change unless the true performance of the employee changes. In contrast, a low coefficient of stability indicates several potential problems with the performance appraisal process.

A low coefficient of stability could indicate that the appraiser does not understand the appraisal process and needs training in the use of the procedure. It could mean also that structural problems exist with the appraisal process. In either situation, remedial actions are warranted by management before sound managerial decisions can be made on the basis of the performance appraisal outcomes.

Procedurally, the coefficient of stability is particularly appropriate for most ranking techniques using a multiple-cutoff model for decision making and seeking to identify persons for awards or persons for layoffs. It is appropriate also for some rating techniques using the multiple-cutoff model, the compensatory model, or the eclectic model when decisions are made on the basis of a single item within the performance appraisal process. The reliability technique is inappropriate, however, when performance assessments are made on more than a single item and results of individual assessments on each item are combined into some type of composite score used subsequently for decision making.

When performance assessments are made on more than a single item and results of individual assessments on each item are combined to form some type of composite score used subsequently for decision making, a more appropriate technique than the coefficient of stability is the coefficient of consistency. A coefficient of consistency measures the internal integrity of a composite score obtained by combining separate performance assessments on numerous items to obtain a global overall performance measure. Unlike the coefficient of stability that requires two administrations of the performance appraisal process for a reliability assessment, the coefficient of consistency requires only a single administration of the performance appraisal process.

Computationally, several different techniques exist for calculating a coefficient of internal consistency. These techniques include the split-half method, the odd-even item method, and the coefficient alpha method. Of these different methods, the alpha technique is by far the most predominant within the professional literature.

The alpha technique, developed initially by Chronbach (see Nunnally & Bernstein, 1994), provides a conservative estimate for the coefficient of consistency. Like the coefficient of stability, the coefficient of consistency ranges between zero and unity. An alpha of at least .60 is needed for making performance appraisal decisions about a group of employees, while an alpha of at least .90 is needed to make performance appraisal decisions about a single individual (see Nunnally & Bernstein).

A high coefficient of consistency suggests that the items used to compute a composite score measure the same underlying construct and it makes logical sense to combine the items. In contrast, a low coefficient of consistency suggests that the items used to compute a composite score fail to measure the same underlying construct and it makes little sense to combine the items. There are several reasons for a low coefficient for internal consistency.

Most often, low coefficients of internal consistency occur when the items measure either different constructs or more than a single construct. For example, some items on a performance appraisal instrument may confound the dimensions of ability and motivation to perform on the part of an employee. Because these constructs are somewhat independent and require different types of remedial activities to remedy, low coefficients of internal consistency will likely emerge when both types of items are combined to form a single composite score of an employee.

Worth noting is the fact that reliability serves only as the first step in the psychometric assessment because reliability establishes the upper limit for validity. Without reliability, a performance assessment process can not be valid.

Validity

Issues of **validity** for a performance appraisal process are concerned with how well the performance appraisal process performs relative to the intended purpose of the procedure. For example, if the purpose of a performance appraisal process is to provide information about the continuation of employment for employees, it is assumed that the process can differentiate between ineffective and effective employees. Similarly, if the purpose of a performance appraisal system is to make merit awards to employees, it is assumed that the process can distinguish between exceptional employees and all other employees.

The degree to which these assumptions are fulfilled relative to these specific examples is the very essence of validity within the performance appraisal process. Although several different types of validity exist, two types of validity are most likely to be encountered within the performance appraisal literature. These types are content validity and construct validity.

Content validity is the only type of validity that is analytically determined. It is analytical in the sense that content validity relies on the subjective opinions of a panel of experts. Experts, as defined for the purpose of content validity, are individuals possessing in-depth knowledge about the content purported to be measured by the performance appraisal process.

To assess the content validity of a performance appraisal instrument, a basic matrix is developed. Each row of the matrix should contain a single item from the appraisal instrument. Listed across the top (columns of the matrix) are the specific content areas purported to being measured by the performance assessment instrument.

Every panel member is requested to evaluate the matrix by placing a check mark in those intersections of rows and columns where the performance appraisal items measure the corresponding content. Results from each panel member should be pooled to form a composite matrix reflecting all the evaluations. An examination of the composite matrix will reveal which items are measuring which content areas and whether all content areas have been addressed adequately by the performance appraisal items.

Unlike the analytical process associated with content validity, **construct validity** is empirically determined. Because job performance is a construct (like leadership, motivation, etc.) that cannot be observed directly, construct validity is inferred on the basis of empirical evidence. Empirical evidence is garnered through several procedures.

For example, the contrast between groups of teachers known to vary greatly in their teaching performance should result in differing performance on the performance appraisal instrument. That is, the highest performing group of teachers in the district should appear distinctly different from the lowest performing group of teachers in the district. If this distinction fails to be met, then the instrument is too insensitive to measure job performance in any meaningful fashion.

Likewise, results from the performance appraisal instrument should correlate with other measures purporting to share some of the same common variance with teaching performance. Other measures might include student ratings, proficiency test scores, work attendance, and/or teaching experience. Failure to detect even moderate relationships between outcomes on the performance appraisal instrument and these other variables purporting to share some of the same common variance brings into question the sensitivity of the performance appraisal instrument for measuring actual on-job behavior.

Unfortunately, validity studies are seldom conducted in the field setting. Without such evidence it is extremely difficult to defend outcomes from the performance appraisal process in the legal setting. As a result, many of the potential advantages expected of and demanded for performance appraisal processes and procedures are seldom realized in practice, and many of the meaningful managerial decisions are relegated to procedural events (seniority, etc.) rather than to substantive outcomes (job performance).

The section that follows proposes a general rather than specific model for appraising the performance of school personnel. This model will: (a) address several phases of the process, (b) note some of the organizational and human obstacles to be encountered in establishing the process, and (c) examine the sequential interrelated steps in its implementation. Again, it is worth noting that there is no ideal performance appraisal process. Some of the steps we discuss will be appropriate to specific appraisal techniques, whereas other steps will be appropriate to different appraisal techniques.

The Performance Appraisal Process

A general model for a performance appraisal process of personnel is presented in Figure 7.3. The model portrays performance appraisal as a process rather than as an event, incorporating several interrelated phases into its design.

Phase 1: Appraisee–Appraiser Planning Conference

Phase 1 consists of a series of steps or activities designed to acquaint or to reacquaint the appraiser and appraisee with the scope, intent, procedures, and expectations of the appraisal process. These steps or activities are addressed generally in the preappraisal planning conference where appraiser and appraisee exchange information about the process. Generally speaking, the conference is designed to perform several functions: (a) enable the appraiser and the appraisee to inform and to become informed about the appraisal process, (b) clarify for the appraisee the organization's expectations for the position, (c) elucidate any differences between present and desired levels of job performance, (d) establish future performance expectations, and (e) allow the appraiser and appraisee to influence each other in planning the appraisal process.

The major goal in Phase 1 of the performance appraisal process is communication. Communication is a two-way process whereby the appraiser and the appraisee review jointly organizational purposes, unit objectives, position goals, performance standards, and appraisal procedures. To ensure adequate as well as systematic coverage of these topics, it is recommended that a performance appraisal manual be prepared and followed during the preappraisal conference.

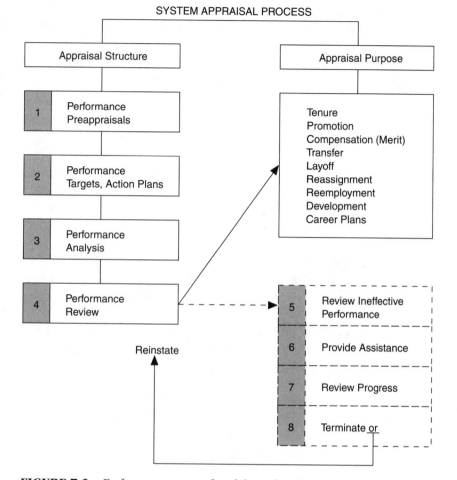

FIGURE 7.3 *Performance appraisal goal-focused model.*

At this point, it is useful to highlight important assumptions about what takes place in a *preappraisal planning conference.*

- Performance appraisal is described as a systematized organizational activity.
- Work standards for the focal position are delineated.
- Job expectations of the employee are discussed.
- Evaluation techniques are explained.

In short, the planning conference should help to inform the employee about desired behavior or performance, how the organization will help the employee to achieve the desired level of behavior, and how it will measure job performance. In addition, the session should be used to analyze the duties of the position and the work behavior necessary to perform effectively, as well as to discover difficulties the employee may have in performing according to plan.

Four major position concepts associated with the performance appraisal process are reviewed by the appraiser and the appraisee in Phase 1: performance effectiveness, performance effectiveness areas, performance standards, and performance targets. These concepts are outlined in Table 7.2.

Phase 2: Performance Analysis

Actual performance assessments begin in Phase 2 of the system appraisal process. In many but not all instances (e.g., reduction in force), performance appraisal at this stage of the process should be a reciprocal activity. This involves a self-appraisal on the part of the employee (Contreras, 1999) and a performance assessment of the employee on the part of the appraiser.

Although both the employee and the employer conduct a performance appraisal focusing on the employee, appraisals of the different sources should be performed independently. With respect to the former, the self-appraisal process has at least three purposes: (a) to assist the employee in analyzing present performance, (b) to provide information for a progress review conference with the appraiser, and (c) to help the employee identify strengths, weaknesses, and potential, as well as to help make plans for improving performance. Figure 7.4 lists the kinds of questions that can be addressed in Phase 2.

Appraisals performed by the appraiser should focus on at least two different dimensions. First, the appraiser should ascertain if the short-range goals associated with the position are being meet. That is, to what extent are the short-term goals or performance targets being achieved by the employee?

Having assessed the short-range goals, attention is refocused on the long-range goals associated with the position. This aspect of the performance appraisal process is future oriented. The task is to determine how well the employee is likely to maintain a course of positive action relative to these goals.

For both observational aspects of the performance appraisal process, detailed records must be compiled. Such records provide the building blocks for subsequent stages of the performance appraisal process. An example of a form that can be used to catalog observations is found in Figure 7.5.

Phase 3: Performance Progress Review

After performance appraisals are completed by the appraiser and the appraisee, the next step in the appraisal process, as shown in Figure 7.3, is the performance review conference, sometimes referred to as the postappraisal interview. The major purpose of the progress review conference is to exchange information between the appraiser and appraisee about the latter's performance. Prior to the conference, several procedural steps must be completed.

TABLE 7.2
Major concepts involved in appraising and documenting the performance of school personnel.

Performance Effectiveness	Performance Effectiveness Areas	Performance Standards	Performance Targets
Performance effectiveness is the extent to which an individual administrator achieves the general and specific objectives of the position to which he or she is assigned. Effectiveness is construed as results actually achieved rather than what activities the position holder engages in to achieve the results.	Key functional areas associated with a position constitute performance effectiveness areas.	Position standards are statements of conditions that will exist when the responsibilities assigned to the position are being carried out effectively. Standards are desired end results the individual is being paid to accomplish; they specify the conditions that exist when the role is being performed satisfactorily.	Position performance targets are specific statements agreed on by appraiser and appraisee that indicate what is to be accomplished to meet a specific position objective. Position performance targets are time bounded, measurable, and focus on what a position holder should achieve (results) rather than on the means by which it is to be accomplished.

---

1. Summarize the overall strengths that you have demonstrated in performing your present assignment.

2. Do you feel that you are well placed in your present assignment? If not, please explain.

3. In what areas of your present assignment or in the way you perform your present assignment do you think you can improve your performance?

4. Do you feel that you have potential beyond your present assignment? How have you demonstrated this potential? What can you suggest as your next assignment?

5. Are there significant facts that you think should be noted about the dimensions of your position that affect your performance and that you think should be brought to the attention of your superior, such as:

   Unit objectives
   Position design
   Human, technical, and conceptual skills
   Social setting
   Situational factors
   Results achieved

6. How effectively do you feel you have met the responsibilities of your position?

Signature of appraisee _____ Date _____

FIGURE 7.4   *A self-appraisal form.*

Preparation for the conference involves reviewing results of the performance appraisal outcomes. A second purpose of the progress review conference is to clarify viewpoints about the appraisee's performance. Differing perceptions of the position's goals, responsibilities, authority, and relationships can be identified, examined, and clarified, while obstacles to progress, whether individual or organizational, are topics for discussion.

The self-development of the appraisee is a third purpose of the progress review conference. As noted earlier, performance appraisal is designed not only to achieve organizational goals but also to help the individual attain personal objectives, one of which should be performance improvement. It is at this stage of the conference that the appraiser attempts to counsel or coach the appraisee to solve any problems affecting performance.

Illustrated in Figure 7.5 are means by which the appraiser can compare self-judgments with those of the appraisee on the latter's performance. The information in this form provides the basis for the progress review conference and the individual development program.

Name of appraisee _____   Organizational unit _____
                                       Position _____

1. What progress does the   What progress does the *appraisee*
    appraiser think the *appraisee*   think he or she has made in
    made during the review period in   closing the gap between actual
    closing the gap between actual   and desired performance?
    and desired performance?

2. In what areas does the   In what respects does the *appraisee*
    appraiser think the *appraisee*   think he or she can improve?
    can improve?

3. Since the last appraisal, in what   Since the last appraisal, in what ways
    ways does the *appraiser* think   does the *appraisee* think his or
    the performance of the   her performance has improved?
    appraisee has improved?

4. What specifically does the   What are the *appraisee's* plans for
    appraiser plan to do to improve   helping himself or herself?
    the performance of the
    appraisee?

5. What follow-up action will be   What appears to be the general reac-
    taken by the *appraiser* on the   tion of the *appraisee* to (a) the
    basis of this review?   performance appraisal and
                                          (b) the ways by which perform-
                                          ance can be improved?

Signature of appraiser _____

Date of review _____

FIGURE 7.5   *Performance progress review form.*

Another aspect of Phase 3 in the appraisal process is the joint development of an action program for the appraisee based on the progress review conference. The essence of the individual development program may be summarized as follows:

• Performance appraisal reports should indicate to both the appraiser and the appraisee how well the latter has done in reaching previously established performance and behavior targets.

• On the basis of the progress review conference (which should make clear both the results achieved and those to be achieved), the appraiser and appraisee come to a common understanding on what performance targets should be reestablished for the next review period.

- During the period set for the individual development program, the appraiser has primary responsibility for guiding and motivating the behavior of the appraisee to achieve performance targets.

Phase 4: Performance Diagnosis and Recycling

As Figure 7.3 indicates, Phase 4 of the appraisal model is the time for diagnosis of performance results and for recycling of the appraisal process. This phase of the process is designed to check the results of the individual development program and to establish new or modified performance targets for the next review period. In effect, the appraisal process is being recycled.

As performance standards are reached, the appraisal process is redirected to other areas of performance where improvement is needed. The purpose of diagnosis is to establish continuity and stability in the individual's development program. Concrete plans should emerge for extending the program in areas where it has been good.

Here is a key point in the understanding of this appraisal program: Hitting the target is not the measure of success. It is expected that some targets will be surpassed, whereas some will never even be approached. The person who sets meager targets and always hits them is certainly of no greater value to the company than the person who sets unreachable targets, falls short consistently, yet in doing so makes substantial improvements in work performance.

If one's "score" in hitting the bull's-eye is not the important thing, then what is? The results achieved by the total process of establishing targets, striving to attain targets, and analyzing what intervenes between planned and actual performance are what count. When a judgment must be made, the individual is evaluated on ability to set targets as well as on ability to attain targets.

Another important aspect of Phase 4 is that in addition to diagnosing individual development, the unit administrator includes in the periodic review the progress being made by the unit toward its objectives and system goals. Diagnosis and recycling of unit objectives and performance are designed to promote coordination and integration of plans and results of plans within the work unit and across the system.

Review and Preview

This chapter has provided an overview of the performance appraisal process. Forces were identified that impact traditional appraisal systems and will continue to influence the appraisal systems used by most educational organizations. Specific suggestions were offered for designing and implementing a performance appraisal system in the educational setting.

When designing and implementing, it is important to focus on the purpose(s) of the appraisal system. Certain operational and behavioral concerns that demand specific choices by those who develop an appraisal system were identified. It was shown how the specific purpose(s) of the system requires different implications.

Because a universal system for effective performance appraisal fails to exist, several different appraisal methods were reviewed. In each of these methods, at least three different evaluation formats were discussed. Each format was linked to certain appraisal purposes, operational concerns, and behavioral concerns.

A four-phase model for implementing a performance appraisal process was presented. Each phase of the model focused on specific responsibilities and tasks to be accomplished. Finally, it was emphasized that performance appraisal should be part of the ongoing life of an employee rather than an isolated yearly event. As a process, every aspect of this important managerial tool must be continually revisited to ensure that the goals of students, parents, employees, boards of education, and taxpayers are being met.

In Chapter 8 the topic of employee compensation will be addressed. Special attention will be given to criteria used to assess current compensation practices within a school district. Procedures will be presented for establishing new compensation methods.

Discussion Questions

1. Compare the performance appraisal process used in your educational organization to the performance appraisal model outlined in this chapter. How does your process differ from the model process? Does your process place greater emphasis on a particular phase of the appraisal process than on others?

2. Has the recent public focus on school accountability impacted the performance appraisal system in your school organization? How *should* this emphasis change the appraisal system?

3. Consider the following statement: "The quality of the appraiser–appraisee relationship considerably influences the effectiveness of the performance appraisal process." How can a manager or administrator improve the quality of the appraiser–appraisee relationship?

4. Compare the advantages and disadvantages of ranking, rating, and narrative systems of performance appraisal for teachers.

5. Consider your current position in a school organization. Which evaluation technique should be used to evaluate you? Why is this more appropriate than other techniques?

6. For what positions in a school organization would appraisal by supervisor be appropriate? Appraisal by peer? Self-appraisal? Appraisal by group or by commitee? Appraisal by parents? Appraisal by students?

References

Arvey, R. D., & Murphy, K. R. (1998). Performance evaluation in work settings. *Annual Review of Psychology, 49,* 141–168.

Contreras, G. L. (1999). Teacher's perceptions of active participation, evaluation effectiveness, and training in education systems. *Journal of Research and Development in Education, 33,* 47–59.

Dressler, G. (1988). *Personnel management.* Englewood Cliffs, NJ: Simmon.

Harris, B. M., & Monk, B. J. (1992). *Personnel administration in education: Leadership for instructional improvement* (3rd ed.). Boston: Allyn & Bacon.

Heneman, H. G. (1998). Assessment of the motivational reactions of teachers to a school-based performance award program. *Journal of Personnel Evaluation in Education, 12*(1), 43–59.

Heneman, R. L., & Ledford, G. E. (1998). Competency pay for professionals and managers in business: A review and implication for teachers. *Journal of Personnel Evaluation in Education, 12*(2), 103–121.

Kelley, C., Heneman, H. G., & Milanowski, A. (2002). Teacher motivation and school-based performance rewards. *Educational Administration Quarterly, 38*(5), 372–401.

Kelley, C., & Protsik, J. (1997). Risk and reward: Perspectives on the implementation of Kentucky's school-based performance award program. *Educational Administration Quarterly, 33*, 474–505.

Painter, B. (2001). Using teaching portfolios. *Educational Leadership, 58*, 31–34.

Peterson, K. D., Stevens, D., & Mack, C. (2001). Presenting complex teacher evaluation data: Advantages of dossier organization techniques over portfolios. *Journal of Personnel Evaluation in Education, 15*(2), 121–133.

Nunnally, J., & Bernstein, I. (1994). *Psychometric theory.* New York: McGraw-Hill.

Supplementary Reading

Berg, J., & Urich, T. (1997, March). A team approach to middle school faculty evaluation. *Middle School Journal, 28*(4), 41–43.

Cook, M. F. (Ed.). (1993). *The human resources yearbook, 1993/1994 edition.* Upper Saddle River, NJ: Prentice Hall.

Danielson, C. (2001, February). New trends in teacher evaluation. *Educational Leadership, 58*(5), 12–15.

Howard, B. B., & McColskey, W. H. (2001, February). Evaluating experienced teachers. *Educational Leadership, 58*(5), 48–51.

Jenkins, G. H. (1994). *Data processing: Policies and procedures manual.* Upper Saddle River, NJ: Prentice Hall.

Kerrins, J. A., & Cushing, K. S. (2000, March). Taking a second look: Expert and novice differences when observing the same classroom teaching segment a second time. *Journal of Personnel Evaluation in Education, 14*(1), 5–24.

Klein, T. J. (1990, May). Performance reviews that rate an A. *Personnel, 67*(5), 38–41.

McGrath, M. J. (2000, October). The human dynamics of personnel evaluation. *School Administrator, 57*(9), 34–38.

Peterson, K. D., Wahlquist, C., Bone, K., Thompson, J., & Chatterton, K. (2001, February). Using more data sources to evaluate teachers. *Educational Leadership, 58*(5), 40–43.

Popham, W. J. (1992). *Educational evaluation* (3rd ed.). Rockleigh, NJ: Allyn & Bacon.

Sawyer, L. (2001, February). Revamping a teacher evaluation system. *Educational Leadership, 58*(5), 44–47.

Schuler, R. S., & Huber, V. L. (1993). *Personnel and human resources management* (5th ed.). St. Paul, MN: West.

Schuler, R. S., & Walker, J. (Eds.). (1991). *Managing human resources in the information age.* Washington, DC: Bureau of National Affairs.

Tucker, P. D., & Stronge, J. H. (2001, September). Measure for measure: Using student test results in teacher evaluation. *American School Board Journal, 188*(9), 34–37.

Werther, W. B., Jr. (1993). *Human resources and personnel management.* New York: McGraw-Hill.

Wilkerson, D. J., Manatt, R. P., Rogers, M. A., & Maughan, R. (2000, June). Validation of student, principal, and self-ratings in 360° feedback for teacher evaluation. *Journal of Personnel Evaluation in Education, 14*(2), 179–192.

8

Compensation

CHAPTER OBJECTIVES

Develop an understanding of current compensation practices and problems.
Provide a model or blueprint for designing the compensation process.
Analyze the compensable factors that comprise the pay structure.
Identify external and internal factors that influence pay policies and levels.
Describe approaches to developing the economic worth of positions.
Stress the importance of assessing compensation process outcomes.

CHAPTER CONCEPTS

Appropriate labor market
Base pay
Benefits
Compensation policy
Compression
Elasticity

Internal consistency
Learning curve
Rationality
Salary
Wage

Human Resource Compensation: Perennial Challenge

Compensation is one of the most visible areas within the human resource domain. With the possible exceptions of proficiency test scores for students and of report cards for school districts and buildings, few other topics command as much interest and as much coverage in the popular press as compensation. Reasons for this popularity are that compensation practices of a public school district impact a variety of different stakeholders including those without children in the school district.

According to Young, Delli, Miller-Smith, and Alhadeff (2001), compensation practices of a school district have important implications for the public, the school board, and the employees. For the public, compensation practices have funding implications related to tax efforts. School boards, elected by public vote, generally act as guardians of public coffers and approve the expenditure of funds for compensation. Employees are recipients of public funds that dictate, to a great extent, the quality of life enjoyed as a consumer.

Given these implications, this chapter views compensation as unfinished business. It provides a perspective on compensation decision making, the goal of which is to solve, effectively and efficiently, compensation issues affecting the community, the school system, and its employees. This perspective includes the components of the compensation process, leading the reader through the steps by which the economic worth of positions and persons is determined, as well as the environmental influences on this issue.

Compensation Strategy

Designing a school system compensation plan starts by considering the link between organizational purpose and compensation strategy. Organizational purpose focuses on the outcomes to be achieved by the system; strategies are the methods used by the system. This perspective, involving the connection between outcomes and strategies, is illustrated in Figure 8.1 and provides the basis for designing a compensation strategy.

Central to the compensation strategy is the mission of the school system. The mission, as noted in Chapter 1, should be based on the purposes of the school district. As Figure 8.1 shows, organizational strategy is anticipatory, future oriented, concerned with emerging environmental conditions, and designed to make education a meaningful experience both for students and for employees. Organizational strategy is a set of plans for moving the school system from an existing state to a desired state, thereby achieving the mission of a school district more effectively and efficiently.

Mission-oriented guidelines are driven by the interaction between human resource strategy and compensation policy. Human resource strategy addresses the number and kinds of positions needed (see Chapter 2) and the skills and abil-

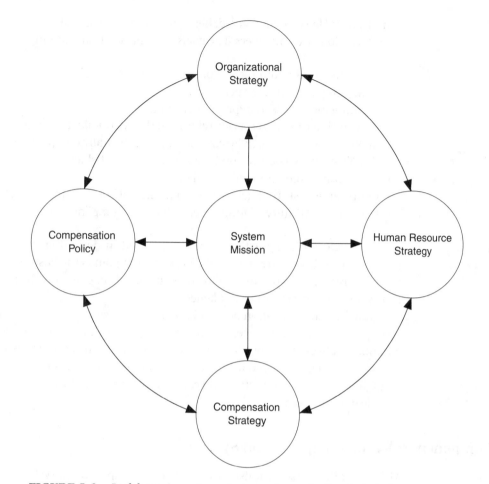

FIGURE 8.1   *Link between system mission and organizational strategies.*

ities required for position holders (see Chapter 3). Compensation policy indicates the system's intent with regard to compensation obligations and responsibilities. This complex web of human resources and **compensation policy,** when integrated into a strategic planning framework, can be used to guide the many administrative judgments involved in creating and implementing a compensation strategy.

A compensation strategy may be viewed as a set of interrelated decisions that allocate fiscal resources to change the system's current compensation status to one that will contribute more effectively to the organizational strategy. This includes plans that direct attention and resources to present and emerging issues related to compensating school employees.

When developing compensation strategies, one central task of educational administrators is to devise plans for allocating funds to employees for services rendered. This should be done through a formal compensation system. Such a system, properly conceived and fairly administered, helps to promote the organization's objectives and the satisfaction of its members. The goals of compensation planning include:

- Attracting and retaining competent career personnel
- Motivating personnel to perform well
- Creating incentives to improve performance
- Maximizing return in service relative to the economic investment
- Making the plan internally consistent and externally competitive
- Establishing a structure conducive to personal satisfaction
- Minimizing union and individual grievances
- Controlling costs that account for four fifths of the system's budget
- Ensuring continuity of funds needed for total compensation

These goals highlight the problems involved in designing the compensation process. In a school system, a good compensation plan is the basic element for employee satisfaction. Without an effective compensation plan, all other system plans, programs, and processes are weakened.

However, compensation plans, like all human resource plans, are subject to external and internal influences, as shown in Figure 8.2. External influences have a cumulative effect and play a large part in determining the characteristics of a compensation system. Internal influences (human and organizational) are frequently changing and require direction and coordination to align the organization with the outside environment.

Components of Total Compensation Systems

Most school systems administer three different compensation systems: those for administrators, teachers, and support personnel. Some of these compensation systems are directly controlled by the school system, which alone is responsible for establishing and implementing them. Other compensation systems are only partially controlled by the school system and require bilateral actions by the school system in the collective bargaining process.

However, regardless of the need for mutual agreement, all compensation systems have several components, each of which is influenced by external and internal factors impacting the school district (see Figure 8.2). One component concerns direct payments to employees; another component concerns indirect payments to employees. Both types of payments consist of several subcomponents, all of which must be considered within the total compensation process.

Direct compensation is the actual dollars paid to employees. The major source of direct payments is the salary or the wage received for services rendered by employees to a school system. Whether an employee receives a salary or a wage depends both on the method used to calculate the source of the direct payment and on

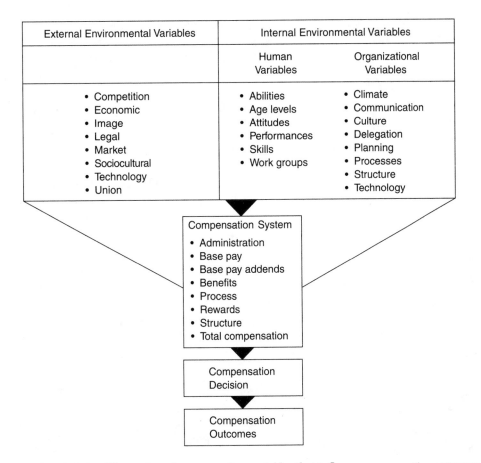

FIGURE 8.2 *Illustration of compensation variables that influence compensation outcomes.*

the employee's job characteristics, as defined by the Fair Labor Standards Act of 1938 (United States Government [M.D.]).

In general, a **salary** is paid to employees who are exempt from the Fair Labor Standards Act of 1938. By being exempted from this act, compensation is related to the job rather than to the amount of time worked on the job. A **wage,** on the other hand, is paid to employees who are covered by this act and who are paid on an hourly basis.

In the school setting, administrators, supervisors, and teachers receive salaries, while custodians, aides, and clerical personnel receive wages. Certain exceptions occur when certain employees are designated as exempted employees due to the confidentiality of their jobs related to collective bargaining.

The expected salary or wage associated with a particular position is referred to as the **base pay** for said employees. Base pay may be supplemented, however, through additional effort on the part of an employee. For salaried employees, additional effort usually involves taking on an extra assignment, such as coaching performed by a teacher. For employees receiving a wage, supplements to base pay involve working overtime.

Indirect compensation refers to certain economic advantages received by an employee beyond salaries or wages and is labeled as **benefits.** These benefits include sick leave, insurance provisions, and retirement incentives and represent a substantial cost for a school district. In fact, benefits usually cost a school district an additional 40% beyond the salary or wage paid to an employee.

Benefits play a very important role in the employment process. For school districts, they serve as an incentive to attract potential employees and to retain current ones. Often, it is this form of indirect compensation, rather than direct compensations of the salary or wage, that gives a school district a competitive edge in the labor market. Because compensation includes both direct and indirect costs, we focus on both types in this chapter.

Direct Cost

The primary direct cost in a compensation system is the base salary or base wage paid to an employee. This base salary or base wage can generally be ascertained from a salary schedule. Salary schedules vary in several ways both between as well as within school systems.

Schedules can be simple or complex and can have fixed or variable dollar amounts associated with a particular position or with different persons holding the same position. The use of any particular type of salary schedule is based on certain assumptions about the position and the employees. These assumptions are often overlooked by school districts, resulting far too often in rigid compliance with past compensation practices.

When assumptions underlying a salary schedule are overlooked, many attempted improvements are stymied and the status quo is maintained. Consequently, we examine several different types of salary schedules. These include the single rate salary schedule, the teacher salary schedule, and the exempted employee salary schedule.

Single Rate Wage Schedule

An example of a single rate wage schedule is found in Table 8.1. This type of wage schedule is frequently used for support personnel paid an hourly wage. As reflected

TABLE 8.1
Example of a single rate wage schedule (hourly rate).

Level I	$13.50
Level II	$14.00
Level III	$14.50
Level IV	$15.00
Level V	$15.50

in Table 8.1, this schedule contains different hourly rates for employees at varying job classifications (I through V).

Each level of a single rate wage schedule pertains either to a single position or to multiple positions. All positions at a particular level are assumed to have the same worth to a school system, and positions at separate levels are assumed to have different worth to the school system. Because the worth assigned to a position by a school system determines the base rate of pay, an employee must change levels or jobs to increase the base rate.

Table 8.1 shows that a single rate wage schedule fails to provide any growth incentive or to reward experience on the job. All employees at the same level receive the same base wage, regardless of their education and experience. Thus, this type of wage structure assumes a similar organizational worth and an equal base rate pay for all job holders at a particular salary level. That is, equal pay for equal work.

Teacher Salary Schedule

In contrast to the single rate wage schedule is the teacher salary schedule (see Table 8.2). Almost all teacher salary schedules provide for a growth incentive and a reward experience. Although the organizational worth of the growth incentive and of employment experience varies considerably among school districts within the same state, this type of teacher salary schedule exists throughout the United States.

TABLE 8.2
A hypothetical teacher salary schedule.

Experience (years)	Education						
	BA	BA+15	BA+25	MA	MA+15	MA+30	MA+45
1	$28,500	$28,550	$28,600	$28,650	$29,000	$29,500	$30,000
2	28,550	28,600	28,650	28,700	29,050	29,550	30,050
3	28,600	28,650	28,700	28,750	29,100	29,600	30,100
4	28,650	28,700	28,750	28,800	29,150	29,650	30,150
5	28,700	28,750	28,800	28,850	29,200	29,700	30,200
6	28,750	28,800	28,850	28,900	29,250	29,750	30,250
7	28,800	28,850	28,900	28,950	29,300	29,800	30,300
8	28,850	28,900	28,950	29,000	29,350	29,850	30,350
9	28,900	28,950	29,000	29,050	29,400	29,900	30,400
10	28,950	29,000	29,050	29,100	29,450	29,950	30,450
11	29,000	29,050	29,100	29,150	29,500	30,000	30,500
12	29,050	29,100	29,150	29,200	29,550	30,050	30,550
13	29,100	29,150	29,200	29,250	29,600	30,100	30,600
14	29,150	29,200	29,250	29,300	29,650	30,150	30,650
15	29,200	29,250	29,300	29,350	29,700	30,200	30,700
20	29,250	29,300	29,350	29,400	29,750	30,250	30,750

The growth incentives associated with teacher salary schedules are defined by education and represent a weak form of competency-based pay. Education may include formal course work, continuing educational units, and/or other approved plans for professional development. Underlying the use of growth incentives to raise the base salary of a teacher is the assumption that additional education increases the teacher's competence on the job. However, "in practice, teachers are often rewarded for taking courses that may have little or nothing to do with the knowledge and skill set needed by the school organization" (Kelley, 1997).

Employment experience is another compensable factor common to teacher salary schedules. The use of employment experience in determining compensation should be based on the learning curve associated with the job. In some jobs, proficiency increases with experience, and salary schedules should reflect this situation by awarding increases reflecting the slope of the **learning curve** depicting proficiency.

Interestingly, little disagreement exists about what counts for appropriate employment experience of teachers. However, there is considerable controversy over the organizational worth of such experience. Depending on whether the teacher is new to the system or an incumbent within the system, the organizational worth of experience may vary within a particular school district.

The organizational worth of employment experience should be based on the learning curve associated with the job rather than on seniority. Nevertheless, some school districts cap employment experience when placing potential job candidates on the teacher salary schedule. This practice has limited economic value to a school system and restricts its ability to compete in the labor market when recruiting experienced teachers.

Although most school systems use the traditional salary structure for compensating teachers, some systems are beginning to explore new strategies. These new strategies require the concurrence of union membership and largely build upon rather than depart from the traditional teacher salary structure. Urbanski and Erskine (2000) label these innovations according to school-based performance awards, National Board for Professional Teaching Standards, and knowledge-and skill-based pay systems.

School-based performance awards programs focus on a bonus system for teachers. Within these types of programs, teachers receive a supplement beyond base pay awarded via the traditional salary schedule based on their obtainment of pre-established goals relating, in most instances, to student achievement. In some instances, supplements awarded on the basis of performance may be used by teachers without restrictions, while in other instances, supplements must be spent for educational improvement of the school.

Unlike school-based performance awards, other districts have awarded teacher salary increases beyond those attributable to the traditional salary schedule on the basis of acquiring certification by the National Board for Professional Teaching Standards. Underlying this type of award program is the assumption that teachers so certified will exhibit the skills and knowledge necessary for effective performance.

In some instances Board-certified teachers receive a supplement beyond the traditional salary schedule, while in other instances, Board-certified teachers are advanced increments within the traditional teacher salary schedule based on board certification rather than on traditional college credit.

Still different are the knowledge- and skill-based pay systems for teachers. Knowledge- and skill-based pay systems assume that education and experience, as awarded by the traditional teacher salary schedule, are poor proxies of their labeled attributes and endorse school district definitions of these attributes (rather than the National Board for Professional Teaching Standards). Only by meeting local school district definitions of skill and knowledge can teachers advance though the traditional teacher salary schedule according to true knowledge- and skill-based pay systems.

Research addressing these new innovative pay configurations for teachers is limited at the present. Whether or not these systems offer a new direction for future compensation is unclear. What the research does suggest, to date, is that performance incentives must be greater than those used by many school districts (Heneman, 1998) and that such pay programs must be enduring (Kelley, Heneman, & Milanowski, 2002). Until further research is conducted that can guide human resource managers, much debate exists in this very important area.

Exempted Salary Schedules

Most exempted salary schedules found within public school districts pertain to administrators and supervisors. However, the mere existence of exempted salary schedules is the exception rather than the rule. It is not uncommon to find school districts that lack any type of exempted salary schedules on which to base the compensation of administrators and supervisors.

For those school districts that do have a formal salary schedule for compensating administrators and supervisors, these salary schedules can be categorized by the compensation policies that govern movement through them by employees. Movement through an exempted salary schedule can be based on time, performance, or some mixture of time and performance. These different categorizations are fixed rate, variable rate, or mixed rate.

A fixed rate salary schedule for exempted employees is modeled after the basic teacher salary schedule. As such, it has certain commensurable factors, such as education and experience, that increase the base salary of an employee each year of employment. An example of a fixed rate salary is found in Table 8.3.

In keeping with this type of fixed rate salary structure, an exempted employee has two avenues to increase one's base salary. The employee can acquire additional education and/or can serve another year in the current position. Movement within this type of salary schedule is automatic and is beyond administrative discretion.

In contrast to the fixed rate salary schedule is the variable rate salary schedule for exempted employees. This type of schedule, as found in Table 8.4, is restricted only minimum and maximum salary rates. Provisions are lacking either for education or for experience in the variable rate salary schedule.

TABLE 8.3
Administrator salary schedule reflecting daily rates.

Classification	Step 1	Step 2	Step 3	Step 4	Step 5	Step 6	Step 7	Step 8	Step 9	Step 10
I Doctorate	$369	$278	$388	$397	$406	$414	$422	$430	$438	$447
Masters	361	370	379	388	397	405	413	421	429	437
II Doctorate	313	321	328	336	344	351	358	365	372	378
Masters	305	313	321	328	336	343	349	356	363	370
III Doctorate	285	292	299	306	313	319	326	332	338	344
Masters	277	284	291	298	305	311	317	323	329	336
IV Doctorate	271	278	284	291	298	304	310	316	322	328
Masters	265	271	278	284	291	297	303	308	314	320
V Doctorate	258	265	271	278	284	290	295	301	307	312
Masters	252	258	264	271	277	283	288	294	299	305

TABLE 8.4
Variable rate administrator salary schedule reflecting daily values.

Classification	Minimum Salary	Maximum Salary
Level I	$369	$447
Level II	313	378
Level III	285	344
Level IV	271	328
Level V	258	312

Movement within the variable rate salary schedule is based solely on administrative discretion. This type of schedule has roots with the pay for performance philosophy. Increases in base salary for exempted employees within a variable salary schedule can be anywhere between the minimum rate and the maximum rate salary points.

Still different from either the fixed rate or the variable rate schedule is the mixed rate schedule. The mixed rate salary schedule contains certain commensurable factors that are fixed and certain commensurable factors that are variable. Within the example as provided, education is fixed and performance is variable.

The mixed rate schedule provides employees with two avenues for increasing their base salary. One avenue is to acquire additional education (vertical), and this acquirement is beyond administrative control. The other avenue (horizontal) is based on job performance and is subject to administrative discretion.

Indirect Cost

Another source of economic concern for a school system is the indirect cost of benefits (*Benefits Next*, n.d.). A benefit is a form of indirect compensation that does not re-

TABLE 8.5
Typical benefits received by employees.

Medical insurance	Dental insurance	Vision insurance
Long-term disability insurance	Life insurance	Annuity
Retirement pickup	Flexible spending account	Sick leave
Personal leave	Vacation	Holiday pay
Tuition reimbursement	Sabbaticals	Conferences

quire additional services beyond those required by the contract, as noted in Table 8.5. Benefits extend compensation beyond base pay and incentives and are intended to be dollar free and to focus on a variety of protective arrangements in addition to monetary components.

It is assumed that benefits enhance the position and personal satisfaction of employees, creating an environment that nourishes personal development and engenders satisfaction associated with a position. Benefits, in general, provide a means of income protection for the employee beyond the direct compensation received. In fact, for many positions, benefits may be more important than salary in that they provide the employee with protection for medical costs when working and provide for income continuity when retired.

Benefit schedules offered to school employees may be categorized as either uniform or variable. Uniform benefits provide the same coverage to all personnel. By contrast, with variable benefits, each employee receives the amount of money the system allocates for benefit purposes and may then spend that money any way the employee chooses.

On the surface, the choice between uniform and variable benefit programs within the total compensation perspective is deceptive. Often overlooked is the scale of economy. Fixed benefits are more cost efficient but may be redundant for certain employees, while variable benefits are less cost efficient and a fixed dollar amount will purchase fewer variable benefits than fixed benefits.

Criticism is mounting and changes are being initiated in the design and administration of benefits. The following points are illustrative:

- Benefit demands are insatiable.
- Benefit costs are often almost half of all personnel costs.
- Benefits do not depend on performance.
- Benefits are not congruent in two-career households.
- Benefits are not designed to motivate high performance.

Consequently, the design of compensation plans should involve careful evaluation of existing or proposed benefits in terms of their impact on base salary, incentive compensation, and performance.

Audit of Compensation Structures

The direct cost associated with salaries and wages and the indirect cost associated with collateral benefits are influenced by both external and internal factors (see Figure 8.2). Because of these influences, direct and indirect costs can become misaligned with the total compensation system. These misalignments fall into three categories: (a) those attributable to the formal structure of salary schedules, (b) those due to the compensation practices of compensation system administrators, and (c) those related to insensitivity to labor market conditions.

To identify potential misalignments of compensation outcomes with the total compensation system, an audit of the system's compensation structure is required. An audit will reveal potential problem areas, indicate remedial actions, and identify sources of inequity. At minimum, an audit should focus on four factors: elasticity, compression, rationality, and market sensitivity.

Elasticity

Elasticity refers to the theoretical earning potential associated with salary schedules. The theoretical earning potential is defined by the minimum and maximum base rates that define a particular salary range or pay grade within a salary schedule. Because these minimum and maximum base rates may not reflect the actual base rate received by a specific employee, the term *theoretical* rather than *actual* is used in the definition of elasticity.

To calculate the theoretical earning potential associated with a particular salary range or pay grade, some simple computations are required. For each level (salary range or pay grade) of the compensation structure, divide the maximum allowable salary by the minimum beginning salary (maximum salary/minimum salary), then subtract 1. The result is then converted into a percentage; this percentage is the theoretical earning potential for a particular level of the salary schedule.

An example involving the elasticity criterion for a group of elementary school principals is provided in Table 8.6. These data reflect a minimum salary rate of $255 per day and a maximum salary rate of $308 per day. The minimum salary is the

TABLE 8.6
Computational procedures for calculating a theoretical earning potential.

Minimum ←									→ Maximum
255	261	267	274	280	286	291	297	301	308

= (maximum rate/minimum rate) − 1 × 100
= (308/255) − 1 × 100
= 20.78%

TABLE 8.7
Examples of elasticity.

	Example A	Example B	Example C	Example D
Level I	25%	25%	10%	25%
Level II	25%	20%	15%	10%
Level III	25%	15%	20%	15%
Level IV	25%	10%	25%	20%

smallest amount that can be awarded, and the maximum salary is the largest amount that can be paid.

The theoretical earning potential associated with this pay grade for elementary principals is derived by dividing the maximum rate ($308) by the minimum rate ($255), subtracting 1 from the result, and converting the final number to a percentage (20.8%). If the same computations are used for all salary levels within a compensation structure, the theoretical earning potential can be assessed for an entire compensation structure involving administrators and supervisors in a public school district.

Table 8.7 presents four potential outcomes relative to elasticity. These outcomes are shown for lack of elasticity (Example A), for elasticity varying according to pay grades (Example B), for elasticity varying inversely with pay grades (Example C), and for elasticity varying unsystematically among pay grades (Example D). Each example has certain implications for the current and future compensation practices of a school district.

If the theoretical earning potential among pay levels within a school district varies substantially, then the compensation structure is elastic because some pay grades have greater earning potential than others. Whether elasticity has a positive or negative effect on compensation practices depends largely on the relationship between the organizational level of pay grades and the size of earning potentials associated with pay grades. Positive effects on compensation practices are most likely to occur either when elasticity does not exist or when it increases according to the organizational level of pay grades.

Lack of elasticity suggests that the theoretical earning potential for employees is a constant percentage throughout the compensation structure (see Table 8.7, Example A). Lower-level employees have the same earning potential as their superiors. Earning potential that is equal or constant across all organizational levels (lacking elasticity) generally has strong appeal to employees and reflects sound compensation practices of a school system.

Elasticity can also have a positive effect when earning potential increases systematically according to the level within the hierarchy (see Table 8.7, Example B). With this type of elasticity, higher-level employees have greater earning potential than lower-level employees. Underlying this type of elasticity is the assumption that higher-level positions are more difficult to obtain through promotion and require employees to remain within a grade for a longer period of time. To compensate for these limitations, earning potentials increase according to the level within the hierarchy.

The negative effects of elasticity often occur when earning potentials vary unsystematically among organizational levels or vary inversely with levels. Earning potentials that vary unsystematically among levels are a problem often found during an internal audit. Because unsystematic variations usually have no logical explanation, they lead to accusations of favoritism benefiting certain employee groups and reflect poor compensation practices by the school system.

The accusation of favoritism is also made by higher-level employees when earning potentials vary inversely with level. In this situation, lower-level employees have greater earning potential than those higher up in the hierarchy. At best, this arrangement creates a competitive rather than a cooperative work environment; at worst, it results in a work environment perceived as inequitable.

The negative effects of elasticity can usually be traced to certain compensation decisions made in the past. With unsystematic variation, barring any actions intended to create a privileged group, market competition for certain groups may have required selective adjustments to attract good employees. If some employee groups receive an adjustment for market fluctuations and other groups do not, the former will have a greater earning potential than the latter.

Elasticity characterized by an inverse relationship between earning potential and organizational level can result from techniques used to update compensation systems. To update compensation systems, school boards can use either a proportional rate technique based on a fixed percentage or a constant rate technique involving a fixed dollar amount. The former technique will maintain the status quo with respect to earning potential, while the latter technique will increase the earning potential for lower-level employees.

Compression

Another criterion for evaluating the compensation structures and practices of a school district is **compression,** which addresses the functional as opposed to the theoretical growth potential for employees within a given pay grade. Compression considers the actual distribution of salaries within a salary grade rather than the theoretical earning potential defined by elasticity.

To assess the actual growth potential for a group of employees, again, some simple calculations are required. For each salary level or pay grade, the base rate of the lowest-paid employee is divided by the maximum allowable base rate associated with the targeted pay grade. The result of this division is then converted to a percentage; the percentage is the actual growth potential within the pay grade.

TABLE 8.8
Computational procedure for calculating compression for elementary principals.

Minimum ←							→	Maximum
255	261	267	280	286	291	297	302	308

Rebecca's rate $297
Jeff's rate $302
Julie's rate $302
Susan's rate $302
= (maximum schedule rate/minimum actual rate) − 1 × 100
= (308/207) − 1 × 100
= 3.7%

TABLE 8.9
Illustration of variations in compression across position.

Position	Compression
Assistant superintendent	15%
Secondary school principal	12%
Elementary school principal	4%
Supervisor	18%

Table 8.8 shows the computations used to assess the compression for a particular pay grade. The table shows the salaries of a group of elementary school principals. In addition to the specific salaries, the anchor points or salary ranges associated with the pay grade are presented.

Rather than using the minimum theoretical base rate, as for elasticity, compression analysis utilizes the minimum actual base rate received by the lowest-paid principal ($297); this is the divisor. The maximum allowable theoretical base rate specified by the schedule ($308) serves as the dividend. After performing the division (maximum theoretical base rate/minimum actual base rate) and subtracting 1 from the finding, the result is converted to a percentage and the actual growth potential is obtained.

The same calculations for assessing compression should be used for each salary range or pay grade (see Table 8.9) within a compensation structure. These calculations reveal the absolute degree of compression for any particular pay grade. The smaller the number, the greater the compression.

Compression, like elasticity, can vary among salary grades. Within a school district, it is not uncommon to find that some salary grades exhibit very little compression, while others exhibit a great deal. An example of variations in compression is presented in Table 8.9.

In Table 8.9, the salary grade for supervisors shows very little compression, as noted by the actual growth potential of 18%. By contrast, the salary grade for elementary school principals exhibits extreme compression, as noted by the actual growth potential of 4%. Because the principals in this compensation system have little room for advancement other than through adjustments to their base salaries, they are likely to be less satisfied with the compensation system than the supervisors.

Compression can be caused by several factors. If the compensation system used with the principals in Table 8.9 awards salary advances based on experience within the district, and if all these principals have been with the district for a long time, then compression may result because of a lack of turnover. If this is the case, and if the compensation structure has been maintained appropriately, compression will be reduced in time by turnover within this group of principals. Replacements for existing employees should have beginning salaries lower than those of continuing employees. Thus, compression will be reduced.

However, a more common cause of compression than workforce stability is failure to update the compensation system relative to market values. When this happens, beginning salaries will be too low to attract quality applicants. To solve this problem, the school district may offer starting salaries that fall in the upper levels of the pay grade or salary range of existing employees.

If new hires have high salaries in the pay range, these salaries encroach on those of long-term employees. This results in compression and produces dissatisfaction among existing employees. As a result of this type of compression, existing employees are likely to question the school board's appreciation for continuous employment in the system and to complain about a lack of economic incentives for advancement.

Rationality

Another criterion for evaluating compensation structures and practices is **rationality,** which addresses the relationship between the salaries of superiors and their subordinates. Underlying the rationality criterion is the assumption that superiors should receive higher salaries.

Although compensation specialists generally agree that rationality assessments should be limited to situations involving direct reporting relationships between superiors and subordinates, two definitions exist for subordinates in education. One definition favors the superior and uses the highest-paid subordinate to assess rationality. The other definition favors the employer and uses a subordinate with like type qualifications relative to the superior.

To illustrate the difference between these two definitions, consider the superior–subordinate relationship involving an elementary school principal and a teacher. For the liberal definition favoring the superior, the subordinate chosen to assess rationality would be the highest paid teacher in the school. In contrast, for the conservative definition favoring the employer, the subordinate chosen for rationality assessment would be a teacher with the same education and the same experience as the elementary school principal.

Choosing whether to use the liberal rather than the conservative definition is largely a policy issue. However, the choice usually has a substantial impact on the outcome of the rationality assessment. Consequently, a choice should be made about the definition of a subordinate before rationality is assessed.

After the definition of a subordinate is selected, the length of the work year must be considered. In the present example involving an elementary school principal and a teacher, the principal's work year will almost always be longer. In many public school systems, the principal's work year is 220 days, while that of the teacher is approximately 180 days.

To control for a work year of varying length, each salary must be converted to a common unit of analysis for rationality assessment. This usually involves using a daily rate of pay. For each position used in rationality assessments, the daily rate is obtained by dividing the base annual salary by the number of days comprising the employee's work year.

An example of a rationality assessment using actual field data is presented in Table 8.10. These data, obtained from a public school district, involve rationality assessments between line administrators who directly supervise teachers in this district. The assessments are based on the conservative definition of a subordinate using a teacher with like type credentials for each line administrator.

As Table 8.10 shows, the rationality assessment reveals an inverse relationship between the salaries of administrators and those of like type teachers. In this district, administrators responsible for the direct supervision of teachers would earn higher salaries if they were paid like teachers. On any given day during the academic school year when both administrators and teachers report to work, administrators earn less money per day than teachers with similar credentials.

The inverse economic relationship between line administrators and teachers shown in this example is not unique. In fact, a survey of over 50 public school districts in a typical midwestern state revealed that the vast majority of those districts

TABLE 8.10
An illustration of rationality using daily rates of pay for line administrators and teachers.

	Administrator Salary	Teacher Schedule	Actual Difference	Rational Difference	Rational Adjustment
Superintendent	$382	$376	6	38	32
High school principal	355	346	7	35	28
Middle school principal	290	284	6	28	22
Elementary 2–4	308	358	−50	36	86
Elementary K–1	284	328	−44	33	77
Assistant high school principal	289	280	9	28	19

had the same problem with respect to rationality assessments involving administrators and teachers. As a result, many of these districts reported problems attracting talented teachers from within the district to fill vacant administrative positions.

Violation of the rationality principle often has several interrelated causes. For rationality assessments involving administrators and teachers, these causes often stem from issues relating to representation of employees by unions and to salary adjustment procedures used to update schedules for different groups of employees.

In many states, unions represent teachers and negotiate their salaries with the school board. Negotiations require an agreement by both sides and have greatly enhanced the economic situation of teachers. However, administrators, unlike teachers, are seldom represented by a union; instead, their salaries are determined solely by the school board.

When establishing salaries for administrators, school boards have used often the percentage increase awarded to teachers through negotiations as a guideline for making adjustments to base salaries. This percentage is usually calculated on increases in the base salary of teachers and fails to consider step increases within the teacher compensation system. Because of this omission of step increases in calculating the adjustment factor for administrators, any preexisting salary difference between administrators and teachers (rationality) is reduced with each budget year.

Assessments of rationality should not be limited to comparisons between line administrators and teachers. These assessments should be expanded to include the economic relationship for all administrators and superior–subordinate reporting relationships within the district. When assessments of administrator–administrator and other superior–subordinate relationships are included, the rationality of a compensation structure can be examined from a between-group as well as a within-group perspective.

Appropriate Labor Market

Market Sensitivity

School systems must compete with other organizations to acquire and retain quality personnel. Success in this endeavor depends, at least in part, on the reward structure of a particular school system relative to the reward structures of competing school systems. To assess the reward structures of other school systems, a market analysis should be performed.

A market analysis requires the identification of an **appropriate labor market.** In reality, many different potential labor markets exist, and each will yield unique results for a market analysis. Defining an appropriate labor market, as opposed to the most appropriate labor market, is a policy decision.

To identify an appropriate labor market for a market analysis, several different factors can be used. Some of the more common factors believed to inform decision

TABLE 8.11
Different criteria that may be used to identify an appropriate labor market.

Geographical area
Student enrollment
District wealth
Athletic conference
Academic performance

making about an appropriate labor market are found in Table 8.11. Underlying each factor are certain basic assumptions about what constitutes an appropriate labor market.

Geographical location, when used to define a labor market, includes the school systems in the immediate area. By being in the immediate area of the target district, potential and current employees, it is assumed, can seek employment in these competing districts without changing their place of residence. With very few exceptions, potential and current employees can always improve their economic position if they are willing to relocate.

Student enrollments are used to define a labor market that contains districts of similar size. Similar-sized districts are assumed to have organizational structures and positions comparable to those in the target district. Comparable organizational structures and positions require comparable skills and knowledge on the part of employees.

District wealth has been defined by factors either for acquiring resources (assessed property value) or for distributing resources (per-pupil expenditures). Depending on the definition of wealth used, this factor assumes a labor market defined by fiscal responsibility. Fiscal responsibility implies that similar resources dictate a similar economic effort on the part of school systems.

In defining a competitive labor market, the district's athletic conference is often used. This factor is somewhat sensitive to geographical area and district size and has general public appeal. If residents of a school district are asked to identify comparable school districts, generally some of the districts in the athletic conference of the target school district are mentioned.

School districts have recently begun to use academic performance to define an appropriate labor market. With many states legislating standardized proficiency tests, the results of these tests have been used to select school districts for a market analysis. The underlying assumption here is that similar academic performance should yield similar compensation packages for employees.

Any single factor or any combination of factors will define a unique external labor market for a particular school district. As such, the results of a market analysis are market specific. For this reason, the choice of factors used to define an appropriate labor market for a school system is a policy decision rather than an administrative decision.

After an appropriate labor market has been determined, the direct and indirect costs of employee compensation within this labor market are analyzed. At minimum, this analysis should focus on the base rates of the positions under consideration, the contractual work year for each position, qualifications of employees occupying these positions, and the amount of money spent for different types of collateral benefits. When information about base rates and the dollar value of collateral benefits is combined, a reasonable assessment of total compensation can be obtained. In addition, the relative worth of education and experience can be factored into the total compensation costs of the school districts within the appropriate market.

Internal Consistency of Compensation Structures

Compensation practices and structures can be assessed according to several different criteria. In the previous section, four criteria were addressed: elasticity, compression, rationality, and market sensitivity. Each criterion provides a standard for gaining important baseline information about certain aspects of compensation systems.

However, these criteria are insensitive to another important compensation principle: **internal consistency**—the relative relationship among all positions within a particular compensation structure. Although the rationality criterion addresses the superior–subordinate relationship, it fails to consider the relationships among other pairs of positions.

For example, in most school districts there is usually some disagreement between elementary school principals and assistant high school principals concerning base rates of compensation. Elementary school principals tend to believe that they should be paid more than assistant high school principals; the latter take the opposite position. To resolve this disagreement, as well as similar disagreements involving other positions, school boards have two options.

One option is to consider all positions to be of equal value and to pay all personnel within the compensation system the same base rate, regardless of their position. With this option, elementary school principals would be paid the same as assistant high school principals. However, this option is seldom used and would probably be unsatisfactory both for boards of education and for school district employees. The other option is to differentiate among personnel within the compensation system in terms of organizational value and base salary. That is, some positions would command higher pay than others. This is the option generally used.

Salary differentiation within the compensation system should be based, however, on the following principle: Positions of similar organizational value should be compensated at a similar rate, while positions of different organizational value should be compensated at a different rate. To determine the organizational value of various positions is difficult but not impossible.

Some school boards might decide to differentiate among positions with respect to base rates of compensation on the basis of budgetary responsibilities. Because most elementary school principals are responsible for administering a building-level budget, whereas few assistant high school principals are involved in budget administration, the disagreement is resolved. Using the budgetary criterion, elementary school principals would be entitled to a higher base rate of compensation than assistant high school principals.

In contrast, other school boards might decide to differentiate among positions with respect to time spent performing work for the district beyond the regular workday. Because most assistant high school principals are involved extensively in extracurricular activities after the regular workday, whereas most elementary school principals are not, again, the disagreement is resolved. Using the extended workday criterion, assistant high school principals would be entitled to higher pay than elementary school principals.

These examples serve both to illustrate a point and to raise an important question. The point is that the solution to the disagreement concerning the base pay of elementary school principals and assistant high school principals depends on the criterion chosen to evaluate the organizational worth of the positions. When the criterion changes, the solution to the disagreement changes.

The important question raised by these examples concerns the choice of criterion (budgetary or extended day) to be used for evaluating the positions. Either criterion is a reasonable choice for a school board. Therefore, the choice is a policy decision rather than an administrative decision.

Policy decisions are required in situations where more than one potential outcome exists and where all potential outcomes are equally appropriate. In these cases, policy decisions depend on the preference of the designated policy group. In turn, the preference for a particular criterion or criteria for assessing the organizational worth of positions depends on the method used to evaluate these positions.

Position Evaluation

Several methods exist for establishing internal consistency relative to organizational worth among positions within a compensation structure. All methods have some common features while varying in important ways. Common to all methods used to establish internal consistency is a focus on positions rather than on position holders.

Positions serve as the unit of analysis for several reasons. First, positions are established to perform certain tasks within the organization, and these tasks determine the relative organizational value of the positions. Second, the organizational worth of these tasks is independent of their actual performance. Tasks can be performed well or poorly, but their worth to the school system remains the same. Third, positions are part of the organizational structure and can be changed only by the organization.

The methods used to evaluate positions differ in complexity. Some methods use only a single global criterion, while others use several different criteria. Although the compensation literature is replete with methods that can be employed to establish internal consistency among positions relative to organizational worth, almost all of them are variants of one of four basic systems: ranking, job classification, factor comparison, and point.

Each of these systems has been used in education and has been applied to districts with as few as four administrators and as many as several hundred. However, because the systems used most frequently are the ranking and point methods, we limit our discussion to these two types.

The ranking method is both the simplest and the oldest method used to evaluate the organizational worth of positions. It uses only one global criterion. The criterion is discretionary and should be chosen by a designated policy group.

Some examples of a single criterion are overall organizational worth, impact on children, extended workday responsibilities, and fiscal responsibilities. Because any criterion for evaluating positions has advantages as well as disadvantages, the choice should be made only after these advantages and disadvantages have been thoroughly discussed. This discussion should focus on organizational implications, rather than on particular positions or position holders, in order to reach a consensus about the single global criterion to be chosen.

If a consensus on a single global criterion has been achieved, the next task is to establish the relative worth of all positions in the compensation system. Relative worth, as defined by the ranking method, involves comparing positions with respect to the single global criterion. The comparison process can use one of the following methods: simple ranking, alternative ranking, or paired comparison. Each method uses a different decisional strategy.

To use any of these methods for assessing organizational worth and internal consistency among positions, a set of 538 cards is needed. On each card, the title of a single position is recorded. In a particular set of cards, the number of cards should equal the number of positions.

Each person in the designated policy group should receive a single set of cards listing all positions under consideration. Members of the policy group are instructed to work independently and to rank their set of cards according to the global criterion. These ranks should be in descending order, with the one position exceeding all other positions on the global criterion being ranked as 1.

After each member of the designated policy group has ranked independently all the positions in the compensation study, the ranks across members should be compiled. Initial results of the rankings will almost always reveal disagreements among policy group members; these disagreements should be discussed in a forum. The members of the designated policy group should explain their rankings and question those of other group members. Afterward, the group should once again rank independently all positions under consideration.

Several iterations of independent rankings, followed by discussions, should be performed to obtain a consensus. However, in many situations, no consensus will emerge. If this happens, the simple ranking method should be abandoned and another method used.

Another derivation of the simple ranking technique is the alternative ranking procedure. This procedure uses the same materials as the simple ranking technique but requires a different decisional strategy. With alternative ranking, group members first select the most important position relative to the single global criterion; next, they select the least important position relative to that criterion. This strategy is used with all positions in the compensation study.

The alternative ranking procedure forces maximum differentiation among the positions in a compensation system. Disagreements on internal consistency are most likely to occur with midrange positions. When these positions lead to problems in establishing internal consistency, one other comparison process may be used. This is the paired comparison process, and it involves still a different decisional strategy.

In the paired comparison process, each position (target position) is compared to all other positions (object positions) in the compensation study. Target positions considered more important than the object position are awarded a plus, and target positions considered less important than the object position are awarded a minus. The organizational worth of any particular target position is determined by assessed net worth reflecting the difference between the pluses and minuses assigned a particular position.

Norm-based systems are often used by school systems to establish the internal consistency of positions in a compensation system. These systems have been used to determine the relative ordering of support personnel in a single wage rate salary schedule and the relative ordering of supplementary assignments for teachers involving extracurricular pay increments to base salary.

In general, norm-based ranking systems are easy to implement, simple to understand, and equitable in application. Thus, employees tend to endorse these systems as a means of establishing the internal consistency of a compensation system. However, the strengths of norm-based ranking systems can be weaknesses when these systems are applied to complex jobs such as those held by administrators and supervisors.

To capture the complexities of administrator and supervisor positions in a compensation system, a criterion-based reference system is generally employed. This system requires a different decisional strategy than a norm-based system. In a criterion-based system, positions are evaluated relative to different criteria rather than relative to other positions, as is the case with norm-based systems.

The criterion-based strategy used most frequently to establish internal consistency is the point method. This method assumes that all positions in a compensation structure have certain underlying factors or common denominators, such as supervision responsibilities, judgment/discretion, fiscal management, community relations, and involvement with parents.

Factors used in the point method can vary both in degree and in weight. For example, supervision could vary in degree by including direct supervision, indirect supervision, and/or the number of work groups supervised. Degrees of judgment/discretion could be analyzed from either a policy involvement perspective or

TABLE 8.12
Results of position ratings across five criteria.

	Judgment Discretion	Parental Involvement	Instruction Leadership	Personnel Evaluation	Extended Day
Department of psychological services	−0.23441	−0.06830	−0.42078	−0.38396	−0.10108
Assistant superintendent	+0.52663	+0.36054	+0.67013	+0.10964	+0.14499
Department of finance	+0.52663	−0.12391	−0.49870	−0.01122	+0.16873
Supervisor building and grounds	−0.10502	−0.17952	−0.49870	−0.17683	−0.10108
Public relations	−0.23441	−0.06830	−1.27792	−0.38396	−0.09229
Transportation	−0.20016	−0.16839	−0.49870	−0.19205	−0.07910
Assistant middle school principal	−0.10274	−0.02359	−0.49870	+0.11343	−0.05712
Food services	−0.23441	−0.17952	−0.49870	−0.17683	−0.10108
Elementary principal	+0.00343	+0.06307	+0.67013	+0.13880	−0.03014
Senior high principal	+0.17465	+0.09098	+0.67013	+0.28218	+0.08300
Director of athletics	+0.03198	+0.18040	−0.49870	+0.05575	+0.14027
Assistant senior high principal	−0.12024	−0.02359	−0.34286	+0.13880	+0.03082
Supervisor of curriculum	+0.03198	+0.06307	+0.67013	+0.26696	+0.05780

an organizational impact perspective. In some positions, the organizational impact may exist only for the immediate work site (assistant principal); in other positions, it may span several work sites (middle school principal); and in still other positions, it may extend across the entire school system (chief financial officer).

The outcomes obtained with the point method are related to the factors selected, the degrees used, and the weight given to each factor. If any alteration is made in factor, degree, or weight, then a different picture of the relative worth of specific positions will be produced. For this reason, the choice of factors, degrees, and weightings is a policy decision rather than an administrative decision.

Once the factors, degrees, and weights have been chosen, each position in the compensation study is evaluated accordingly. Results of the evaluation of positions for one school district using the point method are presented in Table 8.12. The policy group in this example was the board of education, which chose four factors and assigned a different weight to each one.

As Table 8.12 shows, some ratings have a plus sign and others have a minus sign because all ratings are standardized to a normal curve equivalence (z-score transformation) within each criterion. Within any particular criterion, the average performance of all combined position ratings is zero, and the specific rating of any particular position is given in standard units from the average. To illustrate, positions with large plus ratings (high school principal) involve far more supervision than does the average position in this particular district, while positions with large minus ratings (food service) involve much less supervision than does the average position in the district.

Standardization of ratings allows direct comparison of all positions within any criterion and direct comparison of all positions across all criteria. If certain positions are considered undervalued or overvalued, as reflected by standardized ratings, then ratings within any criterion can be used to help redesign positions. For example, the food service position is rated low in supervision; this rating could be increased by shifting supervisory responsibility for cooks and servers from principals to food service.

The overall value of positions using the point method is calculated by summing the weighted ratings across all criteria for each position. The overall value of positions, as calculated on the basis of weighted ratings, is used to order the positions in a classification system, and the classification system reflects the internal consistency among the positions relative to the factors, degrees, and weights selected by the policy group. Once established, a classification system should be linked to a total compensation system containing direct and indirect costs.

The Total Compensation Perspective

The ideal compensation system will be sensitive to both external and internal factors influencing compensation (see Figure 8.2), address the elasticity associated with theoretical earning potentials across pay levels (see Table 8.1), eliminate compression between positions within the same pay level (see Table 8.2), establish rationality for superior–subordinate pairings both within and between compensation systems (see Table 8.9), be sensitive to external market parameters assessed with comparable districts (see Table 8.10), and reflect internal consistency among all positions (see Table 8.12). However, a perfect compensation system exists more in theory than in practice. In practice, the best compensation system that can be obtained by most school systems is a reasonable system.

A reasonable compensation system is derived from informed decisions based on different sources of information. Beyond the different data sources described in this chapter, a reasonable compensation system must be sensitive both to the fiscal constraints of the school district and to the perceptions of employees in the compensation system.

In most cases, the fiscal constraints of a school district are fixed assets. Regardless of the best intentions of those who develop and administer a compensation system, most school districts have fixed economic resources for a compensation system. Consequently, certain choices or compromises must be made when developing and administering a compensation system for a particular group of employees.

Perceptions of particular groups of employees about a compensation system vary on two dimensions: procedural and distributive. Procedural perceptions pertain to the methods used to establish the compensation system; distributive perceptions concern the actual economic incentives provided by the compensation system. Both types of perceptions influence the satisfaction of employees in the public school setting.

When considering all sources of data, a balance between system restraints and employee concerns requires certain compromises. For example, it might be determined that rationality can be established and maintained for employees within the same compensation structure (administrator–supervisor pairings) but not for employees in different compensation structures (administrator–teacher pairings). Likewise, it might be determined that internal consistency can be established and maintained among positions within the same compensation structure at the expense of external market sensitivity, as assessed with comparable school districts.

Compromises based on informed decisions will yield a reasonable compensation system for a particular group of employees. Such a compensation system could involve direct costs associated with a fixed rate salary schedule, with advancement governed by determined factors (education and experience); direct costs associated with a mixed rate salary schedule, with advancement governed by determined and variable factors (job performance); or direct costs associated with a variable rate salary schedule, with advancement governed by job performance alone. Depending on the type of salary schedule (fixed, mixed, or variable rate), the economic value of advancements reflected by a salary schedule must be established.

Indirect costs, involving the collateral benefits of a reasonable compensation system, can be either uniform or variable. Uniform benefit plans fail to consider the needs of specific employees but provide a larger return for a fixed dollar amount due to mass purchasing power. On the other hand, variable benefit plans consider the needs of specific employees while suffering from economy of scale.

Because direct and indirect costs interact to influence the total compensation cost of a compensation system, several different compensation models should be developed. These models should be used to conduct economic forecasts that should provide information about each model relative to total implementation costs and total projected costs in subsequent years. Based on the outcomes of the forecasts, a specific compensation system should be adopted.

The resulting compensation system will be less than perfect. In addition, a reasonable compensation system in one district will not necessarily be reasonable in another district. Consequently, the compensation system adopted by any school system should depend on the unique situation of that school system at a given point in time.

Compensation Control and Adjustment

A reasonable compensation system has a short life expectancy. Major components of a compensation system, such as those involving internal consistency, have a life expectancy of about 5 years. Other components, such as those involving base rates and collateral benefits, become dated with each budgetary cycle.

To maintain a reasonable compensation system requires continuous monitoring by those who develop and administer it. At minimum, monitoring involves realigning the compensation structure with the mission of the school district (see Figure 8.1), keeping abreast of external and internal factors impacting the compensation structure, and assessing changes associated with the direct and indirect costs of an appropriate labor market.

In assessing how well the actual operation of a reasonable compensation plan conforms to standards, goals and audit measures suggested earlier may be used as standards. The ultimate success of a reasonable compensation plan can be judged by the extent to which it attracts competent personnel, motivates them to cooperate voluntarily in achieving the goals of the system, maintains external and internal equity under existing legal constraints and collective bargaining agreements, and results in improved conditions for teaching and learning.

Because the ramifications of any reasonable compensation system are so extensive, checks are required to determine how well compensation plans are reinforcing other plans in contributing to organizational purposes. For example, compensation practices play a key role in determining long-range and operating plans for: (a) recruitment and selection of personnel, (b) appraisal and improvement of performance, (c) design of the organizational structure, and (d) budgeting of expenditures.

The first strategic point considered here is the selection of personnel before assigning them to positions. Every organization, regardless of the nature of its compensation system, should design a selection plan to screen all applicants for system positions. With the help of position guides, qualifications of applicants can be checked against position requirements to determine how well they are fitted to perform the function and to estimate their potential for advancement. At this point, it should be determined whether the base salaries at each level of the compensation structure are adequate to attract qualified personnel. One test of adequacy is how closely compensation at each level conforms to the appropriate labor market. The question to be asked is how much would it cost to replace a current employee with someone else who has the desired qualifications?

The second strategic point concerns performance appraisal after the individual has been assigned. Results of the appraisal, aside from yielding information necessary for making judgments about salary increases, should contribute to plans for the development of employees and for determining whether each employee should be retained in the position, transferred to another position, promoted, or dismissed. Here the test of effectiveness of the compensation plan is whether it provides for systematic appraisal of personnel performance.

The third strategic point concerns the organizational structure. This area is constantly in need of review and, occasionally, revision. As positions are added, eliminated, or modified, these changes should be reflected in the organizational structure and ultimately in the compensation system and the employee's salary. The criterion for this test of the compensation structure is its congruency with the organizational structure. Clearly, a sound organizational structure is indispensable to both the integrity of the compensation plan and to the workability of the appraisal process.

The final point to be considered, control of expenditures for the compensation plan, is essential. One check on the compensation plan is information relating to its impact on the annual and long-term budgets, such as anticipated salary changes by adoption of the compensation plan, annual cost of the plan, and impact of the plan on the community's tax structure.

In a very real sense, then, controlling the compensation plan is as vital to its success as the design of the structure on which it rests. Information yielded by checking the foregoing points, as well as others not mentioned, can be collected, analyzed, and presented periodically to the board of education so that the final step in the control processes—corrective action—can be taken to make certain that the goals of the plan are constantly being achieved.

Review and Preview

In this chapter, we have examined the compensation process and its relationship to the human resource function. Although satisfying the monetary needs of school system employees is not the only responsibility of the administration, absence of a sound compensation plan creates human problems that defy easy resolution. Because the size of the employee's paycheck is related to the satisfaction of both economic and noneconomic needs, the process by which compensation in a school system is determined is crucial to the system's ability to implement an effective human resource plan.

The compensation process presented in this chapter contains various subprocesses, including developing compensation policies, negotiating with unions, establishing the position structure, determining the economic value of positions and position holders, making provisions in the compensation structure for administrative and support personnel, formalizing the compensation plan, and keeping the plan current.

A number of interrelated factors affect an employee's paycheck. These factors include compensation legislation, prevailing salaries, collective bargaining, supply and demand, ability to pay, standard and cost of living, and collateral considerations. Although all of these factors enter into compensation levels established in an organization, one factor or combination of factors may be more important at a given time than others, depending on the circumstances.

Employment may be viewed as an exchange transaction between the individual and the organization in which each gets something in return for giving something. The employment exchanges between the individual and the system are perceived differently by both parties. One of the major problems in compensation planning is to reach agreements between parties by reconciling the nature of the input–output relationship.

In the next chapter we address certain benefits that enhance the earning power of educational employees. Some of the benefits are related to salaries, while others are independent of salary. Collectively, these benefits improve the continuity of the employment process.

Discussion Questions

1. Explain why the following aspects of pay structures have not been widely introduced in school systems: incentive rewards, flexible benefit plans, performance-dependent remuneration, and market-sensitive salaries.

2. Two criticisms of many educational compensation programs are that they are inequitable and that the salaries do not compare favorably with those of other school systems or other professions. Do these criticisms have any basis in fact?

3. Develop the elements of a pay structure that would provide the kinds of rewards that are important to you.

4. Is there any truth to the assertion that pay based on merit rating is only one of many kinds of incentive options? Do incentives have to be based on a *performance appraisal rating?*

5. How do unions influence pay practices directly? Indirectly? How do boards of education influence compensation practices?

6. In what ways are the compensation practices of public school systems influenced by state governments? The federal government?

7. Many states have passed comparable worth legislation for the public sector (ensuring that women and minorities receive payment commensurate with the value of their jobs). Does compensation discrimination exist in female-dominated occupations (clerical, teaching, nursing)? Have teacher unions pursued the comparable worth issue in negotiations? To what extent?

8. Many salary plans include three methods of compensation: (a) automatic increases, (b) pay for performance, and (c) a combination of the above. What are the strengths and weaknesses of each method? Why is method (b) the least popular? What values are lost by strict adherence to a method?

9. Why is the cost of contemporary benefit plans being subjected to stricter controls?

10. Develop a set of guidelines for improving incentive plans.

11. Examine the hypothetical salary schedule in Table 8.2. Respond to each of these questions:

• What are the strengths and weaknesses of the salary schedule?

• Do you agree that experience should be used as a measure of performance effectiveness?

• Does the schedule provide incentives?

• Does the schedule address criticisms of the single-salary schedule generated by the education reform movement?

• Will the average pay raise over 5 years benefit more-experienced or less-experienced teachers?

• If collateral benefits in this school system amount to 35% of total salaries for teachers, what would be the compensation costs for a teacher in 1999 with 16 years of experience? (Assume that all benefits are uniform for all teachers.)

12. Name three comparison sources by which personnel can assess a system's compensation fairness.

References

BenefitsNext. (n.d.). *Human resources answers now—benefits library.* Retrieved August 29, 2002, from the Benefits Next Web site: **http://www.benefitsnext. com/content/view.cfm?articles_ id= 2114&subs_id=136**

Heneman, H. G. (1998). Assessment of the motivational reactions of teachers to school-based performance award program. *Journal of Personnel Evaluation in Education, 12*(1), 43–59.

Kelley, C. (1997). Teacher compensation and organization. *Educational Evaluation and Policy Analysis, 19*(1), 15–28.

Kelley, C., Heneman, H. G., & Milanowski, A. (2002). Teacher motivation and school-based performance rewards. *Educational Administration Quarterly, 38*(5), 372–401.

United States Government Fair Standards Labor Act of 1938. (n.d.). Retrieved May 28, 2003, from the U.S. Department of Labor Web site: **http://www.dol.gov/esa/ regs/statutes/whd/allfair.htm**.

Urbanski, A., & Erskine, R. (2000). School reform and teacher compensation. *Phi Delta Kappan, 81*(3), 367–370.

Young, I. P. (1997). Dimensions of employee compensation: Practical and theoretical implications for superintendents. *Educational Administration Quarterly, 33*(4), 506–525.

Young, I. P., Delli, D. A., Miller-Smith, K., & Alhadeff, A. (2001). The relative efficiency of criteria for establishing salary rates. Paper presented at the California Educational Research Association, Tahoe, CA.

Supplementary Reading

Berry, B., & Ginsberg, R. (1990, April). Creating lead teachers: From policy to implementation. *Phi Delta Kappan, 71*(8), 616–622.

Cook, M. F. (Ed.). (1993). In *The human resources yearbook: 1993/1994 edition* (Chaps. 5 and 6) Upper Saddle River, NJ: Prentice Hall.

Cunningham, W. G., & Sperry, J. B. (2001, February). Where's the beef in administrator pay? *American Association of School Administrators,* 1–7.

Giblin, E. J., Wiegman, G. A., & Sanfillippo, F. (1990, November). Bringing pay up to date. *Personnel, 67*(11), 17–18.

Greenberg, J. (1987). Reactions to procedural injustice in payment distributions: Do the ends justify the means? *Journal of Applied Psychology, 72,* 55–61.

Heneman, R. L., & Ledford, G. E. (1998). Competency pay for professionals and managers in business: A review and implications for teachers. *Journal of Personnel Evaluation in Education, 12*(2), 103–121.

Iseri, B. A., & Cangemi, R. (1990, March). Flexible benefits: A growing option. *Personnel, 67*(3), 30–34.

Lawler, E. A., III. (1990). *Strategic pay.* San Francisco: Jossey-Bass.

Milkovich, G. T., & Newman, J. M. (1996). *Compensation.* Boston: Irwin.

Rock, M. L., & Berger, L. A. (Eds.). (1991). *The compensation handbook: A state-of-the-art guide to compensation strategy and design* (3rd ed.). New York: McGraw-Hill.

Shanker, A. (1990, January). The end of the traditional model of schooling and a proposal for using incentives to restructure our public schools. *Phi Delta Kappan, 71,* 5.

PART III

EMPLOYMENT CONTINUITY AND UNIONISM

Chapter 9
Employment Continuity

Chapter 10
Unionism and the Human Resource Function

Part III is designed to

- Present an approach for designing, implementing, and assessing the content and process of employment continuity.
- Portray the importance of a sound disciplinary system as the basis for procedural justice in public school systems.
- Increase understanding of three aspects of the collective bargaining system in public education: (a) components of the collective bargaining process, (b) the contemporary collective bargaining condition, and (c) strategic school system opportunities inherent in the collective bargaining process and its managerial implications.

9

Employment Continuity

CHAPTER OBJECTIVES

Portray the relevance of school system culture and system equilibrium to employment continuity and its strategic implications.
Identify factors that affect employment continuity and discontinuity.
Present an approach for designing the process and content of employment continuity.
Stress the potential impact on employment continuity of turnover, absenteeism, lateness, layoffs, severance, retirement, and death.

CHAPTER CONCEPTS

Continuity process	Demotion
Defined benefit	Promotion
Defined contribution	Transfers

School System Culture and Employment Continuity

Maintaining the employment continuity of individuals as employees involves considering the importance of a school system's cultural environment. Regardless of the size of a school district or the type of a school district (urban, suburban, or rural), the basic building block is its employees. Collectively, these individuals are immersed in a work environment that has particular characteristics, and these characteristics define the culture of that particular school system.

The culture of a school system is shaped by attitudes, routines, habitual ways of doing things, behavioral norms, rules of conduct, position requirements, and the network of social relationships within which people work. Each of these contributors to the culture can have either positive or negative impacts on employees when fulfilling their assigned job duties and organizational responsibilities. As such, a major human resource goal is to maximize the positive impacts and to minimize the negative impacts associated with every aspect of work life.

In previous chapters, we have examined various processes of the human resource function essential to attracting competent personnel into the system, including human resource planning, recruitment, selection, compensation, and induction. Also, we have addressed ways of helping personnel develop abilities and integrate individual and group interests into the organization that align with the strategic goals of the school district. In short, these processes focused on transforming inexperienced applicants into productive employees.

Within this chapter, we review organizational provisions designed to retain personnel and to foster continuity in the services of all personnel. More specifically, in this chapter, we focus on detailed processes and procedures for enhancing the work life of employees. Attention is afforded to processes and methods by which such plans can be designed, implemented, and controlled.

Human Problems in School Systems

The importance of systematic planning relative to the continuity of school personnel cannot be overemphasized by the modern-day organization. Even in institutions where the planning concepts are subscribed to and implemented accordingly, things do not always run smoothly. A sustained effort must be made to keep any organization operating effectively on a day-to-day basis.

Indeed, employees have a way of interfering with plans, violating rules, and behaving in other ways inimical to the interests of the organization and in some instances the interests of self. So long as individuals fill positions in organizations and are required to work with others in satisfying the goals of the organization, there will be problems. Examples of some of the more common problems encountered by public school districts include the following:

- Some employees will become physically ill.
- Some employees will become mentally ill.
- Some employees will become obsolescent.
- Some employees will need to be absent from work.
- Some employees will have work-connected accidents.
- Some employees will be affected by the physical conditions of employment.
- Some employees will have home-related stresses.

Many of these problems encountered by the modern school district may stem from or be related to sources of employment insecurities either actual or perceived by the employee. Perceptions of threats about losing one's position, being reduced in status, or losing one's job freedom have existed always in organizations. Real or perceived, the toll of organizational insecurities is immense for the operation and administration of a public school district and has important implications for the human resource function in public school districts.

Because of these reoccurring conditions within the public school setting, a school system must address personnel problems from a humanistic viewpoint. Due to the fact that such problems affect two of the district's strategic goals (stability and development), the system needs healthy, productive people continuously on the job who are physically and mentally able to contribute maximally to the work of the enterprise and who maintain a favorable attitude toward their roles and the environment in which they function. Without such people, the probability of achieving the strategic goals of the system is almost nonexistent.

The nature and scope of provisions for maintaining continuity of personnel service is determined, at least in part, by the system. A school system determines, to some extent, what provisions should be made for enhancing continuity of service, what types of programs are needed, and how they will be organized and administered. Next, we will examine the process by which such plans for continuing employment are designed and implemented.

The Employment Continuity Process

Keeping the school system staffed continually with competent personnel involves consideration of and action on problems encountered by personnel in the conduct of their assigned duties. The employment **continuity process** by which the foregoing problems are dealt with varies from, but has much in common with, arrangements for making and carrying out other organizational decisions within the ongoing educational enterprise. In this case, it consists of making a series of decisions about continuity of service, including: (a) what the plans are expected to achieve, (b) what types of plans are needed to realize expectations, (c) who will be responsible for each phase of the program, (d) what are the specifics of each type of program, and (e) how the results of the process will be determined.

Expectations or results that the system intends to achieve from plans for service continuity are both long- and short-range and include the following:

- Improve the ability of the system to perform its function
- Enhance the system's work environment
- Prevent and control occupational stress
- Control personnel costs
- Provide position security for personnel
- Control avoidable absenteeism and lateness
- Furnish financial protection against risks such as illness and accidents
- Reduce personnel turnover
- Facilitate change within the system
- Improve individual and system effectiveness
- Prevent accidents
- Maintain position and system performance standards
- Comply with statutory requirements
- Provide opportunities for personnel self-development and self-renewal
- Establish program limits
- Attend to preretirement problems of personnel adjustment.

Once the goals for maintaining continuity of personnel service have been set forth, implementation by school officials follows. Early in the planning stages, at least two actions are necessary. One of these actions is the preparation of a series of policy statements to guide members in designing and implementing specific programs.

The other action is a set of specific plans needed to carry out the intent of the policy. This includes the manner in which personnel continuity programs will be organized and administered, as well as the controls essential to the resolution of personnel problems. An example of these actions for the Riverpark school system is illustrated in Figure 9.1.

The employment continuity policy presented in Figure 9.1 illustrates an approach to reducing undesirable outcomes throughout the continuity process. This policy's intent is to: (a) exercise continuous direction while guiding action and maintaining control over the planning and implementation of the process, (b) influence action and conduct of system members regarding employment continuity, and (c) serve as a guiding principle for the growth of the workforce and its organizational entity. The supporting statements are employed to interpret and to translate the Riverpark school system's continuity policy into more specific operational plans and procedures.

Provisions Conducive to Employment Continuity

Provisions essential to employment continuity described in this chapter are defined as certain direct or indirect forms of compensation that do not require additional services to be performed beyond those required under the basic compensation struc-

It is the policy of the Riverpark school system to

- Provide continuity of personnel employment insofar as this is economically feasible.
- Control reduction in force on the basis of performance, ability, and length of service. When these factors are approximately equal, length of service with the system will govern.
- Grant leaves of absence for acceptable reasons.
- Provide assistance to individual staff members in maintaining and improving physical and mental health.
- Provide an attractive and efficient environment by maintaining good physical working conditions.
- Install every practical safety device, take every measure to prevent accidents, guard against mechanical failure, and provide adequate equipment for accident and fire prevention.
- Make available adequate substitutes for absentees.
- Fill vacancies by upgrading or promotion from within whenever present employees are qualified.
- Encourage reassignment when it is in the interest of the individual and the system.
- Protect personnel against unfair separation from the system.
- Assist personnel to plan for retirement.

FIGURE 9.1   *Illustration of an employment continuity policy.*

ture or union contract. Employee benefits have been classified as either entitlements or privileges. These benefits associated with entitlements and privileges vary in degree with the amount of discretionary prerogative exercised by the school system in actual administration.

Entitlements

To enhance the continuity of the employment experience for public school employees, certain legislative acts have been passed by state governments. The intent of these legislative acts is to supplement the employment benefits granted by individual school systems and to provide public employees with a basic level of job security. In most instances, these legislative acts provide employees with a minimum foundation relative to a specified benefit but allow considerable discretion on the part of school boards in the implementation and administration of said benefit.

Some of these acts are designed to provide public school employees with a certain level of employment protection while fulfilling their assigned duties in a satisfactory manner. Others are designed either to provide employees with rewards for the service rendered to a public school district or to protect the income of employees while working in a public school district. Examples of each type of employee continuity incentive are discussed next.

Employment Protection Entitlements

In the broadest sense, employment protection embodies a system designed to provide educators with continuing employment during efficient service and establishes an orderly procedure to be followed prior to termination of services. Employment protection clauses have been enacted for teachers and for civil servant employees through specific legislation. For other employee groups, employment protection clauses may be established through written policies or inferred through administrative practices.

Salient features of employment protection include the following:

- Completion of a specified probationary period, construed to mean a temporary appointment during which time the individual is carefully supervised and appraised in terms of ability to render efficient service to the school organization.
- An orderly procedure for dismissal of personnel. This includes provision for notifying the individual that his or her services are unsatisfactory, as well as a reasonable opportunity to show improvement before notification of intent to dismiss is given.
- Notification of the intent to terminate the services of the individual in the event that desired improvement in performance has not been attained. Written notice of the intent to dismiss details specific reasons for the contemplated action.
- A hearing before local school authorities that provides an opportunity for the affected staff member to defend self against the charges.

The implications for employment protection clauses are not always understood by some professionals or by many laypersons. Perhaps this misunderstanding has given rise to the relatively high incidence of litigation on the part of involved parties. In general, employment protection, as defined by legislation, written policy, or administrative practices, is a process rather than an absolute right granted to an employee.

Employees have no inherent right to permanent employment merely because of complying with formal requirements or serving a probationary period during which satisfactory service has been rendered in the eyes of the employer. Employment protection clauses require certain actions on the part of the employer rather than an inert right of the employee to the job. Such actions or requirements on the part of the employer should not be interpreted to mean that the local board of education has no authority to make changes affecting persons who have gained employment protection.

Indeed, the phrase *permanent employment* can be misleading and is frequently the cause of many misinterpretations of tenure legislation. If the board decides to reduce the size of the staff because of declining enrollments, existence of employment protection legislation does not prevent the board from taking such action.

It is generally not the intent of employment security provisions to prevent boards of education from making necessary changes involving personnel. Permanent employment does not mean an absolute absence of change in conditions of employment. If this were so, administrators would be powerless to cope with the day-to-day personnel problems with which they are confronted when trying to manage the public school district.

Worth noting is the differentiation between employment status and job assignment for employees. These terms are not synonymous within the human resource domain as the terms relate to employment security. Employment security clauses address the former but not the latter, and the school board retains the right to reassign personnel at will unless restricted by other sources such as school board policy or labor contract that forbids such actions on the part of the school board.

Rationale for establishing employment security provisions is multifaceted. Among the more common reasons for these employment security clauses are those listed here:

- Security of employment during satisfactory service.
- Protection of personnel against unwarranted dismissal.
- Academic freedom in the classroom.
- Permanent employment for best-qualified personnel.
- Staff stability and position satisfaction.
- Freedom outside the classroom commensurate with that of any other citizen.
- Liberty to encourage student freedom of inquiry and expression.

Legislative activity relating to employment security is defended generally on the basis of social benefit. The state seeks to improve the school system through the instrumentality of employment security, which is designed in part to protect the public and pupils from incompetent employees. Employment security legislation is not intended to establish an occupational haven for the unqualified or unsatisfactory employee.

Much attention has been given to the validity of employment security clauses especially as these clauses relate to tenure for teachers. Even though many oppose the concept of tenure, all states have some form of tenure legislation for teachers (LaRue, 1996). Although there is widespread discontentment with tenure systems, part of the dissatisfaction arises from the assumption that tenure protects incompetents.

The existence of incompetents in any organization, however, cannot be blamed totally on legislative provisions designed to protect the position security of teachers as well as to protect the school system. Evidence indicates that inaction of school boards and administrators in dismissal and supervisory efforts deserves substantial blame (Pennsylvania State Teachers Association, 1996). Tenure systems do not prevent school systems from designing effective appraisal and personnel development processes and do not prevent the administration from taking action against incompetents.

Unions, courts, state governments, and school systems have gone to considerable lengths to provide for personnel security, which is one of the basic psychological needs of employees. Tenure for educators, protection under civil service for many classes of noncertified personnel, contracts with seniority provisions, due process, and grievance systems are illustrative of these efforts. Complete security for any individual, however, is an illusion in modern-day school systems.

Retirement Incentive Entitlements

Like employment protection clauses, retirement incentives are another form of entitlement awarded public sector employees by state legislation. With respect to retirement incentives, it is not unusual for states to have three different public employee retirement systems to cover separate groups of personnel employed by public school districts. By far, the largest of the retirement systems is the state teacher retirement system (STRS) followed in size by the state employee retirement system (SERS) for noncertified employees and by the public employee retirement system (PERS) for administrative personnel.

Although salaries and wages received by educational employees tend to be less than the salaries and wages received by their counterparts in the private sector, the same is not necessarily true for retirement incentives. Public school employees tend to enjoy a retirement system far superior to the retirement systems of most employees within the private sector. Types of retirement systems falling under entitlement clauses can be classified as a defined benefit system, a defined contribution system, or some combination of these two types of retirement systems.

Most of the state retirement systems are **defined benefit** systems. Characteristics of the defined benefit retirement system found in most states are shared levels of funding for the system and a fixed amount of retirement income for the employee following retirement. To fund defined benefit systems administered by a state, both the school district as an employer and the individual as an employee must contribute funds to the retirement system.

Actual amounts contributed to a retirement system by employers and by employees vary from state to state. Employers contribute usually a fixed amount that is a percentage of the employee's salary. The employee's obligation is generally equal to or less than that of the employer's contribution and is based also on a percentage of the salary received by the employee.

Although the employee's obligation is for a fixed amount relating to salary, certain states allow the employer to pay part or all of the employee's obligation to the retirement system. When the employer pays on behalf of the employee, the payment is called a "pick-up." A retirement pick-up by a school district on behalf of the employee can be either partial or full payment of the employee's obligation.

To illustrate the pick-up principle, within the state of Ohio the individual's obligation to the retirement system is 9.3%, while the school district's obligation to the retirement system is 14% (Ohio State Teachers Retirement System, n.d.). The school district may pay part of or all of the 9.3% employee obligation on behalf of the employee. If only a portion of this obligation is being paid, then this level of compensation reflects a partial pick-up; when all of this obligation is being paid (9.3%), this effort reflects a full pick-up.

Many school districts use the managerial technique of a pick-up as a means to control salary levels. By using the pick-up process to pay either part or all of the employee's obligation within the retirement system, the employee's net income is increased because of the reduced liability for that payment. Although overall cost to the school system is increased proportionate to the pick-up provision, this type of cost is less visible to the public than changes in cost associated with increasing dollar amounts within the schedule.

Another unique aspect of a defined benefit retirement system for public school employees is that this type of retirement system yields a fixed income for the employee postretirement. Postretirement income is calculated on the basis of an employee's earnings. Earnings have been defined, for the purpose of retirement systems by different states, as average annual earnings: the average of the last 3-to-5-year earnings, or the average of the highest 3-to-5-year earnings.

Other factors that influence the actual payout under a defined benefit system are years of service in the retirement system and chronological age of the employee. To protect the buying power of a retiree, these types of retirement systems have a cost of living provision. A cost of living provision adjusts upward an individual's retirement income to offset inflation.

In contrast to the defined benefit retirement system is the **defined contribution** retirement system found in some states. "Defined contribution plans require specific contributions by an employer, but the final benefit received by employees is unknown; it depends on the investment success of those charged with administering the pension fund"(Milkovich & Newman, 1996, p. 461). Reasons for defined contribution plans in education are twofold.

According to some sources (National Conference on Public Employee Retirement Systems, 2002) public employees during the 1980s and 1990s witnessed many of their counterparts in the private sector reaping major gains in their retirement portfolios through market increases in stock investments. During these periods, double-digit increases within the same year were not unusual for investments. As a result of their observations, public sector employees campaigned for more discretion in the management of their retirement investments than afforded by a defined benefit plan.

Another problem associated with the defined benefit retirement systems is the lack of portability afforded employees in their professional life. Although employees could change jobs and job locations within the same state, different states had different plans and reciprocity among defined benefit plans was nonexistent between states. To offset these problems and to quench the investment thirst of public sector employees, many states initiated defined contribution plans for public school employees.

Today, new employees to a public school district have a window of choice in many states for deciding which type of retirement system to select. If the employee selects the defined contribution, then the employer contributes a fixed amount to a particular source. The most frequently used source for defined contributions in the public school setting is the Teachers Insurance and Annuity Association (TIAA; **http//www.tiaa-cref.org**).

Most of the sources of investment used for defined contribution plans provide the employees with investment options. With many employees losing considerable amounts of their retirement due to a drop in specific stock market investments during recent years, it will be interesting to see how durable the defined contribution plans will be. No longer are these types of plans viewed with the same level of confidence as they were only a few years ago.

Complementing either defined benefit retirement funds or defined contribution plans for some employees in the public sector is the Social Security Act established by the federal government (U.S. Social Security Administration, n.d.). Social Security is a defined benefit plan administered by the federal government and has four types of payments for participants: payments for old age, for dependents of workers with disabilities, for surviving family members, and for lump sum death payments.

However, the Social Security Act is not universal across states with respect to public school employees. Some states have optioned not to participate in social security, and educators in these states have their earnings exempted from the social security tax. In those states where educators fail to contribute to social security (see Ohio, for example), the organizational and individual contributions for defined benefit plans as well as the organizational contribution for defined contribution plans are higher in exempted states than in those states where educators participate in social security.

Leave Incentive Entitlements

To enhance the employment continuity of public school employees, certain types of leaves have been developed by state and federal governments. Some of these leave provisions pay employees for time not worked, whereas others protect the job security of the employee during times away from the job.

Most states have legislated sick leave provisions for public school employees. Sick leave provisions were designed initially to be an income protection for the employees when they miss work. That is, sick leave was designed initially to protect the income flow of an employee from any disruption in the work schedule due to a temporary illness.

Within the public sector, a minimum number of sick leave days are granted to each employee by the state, and these days are administered by the local school district. Actual number of sick leave days granted by the state follows a basic accrual system whereby teachers earn a specified number of sick days for each month worked. These earned days of sick leave accrue and unused sick days are carried over into sequent school years.

Because sick leave days accrue and are carried over, some school districts in conjunction with labor unions have developed sick leave banks for employees (Westfield Classroom Teachers Association, n.d.). Individuals "deposit" some of their unused sick leave days in a so-called bank. Other employees that lack adequate accumulation of sick leave to cover their illnesses can borrow sick leave days, which must be repaid from sick leave earned in subsequent months or years.

Although the basic purposes for which sick leave may be used are addressed in some state laws, school systems have great latitude in the administration of the sick leave program. School districts can expand the permissible scope for sick leave usage and can develop administrative processes for managing the sick leave program.

To aid in the administration of sick leave programs, some school districts have elected to pay employees for unused sick leave at the end of their career with a public school district. This practice of paying for unused sick leave changes the very purpose of sick leave provisions from an income protection procedure to an income generation procedure. Still other school districts have paid the medical insurance of retired employees by using funds from the purchase of unused sick leave.

However, not all leave entitlements awarded employees compensate individuals for time away from the job. Some types of leaves offer protection for employment but not protection for income. An example of such a leave provision enjoyed by public school employees that protects the job rather than the income is the Family and Medical Leave Act (FMLA).

The Family and Medical Leave Act (U.S. Department of Labor, 1993), passed in 1993 by the federal government, permits public school employees to take unpaid leaves of absence. These leaves, as ensured by the Family and Medical Leave Act, can be used for certain personal and family reasons: (a) birth of a child, (b) adoption or foster care, (c) serious health problem of a family member, and (d) serious personal health problem. FMLA leaves can be up to 12 weeks per calendar year for qualified employees.

Privileges

Previous sections of this chapter addressed entitlements granted by state and federal governments to enhance the employment continuity of public school employees. Within this section we discuss some of the more important privileges that most public school districts use to complement the entitlements extended to employees. These benefits are privileges in the sense that employees lack any statutory rights relative to the benefit discussed in the following sections of this chapter.

Medical Coverage

One of the most important benefits offered public school employees within the employment continuity process by a local school district is medical coverage. In fact, for many of the lower paid positions in the school system, medical coverage is just as important as salary for attracting and retaining employees. This coverage is especially important for bus drivers and for food service workers as well as single wage earners in any job category.

When placing this type of coverage in perspective, until the 1980s, medical coverage was viewed almost as an entitlement rather than as a privilege because most public school districts provided employees with full coverage with no out-of-pocket expense. Little differentiation was made during this time period between employee coverage for the individual and family coverage for the employee. However, following this period in time, the cost for health care coverage became one of the most expensive benefits provided employees of public school districts.

To control these costs associated with medical coverage for public school employees, several steps were taken on the part of human resources. Initially, employees were requested to pay only a deductible each calendar year. Deductibles were fixed costs incurred by the user of the service and paid in full by the employee before the insurance company contributed funds to the provider.

With medical costs continuing to increase, school boards began to require employees to pay a percentage of their medical premium in the late 1980s. Although the family coverage was more expensive than the single coverage, the employee's percentage was usually a fixed dollar amount regardless of the type of coverage opted for by the employee (individual or family). During the 1990s, however, most school districts changed the way that medical benefits were managed in an effort to reduce the increasing costs associated with this privilege.

School districts adopted many different types of management plans in an effort to control medical cost for employees. Some of the more common plans in existence then and today are the health maintenance organizations (HMOs), the point of service plan (POS), and the preferred provider organization (PPO). Each of these plans has some unique characteristics and some common characteristics.

All these plans are very similar and share some common characteristics. One characteristic is that these plans restrict, to varying degrees, the employee's choice of medical providers, and limit the choice of providers to only those preapproved medical professionals. Another common characteristic is that these types of plans require, generally, that the employee pay a copayment with each visit to the medical provider.

Although employees continue in most school districts to pay a proportion of the insurance cost and to pay a copayment for each visit to the provider, medical insurance is still an important factor for recruiting and retaining public school employees. In fact, because healthy employees are necessary for the school to operate in an efficient and effective mode, public school districts have become even more proactive in this area. Rather than operating from a reactive position of helping ill employees seek and pay for treatment, school districts operate now in a proactive mode by helping to prevent illness on the part of employees though implementation of employee assistance programs.

Employee Assistance Programs

Knowledge concerning the prevention of certain kinds of health problems affecting employees in their performance of assigned duties and organizational responsibilities has emerged from within the health care industry. In response to this knowledge about prevention, many school districts have taken steps to develop employee assistance programs. Underlying the need for such support systems are data indicating more employees than ever before are showing signs of performance dysfunction within the work setting.

Sources of deterioration in work performance stem from both internal and external environmental factors, such as changes in work load or work relationships, perceived discrimination, marital adjustment, stressful superior–subordinate conditions, and various forms of substance abuse. Organizational consequences resulting from these conditions are numerous and far-reaching for the school district and for the employee.

Consequences of dysfunction on the part of an employee within the work setting can be exhibited in several ways, including personal disorganization, absenteeism, tardiness, increased costs for health insurance, grievance filing, litigation, and, most important, erosion of the relationship of the school system to personal well-being. Because of these outcomes, at least three reasons exist for developing effective employee assistance programs: (a) humanitarian considerations basic to assisting members in dealing with problems affecting performance, (b) cost-containment-associated remedial actions, and (c) maintenance of performance continuity and strengthening of the link between individual and system effectiveness.

With the cost of health insurance premiums rising annually, controlling health-related expenditures has become a key factor for managing the human resource function in the public school setting. Management of the human resource function in public schools involves focusing on reducing insurance claims while increasing the system's ability to develop a viable support system for its members. Regardless of system size, common behavior problems of various kinds are inevitable for employees of a public school system and warrant carefully designed plans to meet the objectives of the human resource function.

Employee assistance programs within the public school setting should include these options: (a) *wellness* programs, which stress preventive health maintenance; (b) programs focusing on personnel behavior problems that stem from *work assignments* or *work relationships;* (c) programs designed to treat *personal problems* that affect member performance; and (d) any combination of these options. The kinds of and extent of programs offered by a public school district depend on a variety of factors, including program objectives, system size and resources, problem prevalence, and organizational recognition of the existence of a problem and commitment to its resolution. In general, there is a positive relationship between system size and program breadth: the larger the system, the greater the likelihood that the program services will be more extensive.

To design, implement, and monitor an employee assistance program properly, certain issues must be addressed. These issues are brought into focus through questions such as:

- To what extent have personnel problems been identified that warrant initiation of an employee assistance program (e.g., absenteeism, tardiness, gambling, stressful work-related conditions, personal problems affecting individual performance, and substance abuse)?
- Of the four options regarding employee assistance programs described previously, which is most suitable as a planning strategy? This issue involves enlisting employee participation in decisions concerning courses of action designed to maintain their well-being as well as that of the system.

Some of the factors considered important to the success of health-related programs include:

- *Policy*—A policy statement forms the bedrock on which to establish both wellness and assistance programs. Policy is intended to make clear program objectives; board of education commitment; the scope, type, and extent of assistance eligibility (e.g., salaried, nonsalaried, or contingent personnel); and internal and/or external provisions for referral, counseling, and treatment stipulations.
- *Procedures*—Programs that center on dysfunctional behavior require established procedures. These include such steps as problem identification, referral (system or self), diagnosis, intervention, and follow-up.
- *Sponsorship*—Costs of assistance programs remain a disturbing issue: the extent to which expenses should be borne by the employer, the union, the individual, or a combination of these stakeholders. Because expenditures for all forms of benefits are reaching new heights, and because more personnel seek or are urged to seek various forms of treatment, cost considerations enter into policy and program decisions. System trends in health maintenance costs and forecasts of health risks are among the kinds of information that should become part of the system's personnel database.
- *Education*—Educating all supervisory personnel about procedures for dealing with both wellness and assistance programs is deemed an integral component of program implementation. Program objectives, procedures, confidentiality of information, and forms of treatment and care are examples of program elements about which personnel need to be informed and educated.
- *Flexibility*—Due to the size range of school systems in the United States, both wellness and assistance programs must be modeled to fit the experiences, conditions, trends, and needs of each system and the individuals within the system. Need identification is diagnosed through such sources as insurance claims, medical records, surveys, performance appraisal information, and budgetary indicators.

In sum, examination of the contemporary social scene, changing member expectations, and stressful conditions in both internal and external environments lead to the realization that wellness and assistance programs are no longer only theoretical issues. The school system's concern in this regard is how to position the organization and the human resource function so that whatever health maintenance strategies are adopted, they will result in closing performance gaps at individual, group, and organizational levels.

Employee Conveniences

With the exception of certain central office personnel and certain support staff, most public school employees work less than the standard work year followed by employees in the private sector. Many of the employees that comprise a public school district's workforce have work schedules that follow closely the school calendar for students or extend the basic school calendar for students by a specified number of days or weeks. Although variations exist among school districts, the calendar followed by most students will average approximately 185 days across the nation.

Because most of the public school employees work less than the standard work year (260 days), most school employees fail to earn vacation. Without vacation time many school employees may encounter difficulty in managing certain aspects of their personal lives that requires attention during their scheduled work times. To address these contingencies, public school districts have developed certain types of leave provisions in an effort to facilitate the employment continuity process for employees.

These types of leave provisions are a privilege rather than a legislative right and are designed to protect the income flow of an employee when the work schedule is disrupted temporally through no fault of the employee. As such, school districts should have great latitude in the development and administration of these types of leave provisions. However, far too often, school boards and school administrators have forfeited the school district's authority with respect to these types of leave provisions either through poorly written polices or inappropriate concessions at the bargaining table.

The most common mistake made by school boards and school administrators in this area of human resource management is to develop in policy or agree to in contract a single leave procedure that purports to cover the array of contingencies that employees may encounter during their work year. This single leave provision is labeled generally as "personal leave" and is applicable to a wide range of situations. To qualify for global personal leaves, employees must satisfy generally only regulatory provisions.

A review of many policies and contract provisions reveals several common regulatory provisions governing the usage of global personal leave procedures. Examples of the regulations are as follows:

- Employees must apply a specified number of days before the leave.
- Leaves cannot be taken the day before or the day after a holiday.
- Leaves cannot be taken either the first week or the last week of the school year.

- Leaves cannot be taken the last day of a grading period.
- Leaves cannot be taken if a certain percentage of the employees at a work site are absent.
- Leaves cannot be taken to pursue other employment opportunities.

If an employee satisfies the regulatory conditions, then personal leaves are granted by management usually without question. By following only regulatory provisions for granting personal leaves, school administrators relinquish managerial prerogatives that have an important administrative and economic implication for a public school district. Time away from the job by employees has profound operational and economical implications that should be controlled whenever possible.

However, regulatory requirements, as cited previously, defeat, in many instances, the basic purpose of leaves as a means of enhancing the employment continuity process for employees. Events occur within the lives of employees that fail to fit within the confines of such regulations. Failing to satisfy regulatory requirements, employees are ineligible for personal leaves.

In contrast to this singular approach for personal leave as practiced by many public school districts, we advocate that personal leave be decomposed and that several different types of leave be made available to employees. By decomposing personal leave into different types of leave provisions, more latitude is granted the employee in the use of leaves and more authority is granted the employer in the operation of a public school district. We suggest that personal leave be decomposed to include the following three categories rather than a single category: (a) emergency leave, (b) business leave, and (c) personal leave.

Emergency leave should be requested only in specific situations by employees. Situations warranting emergency leave are those that require an employee's immediate attention and failure to afford such attention would result in irreparable harm. Examples of incidents requiring emergency leave are broken water pipes in the home and an injury or automotive accident involving the employee or an immediate family member.

To qualify for a business leave, employees must be involved in some type of economic transaction. An economic transaction involves situations where each party stands either to lose or to gain something of economic value as the result of the interaction. The most common example for a business leave with public school employees is closing on a house.

Personal leave, within our scheme of leave provisions, is more narrowly defined than typically found in most school districts. We define personal leave as a nonrecurring event that is somewhat unique to an individual. Examples of situations where personal leave would be appropriate include graduating from an educational institution and attending the wedding of an immediate family member.

By decomposing a global personal leave provision into more specific types of leave provisions, several advantages can be realized in the employment continuity process. Most important, individuals as employees will have greater liberty in using leave and will be less restricted by the leave process than some employees encounter with global personal leave previsions governed by regulatory provisions. Equally as important is the ability of school administrators to manage more efficiently and effectively the educational organization with separate leave provisions than with a single leave provision strictly regulated.

Administrative Incentives for Employment Continuity

School districts as employers can develop and administer certain processes and procedures that enhance the employment continuity of employees in their assigned duties and organizational responsibilities. Foremost among these processes and procedures are mechanisms that allow employees the opportunity to change positions within the organization. Employees can move vertically or horizontally, and these moves can be initiated by the employee or by the employer.

Movement Within an Organization

Individuals accept employment with a public school district for many reasons. Among these reasons is the need for gainful employment that will yield compensation for services rendered that can be used to fund a certain level of life's pleasures. Once the need for gainful employment is satisfied, other needs may become potent for some employees.

Among these other needs that may become potent is a desire to change work assignments within the public school district. A desire to change work assignments can be attributed to several reasons, both psychological and economical. Employees may seek novelty within the work environment, may seek avoidance of an unpleasant working situation, and/or may seek to improve their organizational status within the public school district.

School employees, like any other employees, are not exempt from the psychological phenomenon of burnout. Working at the same job for many years can result in levels of performance that are less than the employee is capable of performing. Seldom do dysfunctional employees fail to know what to do, but lack, in most instances, the motivation to perform at their capacity in assigned duties.

What may have been a desirable work environment for some employees upon entrance to the school district workforce could have changed. School districts are dynamic entities and evolve over time. Leadership changes and work group composition changes can both change what was an ideal working situation into one that is no longer desirable for some employees.

Still other employees may desire to enhance their position within the organization. These employees may have been underemployed on their entrance into the workforce of a school district or may have upgraded their job skills after being employed by a school district. In either situation, this group of employees seeks to capitalize on their occupational skills through obtaining a higher-level position within the public school district.

Regardless of the reasons underlying the desire for employees to seek different work assignments within a school district, it behooves the organization to provide means for employees to satisfy their desires. Public school districts that ignore these needs are to experience likely turnover rates in excess of those normally expected in the operation of a school district. Many of the employees electing to leave a public school district because of restricted opportunity are likely to be the type of employees that the school district should retain within the workforce.

To retain satisfactory employees desiring changes in work assignments, school districts can develop transfer and promotion provisions. These provisions provide employees with a means for changing their immediate work environment while maintaining their continuity of employment with a public school district. Through changing their immediate work environment, satisfaction and performance on the part of the employee may be enhanced.

Transfers are linked closely to one aspect of human resource planning: the need to shift position holders within the system to staff vacancies, place personnel in positions in keeping with their interests and abilities, and correct staffing errors in the current workforce. The term *transfer,* as used here, refers to the movement of personnel from one position, office, department, or school to another position, office, department, or school within the same school district. Movement involved with transfers is horizontal generally and may or may not involve increases in responsibilities or compensation for the employee.

In general, transfers are initiated either by the administrative staff (involuntary) or by the employee (voluntary). Because of the implications associated with transfers, transfer of personnel is an important aspect of school administration for enhancing the work continuity process for many employees. Indeed, transfer provisions deserve more attention from a policy standpoint than is usually afforded by most public school districts to this important administrative process.

When formulating a transfer policy for a public school district, certain issues must be addressed. To help in addressing these issues, a series of questions are proposed for consideration by those responsible for developing and implementing a transfer provision. These questions include the following:

- What forms of employee transfer will be recognized in the system's transfer policy (employer initiated and/or employee initiated)?
- What criteria shall apply in evaluating employee transfer requests?
- What contractual considerations are involved in employee transfer?
- What arrangements exist to consider personal reasons of employees who request or refuse transfer?
- What are the reasons for making involuntary transfers?

Answers to these questions should be addressed in the transfer provisions of a public school district and should form the framework of a transfer provision. By addressing these issues in board policies and in labor contracts, many potential problems can be avoided. Most important is that transfers should be encouraged whenever they are in the interest of the individual and in the interest of the system, and that transfers are a valuable administrative process for improving staff development and flexibility.

A related but somewhat different administrative process for changing the employment status of individuals within the workforce is **promotion.** Promotion is taken generally to mean vertical movement for employees within the organization, while transfer is taken generally to mean horizontal movement for employees within the organization. Most often, promotions involve changes in compensation and in job duties that seldom accompany transfers.

Throughout this text, the importance of designing and implementing a proactive human resource strategy has been stressed. One aspect of this strategy is getting the right people into the right positions. An administrative mechanism for facilitating this strategy is sound promotion polices and procedures.

Promotion policies and procedures should be shaped to advance individuals who have the abilities, skills, attitudes, and commitment to enhance organizational efficiency and effectiveness. Under this arrangement, promotions are bestowed on those who meet and exceed minimum performance standards. Promotion criteria are needed for helping to identify people whose strengths are needed to achieve position and system aims and to place such individuals where their strengths can be exercised fully to the advantage of the individual and the school system.

A major issue for promotion, like for transfer, is the potential impact of seniority on promotion decisions. Promotion policy should avoid practices that place a priority on seniority when filling a vacant position. Seniority should become an issue only when candidates for promotion are equally qualified relative to the vacant position requirements; otherwise, promotion decisions should be made on the basis of merit.

Although policies of the school board and labor contract procedures for transfers and for promotion require considerable planning on the part of school boards and system administrators, the contingencies addressed in these types of reassignment provisions are more easily dealt with than those required of still another type of reassignment provision encountered by most school districts. This last type of reassignment provision is **demotion.** Demotion is a special type of reassignment that involves moving to another position that commands less salary, is lower in status, has less responsibility, offers fewer privileges, and/or affords less opportunity than the current position of an employee.

Demotions, like transfers, can be either voluntary or involuntary. Voluntary demotions are sought by the individual, while involuntary demotions are initiated by the school district. Depending on the initiating source for demotions, different processes and procedures may be evoked.

Individuals seeking to be demoted do so for several reasons. It is not uncommon for certain service employees to seek a lesser job to obtain a more accommodating work schedule, especially if the latter schedule adheres more closely to that followed by their children. Central office clerical personnel may seek building-level secretarial positions to have summers off when their children are home.

Other personnel may have accepted promotions only to find that the newly assigned position fails to fulfill previous personal expectations anticipated with a reassignment. It is not unusual for newly assigned assistant principals to desire to return to a former teaching position after the first year of administrative service. In large school districts, some employees may desire to obtain a work assignment closer to their home than their current higher-level assignment that requires greater commute time to the primary work location.

When employees seek actively a demotion for personal convenience, employees should accept fully all consequences of the reassignment. If the new position commands less salary than the previous position, then the employees should be expected to take a reduction in compensation. However, when the change in job assignment involves involuntary demotion, other factors may come into play.

Involuntary demotions can come about for any number of reasons. Declining enrollment may require that certain school buildings be closed and that school personnel be reassigned. For some personnel, the reassignment may involve an involuntary demotion. An involuntary demotion for administrators is likely when other principalships are unavailable within the school system.

Some other position holders may encounter an involuntary demotion as a result of an organizational realignment. Results from organizational studies may reveal that certain positions have been overclassified and overcompensated. When such results surface through no fault of the employee, the school district may have certain obligations to the employee that fail to exist when demotions are sought on a voluntary basis.

From the standpoint of the public school system, one of the most important aspects of involuntary demotion is that appropriate procedures for such action are established and adhered to scrupulously. For many individuals, work is the most important element in their lives. To be subjected to an involuntary demotion is, to most persons, a rejection, a crushing blow, one that is likely to generate the severest kind of antiorganizational behavior.

For certain employees that have performed faithfully and effectively, involuntary demotions may not be the appropriate action if certain responsibilities of such individuals can be shifted temporarily to other positions. Other alternatives include transfer to a less demanding position without loss of pay or status or providing incentives for early retirement. Such solutions are preferable when they can be arranged without interference with system operations and without creating role inequities that may lead to conflict.

Whatever the reasons for an involuntary demotion, the decision should be based on clear procedures and processes. Given adequate school board policies and labor contract provisions, the system is in a sound position to use involuntary demotion appropriately. At minimum, an involuntary demotion should include: (a) informing the employee of the intent to demote; (b) providing options, where feasible, such as transfer to a position of lower status, responsibility, and salary readjustment; (c) endeavoring to negotiate a settlement acceptable to both parties; (d) formalizing and informing the individual of the reasons for demotion; (e) notifying concerned parties of the official starting date; and (f) prescribing new position responsibilities.

Review and Preview

This chapter has dealt with organizational provisions designed to retain personnel and foster continuity in personnel service. Analysis of the personnel continuity process indicates there are two clusters of activities: one is concerned with the health and mobility of continuing personnel; the other is focused on members who leave the system voluntarily or involuntarily.

As outlined in this chapter, the process for maintaining continuity of personnel service stresses the need for a projected course of action based on a series of decisions relating to what plans for personnel continuity are expected to achieve; types of plans needed to realize expectations; and program organization, administration, and control. Expectations or results that the system derives from plans for service continuity are both long- and short-range and include improvement of the system's ability to perform its mission; improvement of individual effectiveness; and improvement of the system's physical, psychological, and organizational environments. Models have been included to examine the employment continuity process, continuity policy, time-related benefits, absenteeism and lateness, reduction in force, and retirement. Other continuity aspects treated include employee assistance programs, health maintenance, temporary personnel, promotion, transfer, and demotion.

Discussion Questions

1. Most school organizations utilize a form of limited illness plan that provides for a limited number of authorized days of absence. Some employees use all of these days, while others rarely use one day. Given that even authorized absences result in a loss to the organization (e.g., of quality classroom instruction), how can a school organization minimize the impact of absent employees?

2. Most school systems have limited opportunities for advancement for teachers. The most common step up for teachers is to the ranks of administration. This step generally means the loss of an experienced and capable teacher. What other advancement opportunities can be developed for teachers that promote retaining excellent teachers in the classroom?

3. What are the advantages to the organization of internal staffing in the form of promotion or transfer? What are the advantages to the individual of internal staffing?

4. Employee assistance programs are viewed as devices that aid in cost containment and the maintenance of organizational effectiveness. How is it possible to gauge the effectiveness of these programs?

References

LaRue, A. (1996). *Summary of state teacher tenure laws: The changing face of teacher tenure.* Retrieved July 30, 2002, from the American Federation of Teachers Department of Research Web site: **http://www.aft.org/research/reports/tenure/Laruetab.htm**

Milkovich, G. T., & Newman, J. M. (1996). *Compensation* (5th ed.). Boston: Irwin McGraw-Hill.

National Conference on Public Employee Retirement Systems. (2002, May). *The evolution of public sector pension plans.* Retrieved July 30, 2002, from the National Conference on Public Employee Retirement Systems Web site: **http://www.ncpers.org/news/pension.pdf**

Ohio State Teachers Retirement System. (n.d.). *About STRS Ohio.* Retrieved July 30, 2002, from the Ohio State Teachers Retirement System Web site: **http://www.strsoh.org/aboutstrs/1.htm**

Pennsylvania State Teachers Association. (November, 1996). Issues-research-testimony: *What the public wants to know about teacher tenure.* Retrieved July 30, 2002, from the Pennsylvania State Teachers Association Web site: **http://www.psea.org/pseafrontpage/news/issues/tenure.htm**.

U.S. Department of Labor. (n.d.). *Family and Medical Leave Act of 1993.* Retrieved July 30, 2002, from the U.S. Department of Labor Web site: **http://www.dol.gov/asp/programs/handbook/fmla.htm**

U. S. Social Security Administration. (n.d.). Social Security Act of 1935. Retrieved May 28, 2003 from the Social Security Administration Web site: **http://www.ssa.gov/about. htm**

Westfield Classroom Teachers Association. (n.d.). *Article XIV–Sick leave bank.* Retrieved July 30, 2002, from the Westfield Classroom Teachers Association Web site: **http://www.wwcta.org/article-xiv. htm**

Supplementary Reading

Andrew, L. D. (1985). *Administrator's handbook for improving faculty morale.* Bloomington, IN: Phi Delta Kappa.

Flygare, T. J. (1978). Mandatory retirement is fading fast: Will tenure be next? *Phi Delta Kappan, 59*(10), 711–712.

Friewald, J. L. (1978). Tenure: Another sacred cow about to bite the dust. *Phi Delta Kappan, 59*(10), 711–712.

Hazard, W. (1975). Tenure laws in theory and practice. *Phi Delta Kappan, 56*(7), 459–462.

Lang, T. H. (1975). Teacher tenure as a management problem. *Phi Delta Kappan, 56*(7), 451–454.

Masters, F. W. (1975). Teacher job security under collective bargaining contracts. *Phi Delta Kappan, 45*(7), 455–458.

National Institute of Education. (1984). *The culture of an effective school.* Research Action Brief Number 227. Washington, DC: Author.

Nilsen, A. P., & Leuhrsen, S. (1990). How to keep even your best friend from getting tenure. *Phi Delta Kappan, 72*(2), 153–154.

O'Neill, J. M. (1998). Pressure to cut costs puts tenure on the block. *Philadelphia Inquirer,* E4.

Prince, J. D. (1989). *Invisible forces: School reform versus school culture.* Bloomington,

IN: Phi Delta Kappa Center on Evaluation, Development, and Research.

Reeder, L. S. (1986). The price of mobility: A victim speaks out. *Phi Delta Kappan,* 67(6), 459–461.

Skinner, D. C., Edwards, W. T., & Gravlee, G. L. (1998, September). Selecting employment practices liability insurance. *HR Magazine,* 146–152.

10

Unionism and the Human Resource Function

CHAPTER OVERVIEW

Historical Perspective
Purpose Perspective
The Regulatory Anatomy of Bargaining
Collective Bargaining and the Human Resource Function
Collective Bargaining Developments in Public Education
The Collective Bargaining Process
    Prenegotiations Planning
    Ten Prior Planning Premises
    Organization for Negotiation
    The Planning Committee
    The Negotiating Team
    Shaping the Human Organization Through Contract Design
    Determining the Scope of Bargaining
    Contract Negotiations
    Impasse Procedures
    Contract Contents
    Organizational Security
    Compensation and Working Conditions
    Individual Security
    Contract Administration

CHAPTER OBJECTIVES

Overview the historical basis and attendant developments of 20th-century collective bargaining in public education in the United States.
Portray the importance of the human resource function in coordinating, systematizing, and administering the collective bargaining process.
Indicate why teacher unions should be a dynamic part of resolving public education problems in the 21st century.
Depict the elements of a model for the collective bargaining process.

CHAPTER CONCEPTS

Arbitration
Collective bargaining
Collective bargaining process
Contract administration
Contract design
Exclusive representation
Grievance procedure

Impasse procedures
Negotiating modes
Negotiations
Prenegotiations planning
Scope of bargaining
Strike

Historical Perspective

Few other organizational phenomena have influenced the practice of human resource management in public school districts more than the advent of collective bargaining in education. Collective bargaining has changed the entire scope of the human resource management process in public education. What was once a unilateral decision-making process on the part of management has changed to a bilateral decision-making process involving the input of labor for managing many employee groups.

Collective bargaining within the public school setting is an evolving process that has spanned several decades. Initially, collective bargaining within the public school setting was modeled after collective bargaining in the private sector; however, more recently some very important differences have emerged between public and private sector collective bargaining practices. These differences have and will continue to have implications for the practice of human resource management for public school districts.

One major difference between the public and the private sectors concerns the enabling source for collective bargaining. Within the private sector, the enabling source for collective bargaining is the federal government. For public education, the enabling source for collective bargaining is state government.

Because collective bargaining within the private sector is a federal concern, a single set of laws, procedures, and administrative rules transcends state boundaries. Regardless of the type of union (truckers, mine workers, automotive, etc.) or the location of the union activity within the United States, the same rules apply for all collective bargaining activities. Oversight of all collective bargaining in the private sector falls under the same legislative acts and is administered by a single regulator agency, the National Labor Relations Board (NLRB; **http://www.nlrb.gov/**).

Unlike the consistency for collective bargaining within the private sector, considerable variations exist for collective bargaining within the public sector. In some instances, states have authorized collective bargaining for public school districts through the passage of specific legislation, while in other instances, states have failed to enact legislation pertaining to collective bargaining in the public school setting. Since the first enabling act was passed by Wisconsin in 1959, 34 other states have passed similar enabling legislation, with 15 states lacking enabling legislation for collective bargaining in the public sector (American Federation of Teachers, n.d.).

Of those states passing enabling legislation, many variations exist about the practice of collective bargaining within the public school setting. For example, some of the states have established state employment relations boards (SERB) similar to the NLRB to administer the public sector bargaining laws; some of the other states have no such mechanism for administering the bargaining laws pertaining to public school districts (American Federation of State, Country & Municipal Employees, n.d.). States without enabling legislation for collective bargaining may still have collective bargaining in the public school setting but do so without the benefit of legal sanction.

For those latter states failing to sanctify collective bargaining, collective bargaining is viewed as a privilege rather than a right. It is a privilege in the sense that collective bargaining exists only because the school board agrees to extend the bargaining process to the employees. Without the existence of enabling legislation for collective bargaining, employees fail to enjoy any basic rights relative to the collective bargaining process other than those rights granted by the local board of education.

The general notion of extending the privilege of collective bargaining to employees has expanded beyond the scope of existing legislation in several instances. To illustrate, certain school districts in Wisconsin and Ohio have extended bargaining rights to certain managerial groups exempted from the public sector bargaining laws within these states. More specifically, school districts in Milwaukee, Wisconsin, and in Toledo, Ohio, afford collective bargaining rights to principals and to managers even though these groups have been excluded specifically by state legislation within the respective states.

As a result of the growth of collective bargaining in general, school boards and human resource administrators have become increasingly cognizant of the need for continuing education relating to collective bargaining in the public sector to keep abreast of rapidly changing conditions and to learn to deal more effectively with the organizational impact of collective behavior. This phenomena, considered to be one of the most significant legal developments in the 20th century, has forced school systems to master collective bargaining procedures, just as school boards and school administrators have learned to master other organizational problems imposed on them by a world in transition.

School boards and human resource administrators are rapidly gaining greater sophistication and acquiring those skills essential to cope with numerous complex issues posed by unions. The initial collective bargaining movement in education found school boards and human resource administrators unprepared generally to engage in the collective bargaining process. With the passage of time, however, there has been increasing awareness by school officials that the application of collective bargaining techniques to school personnel problems requires boards and administrators to adjust to new and changing roles in order to establish conditions of employment for personnel under their jurisdiction.

Purpose Perspective

Collective bargaining may be defined as a bilateral process in which representatives of school personnel meet with representatives of the school system to negotiate jointly an agreement defining the terms and conditions of employment covering a specific period of time. The following information identifies important purposes and elements of the transactional relationship by which conflicting demands and requirements of both parties are reconciled within the collective bargaining process. It is useful to review these propositions and to show their relevance to the human resource function before going on to a discussion of various steps in the conduct of the collective bargaining process.

Worth noting is that the employees of school systems join unions for many reasons. These reasons include economic, psychological, political, and social. The major goal of unions is to maximize opportunities and security for their membership, including a higher standard of living, financial protection, position security, employment rights, opportunity for advancement, maintenance of individual integrity, and attainment of status and respect warranted by members of any profession.

A major objective of the administration of a school system is to operate the system effectively and efficiently in the public interest and to maintain the authority and the rights it needs to accomplish these purposes. In contrast, unions seek to restrict unilateral decision making by the board of education and to modify decisions so that outcomes are in accord with the needs and desires of the membership. Many times these differences encroach on the prerogatives of each party and must be reconciled through the collective bargaining process.

The collective bargaining process in the public sector is influenced by a variety of interests that are portrayed graphically in Figure 10.1. The contract ultimately agreed to by both parties will be the result of the combined interaction of various forces, factors, and conditions. Over the years, the public, courts, media, government officials, pressure groups, and students have become acutely interested in, drawn into, or have attempted to influence the settlement of disputes between employees and employers in the public sector.

Collective bargaining goes beyond willingness of a board of education to hear from, listen to, or be consulted regarding conditions of employment. The willingness of a school board to hear from, listen to, or be consulted about conditions of employment follows a *meet and confer* model rather than a collective bargaining model. The meet and confer model requires only that the board of education listen to the demands of employees rather than react to their demands.

In contrast, the collective bargaining model requires *codetermination* of the terms and conditions of employment, which, when mutually agreed to, bind both parties to those terms and signals the end of individual relations and the beginning of group relations between employee and employer. Often, the collective bargaining process involves new and emerging responsibilities for the system, modification of the administrative structure, extension of the human resource function, and different styles of leadership to deal more effectively with emerging employer–employee relationships, the new work ethic, and changing criteria for individual effectiveness in the world of work. Collective bargaining in the public sector gives the public employee the right to participate through a chosen representative in the determination of policies and practices that affect conditions of employment.

Often overlooked is the fact that collective bargaining imposes restrictions on the system, the union, and the employee. Unilateral action is prohibited on the part

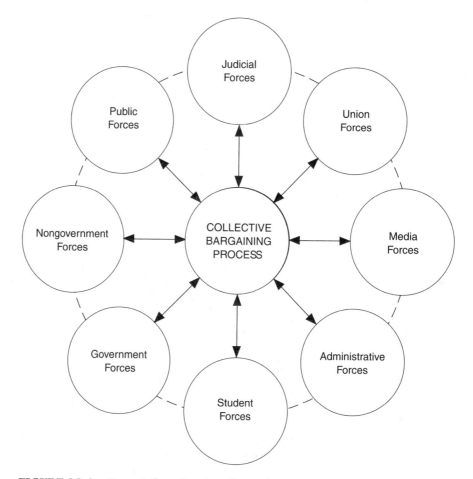

FIGURE 10.1   *Forces influencing the collective bargaining process.*

of all stakeholders. The system must bargain with the official bargaining unit and not with individuals as employees. Once organized, employees forfeit their rights as individuals to negotiate with the school board and school administrators and delegate this right to their chosen bargaining agent.

Existence and acceptance of the collective bargaining principle by a school system does not imply abandonment of the twin objectives of organizational efficiency and effectiveness so legislatively charged. The investment that a system makes in its human resources is considerable. The system should, therefore, focus its attention on controlling costs and maximizing the productive contribution of each of its members in exchange for the system's investment in pay, benefits, opportunities, and position-related satisfactions.

A major goal of collective bargaining is to establish a sound and stable relationship between the system and the chosen representative of the employees. Only by participation of both parties in resolution of disagreements and by good faith on either side in yielding to reasonable demands can this end be achieved. Adherence of the board to its responsibilities to constituents is an essential ingredient of harmonious personnel relationships.

The Regulatory Anatomy of Bargaining

Public employment practices within each state are shaped by specific labor laws and are enforced by different administrative agencies and by various court rulings. The structure of the external regulatory anatomy governing teacher union–school system employment relations, the policies by which they are shaped, the manner in which legislation is enforced, and the judicial interpretations of such policy are of primary importance to the human resource function in the public school setting. Knowledge of each authority is a necessity for the effective human resource manager.

As noted earlier within this chapter, collective bargaining laws vary greatly across states. Even though most state collective bargaining laws cover many universal topics such as **recognition procedures, impasse procedures,** and **contract administration,** they do so from different perspectives. However, there are some basics associated with each of the topics.

Most public sector bargaining laws address recognition procedures. This section of the law provides answers to the important questions of who represents whom and how this recognition takes place in the field setting. Individuals have the right to be represented by organizations of their choice free from the influence of employers.

Without exception, all public sector bargaining laws adopt the principle of exclusive representation for employees. Exclusive representation implies that all employees within a defined bargaining unit be represented by a single representative or bargaining agent. Although it is a single bargaining agent, this representative has typically a three-tier organizational structure in education.

These tiers are national level, state level, and local level. In most instances for teachers, the national organization is either the American Federation of Teachers (AFT; **http://www.aft.org**) or the National Education Association (NEA; **http://www. nea.org**). Each of these national organizations has a state counterpart, and each state counterpart has many local educational associations (LEA). For the many other school district employees who are not teachers and are also organized for the purpose of collective bargaining, municipal employee structures exist for exclusive representation by a parent organization (American Federation of State, Country & Municipal Employees, n.d.).

Employees being represented by an exclusive agent are referred to as members of a bargaining unit. It is common for state bargaining laws to exclude certain groups of individuals, such as managers, from representation and to use the term *appropriate bargaining* unit for those being represented. An appropriate bargaining unit is one that has been certified by a state employment relations agency and one that recognizes the fact that a perfectly construed bargaining unit fails to exist in practice.

Within the bargaining process, an impasse exists when either labor or management feels that no further progress can be made toward reaching an agreement. An impasse can occur either when one party refuses to negotiate a specific item proposed by the other party or when both parties fail to concur about the disposition of an item being negotiated. To resolve these types of stalemates, most public sector bargaining laws address impasse procedures.

Impasse procedures pertaining to stalemates in the negotiation process can take several forms. They can range from mediation to fact finding through arbitration, and these techniques vary in degree to which third-party intervention supplants labor–management decision making at the local level. At this stage of the negotiation process, these techniques are referred to as interest impasse procedures.

In addition to the interest impasse procedures for resolving an impasse during the bargaining process, some states provide the employees with the right to strike. The right to strike is addressed by state bargaining law and differentiation is made within these laws between legal and illegal strikes. Interestingly, even when employees utilize their right to strike and perform a legal strike, they can be discharged by the board of education for failing to fulfill their contractual duties.

After the contract has been ratified by both parties, there may be disagreements over the interpretation and application of the contract. These disagreements are resolved generally through a **grievance procedure**. The grievance procedure can be resolved within the school district or can be submitted to an outside third-party neutral for an arbitration ruling.

Arbitration to resolve a dispute for an existing contract is referred to as rights arbitration in contrast to interested arbitration. Rights arbitration can be mandated by state bargaining law whereby it becomes compulsory arbitration, or state bargaining law can be silent to rights arbitration whereby it becomes voluntary arbitration if so utilized as an impasse procedure to resolve contract disputes. In either instance, depending on the state bargaining law, rights arbitration can be either binding, which requires parties to follow dictates of arbitration outcomes, or advisory, which requires parties to consider recommendations from arbitration outcomes.

Relationships among existing laws, administrative interpretations, and court rulings are often contradictory. Many labor laws were passed before collective bargaining statues were enacted and conflicts often arise when trying to administer the human resource function in the public school setting. As an example, consider the human resource function involved in awarding tenure to probationary employees.

Tenure, in general, implies both that an employee has a property right for the job and that a person should not be released from employment without just cause. Many states have a statutory requirement for tenure that requires serving as a probationary employee for a specific period of time before tenure is awarded (e.g., 27 months within a 5-year period). However, a labor contract may state that no employee can be released without just cause, and, thus, provide all employees within the bargaining unit with instant property rights for their position regardless of their length of employment in said position.

Collective Bargaining and the Human Resource Function

As we examine the relationship of the human resource function to the collective bargaining process, it is worth remembering that negotiations result in economic decisions that have considerable significance for the system, personnel, clients, and community members. As such, the human resource function should be designed to facilitate the collective bargaining process.

Personnel administration must be concerned not only with protecting the interests of the organization so that established goals can be met but also with *taking advantage of opportunities* in the collective bargaining process to satisfy needs of individual staff members and to create a framework conducive to goal achievement. To address these separate but related concerns and obligations, the personnel office must serve several functions.

One function involves coordinating the collective bargaining process by maintaining a diligent focus on bargaining goals, strategies, and tactics. Monitoring of activities is necessary to ensure, as much as possible, outcomes from the bargaining process are aligned to strategic plans of the school district. When coordinating the collective bargaining process, management must set aside antiunion sentiments and remain in a problem-solving mode.

Another function served by the personnel office involves data management. Data must be collected, refined, stored, retrieved, and analyzed for many different topics being negotiated within the collective bargaining process. Only by using current and relevant data can serious omissions within the collective bargaining process be avoided by boards of education and functional agreements between management and labor be obtained in the collective bargaining process.

At the conclusion of the bargaining process and following the ratification of the master contract both by labor and by management, the personnel office assumes much of the responsibility for administering the contract. Often, contract language must be interpreted for those at the school building level and certain management personnel must be trained with each new contract. Part of the contract administration process involves keeping records about the existing contract and developing strategies for upcoming negotiations for successor contracts.

As a process, collective bargaining is interrelated with other processes included in the human resource function. Human resource planning (discussed previously) is a primary area of concern for collective bargaining because it establishes the future organizational structure, the number of positions, the rules for promotion from within, transfers, staff curtailment, and the nature of the work to be performed. Similarly, matters pertaining to salaries, wages, and collateral benefits are of prime concern to both parties in the bargaining process.

In attaining the goal of a competent and adaptable workforce, system members are to be regarded as the school system's core constituency. If there is one defining reason for the operation of the human resource function, it is to contribute to the generation of strategies and practices to improve the quality of work life. This means exerting effort, through collective bargaining and other processes, to make the school environment more acceptable to those who render system service.

Collective Bargaining Developments in Public Education

To understand the current direction, key issues, and continuing problems in the evolution of collective bargaining in public education, it is helpful to review some of the salient developments that have occurred over the past decades. These changes are noteworthy and include the following:

- A majority of states now permit collective bargaining for local and state government personnel, the laws for which generally follow the format of laws governing private sector bargaining.
- Membership in national organizations for educational personnel (e.g., the National Education Association and the American Federation of Teachers) has increased significantly, as have their resources and political influence. National organizations that focused almost exclusively on certificated personnel have expanded recruitment efforts to include noncertified school personnel.
- Negotiated agreements between school boards and teaching personnel as well as between school boards and noncertified personnel have become commonplace.
- Growth of unionization and collective bargaining in the public sector has been accompanied by a substantial increase in strike activity.
- Movement toward unionism for school administrators has been spurred by: (a) a concern that school boards are bargaining away the rights of middle-level school management, (b) fluctuating enrollments, (c) the desire of administrators for greater employment security, and (d) economic pressures.
- Statewide, regional, council, multilevel, and multilateral collective bargaining notions have been introduced as solutions to personnel issues in education.
- The scope of negotiations, whether the subjects are mandatory or permissive bargaining issues, continues to be controversial. Major trends in teacher agreements include provisions relating to compensation, grievance procedures, school calendar and class hours, class size, supplementary classroom personnel, evaluation of teachers, assignment of teachers, transfers, reductions in force, promotion, in-service and professional development programs, instructional policy committees, student grading and promotion, student discipline and teacher safety, and federal programs.
- Using a dual strategy of collective bargaining and political action, organized teachers have secured contractual gains locally and simultaneously have achieved political success at higher levels of government. Although these gains are neither total nor universal, teachers have acquired a number of noncompensation items that limit the flexibility of school management and

increase the cost of public education. At the same time, collective bargaining emerged as a tool for remedying decades of low salaries and arbitrary treatment by school officials.

- One emerging pattern immediately discernible is the continually strengthening pressure for citizen involvement in the entire public school collective bargaining process.
- Collective bargaining has a significant impact on the allocation of resources in school districts. The link between inputs and student outcomes, however, is less than satisfactory.

Teacher groups, once organized, seldom decertify their bargaining agent. The resulting influence of teacher unions in the United States must be regarded as substantial. Its power goes beyond union membership. Union tactics and negotiated contracts are emulated across the nation, and federal, state, county, and municipal governments are helping to shape employment relations in education.

The Collective Bargaining Process

The text that follows considers the actual steps in the **collective bargaining process** by which the board of education and the authorized negotiating unit move from prenegotiation activities through the collective bargaining process to obtain a master agreement. The framework in which the content of this section is presented is based on a model of the collective bargaining process illustrated in Figure 10.2. This model depicts the bargaining process as embodying three phases: *prenegotiations, negotiations,* and *postnegotiations.* Although the discussion that follows focuses on the various facets of prenegotiations preparation (Phase 1), reference will be made to the interrelationship of each phase to the entire bargaining process.

The terms *collective bargaining* and *collective negotiations* are employed interchangeably in the literature. The term *bargaining,* as used here, refers to the total *bargaining process,* one phase of which is *negotiations.* At-the-table activities, as well as those directly relevant to them, are viewed as negotiations.

Prenegotiations Planning

Prenegotiations planning (Phase 1 in Figure 10.2) is a continuous activity within the collective bargaining process. It begins for a successor contract during the negotiation phase for the current anticipated contract being discussed at the bargaining table. Many items and issues discussed for inclusion in one contract are revisited for inclusion when negotiating subsequent contracts.

One of the major reasons for the now generally recognized need for increased negotiation planning time is the complexity and number of issues to be negotiated. Although *economic issues* (such as salaries, wages, retirement, leaves of absence, group insurance, extra pay for extra work, and compensation incentives)

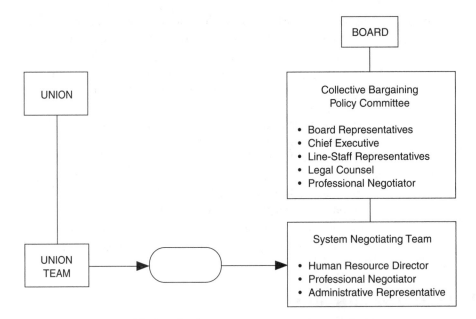

FIGURE 10.2   *Model of a school system organization for negotiations.*

once constituted the core of agreement discussions, *noneconomic issues* (such as organizational justice, performance appraisal, nonteaching functions, and class size) have become equally important to union members in recent times. In many instances, these latter areas of concern may be just as expensive as actual economic items because of the restrictions they may place on the ability of school administrators to manage the school district.

In addition to the costs associated with traditional benefits enjoyed by school personnel, the relative cost of many of these benefits has increased substantially due to inflation. Many of these benefits were awarded initially only to the working employee but have been expanded to cover family members and significant others. Little doubt exists that the list of benefits provided for school personnel will multiply as the number and amount of benefits increase in the private sector of the economy.

Finally, some recent social issues related to education are being addressed at the negotiations table, especially those involving student testing, integration, decentralization, transfer of teachers to inner-city schools, and community control of local school attendance units. Accordingly, the need for sophistication at the negotiations table, based on extensive and careful preparation, is no longer debatable for boards of education; time is needed to gather facts, relate facts to issues, decide strategy, and complete budget planning after contract settlement. Those boards of education that fail to plan will forfeit many of their managerial rights at the bargaining table.

Ten Prior Planning Premises

Planning premises are listed here to stress the importance of developing a system of plans and a planning process that will: (a) strengthen the relationship between collective bargaining and student learning and (b) lead to an organizational planning culture that methodically pulls together all of the strands of collective bargaining, which when entwined will lend substance to system purposes, direction, and the future generation of effective educational programs and services (see Table 10.1). Planning premises include the following:

- *Premise 1*—The organization's information system should be designed to facilitate effective strategic planning for collective bargaining (see Table 10.1).
- *Premise 2*—Political, governmental, technological, economic, and legal factors that affect the administration of modern educational organizations are rather complex and not readily resolved by simple, short-range plans (see Figure 10.2).
- *Premise 3*—The collective bargaining process encompasses a group of activities with considerable potential for exploring the broad range of opportunities and strategies in contriving to move the system from where it is to where it ought to be (see Figure 10.2).
- *Premise 4*—A collective bargaining planning structure is an effective mechanism for implementing the strategic aims of the system (see Figure 10.2).
- *Premise 5*—One of the objectives of prenegotiations planning is to generate plans for (a) development of new programs and services, (b) improvement of existing programs and services, and (c) divestment of nonproductive programs and services.
- *Premise 6*—A collective bargaining policy, as illustrated in Figure 10.3, serves as a guide to thinking, discretionary action, and decision making, and provides a common premise for action and policy implementation.
- *Premise 7*—The organizational right to engage in public bargaining is a long-standing public policy in the United States since 1959.
- *Premise 8*—Responsible players in collective negotiations include three parties—employees, employer, and government. Each engages in protecting and promoting its fundamental objectives.
- *Premise 9*—Gaining a thorough knowledge of the board's statutory powers and duties, and of laws and regulations that apply to bargaining, is an indispensable obligation of the board (National School Boards Association, 1996).
- *Premise 10*—Cultivate sources of expertise and seek these sources as needed throughout the negotiation process.

Organization for Negotiation

In the preceding section, we explored the planning aspects of collective bargaining. Illustrated were activities that relate to the assembly, summary, and organization of

TABLE 10.1
Outline of information related to prenegotiations planning.

Illustrative Questions for Fashioning Bargaining Strategy	Bargaining Information Subsystems	Illustrative Information Sources
What is our current school productivity situation?	Pupil, teacher, work group, and organizational productivity subsystems.	Local, state, and federal achievement data (pupil, teacher, work group, and system).
How effective are our current plans and programs for student learning?	Program evaluation subsystem.	Accrediting association reports, state agency reports, and evaluations of programs and services by central administration and work units.
How effective has the current union–system agreement been in achieving strategic aims for pupils and staff?	Contract assessment subsystem.	Policy committee appraisals, reports of chief executive and staff, and system intelligence sources such as media, union, staff mediators, and arbitrators.
What strengths and limitations exist in the current contract?	Contract assessment subsystem.	Evaluations by union and system regarding actual versus desired outcomes.
What changes should we anticipate in our internal situation? Our external situation?	Internal assessment subsystem. External assessment subsystem.	Community responses to contractual efficacy.
What major issues can we anticipate in the forthcoming negotiations?	Contract assessment subsystem.	Prenegotiation issue exchanges between union and system.
What do we want our future situation to be?	Strategic planning subsystem.	Strategic plans approved by the board of education.
What internal and external constraints may affect achieving the future we desire?	Internal and external subsystems.	Financial, demographic, political, economic, legal, and technological data having a bearing on system change.
What actions should we take to achieve the future we desire?	Strategic planning subsystem.	Strategic decisions approved by the board of education.
How shall we program the actions necessary to implement our plans?	Strategic planning subsystem.	Plans allocating responsibilities for implementing strategic decisions.

information needed by the policy committee and the negotiating team. Concurrent with or prior to these planning activities, a decision is needed to determine what agents will represent the system in negotiating with the association representing bargaining unit employees.

Before representatives of both management and labor sit down at the negotiations table, it is essential that the school system organize activities relating to col-

Riverpark School System's Strategic Aims and the Collective Bargaining Process

Planning aspects of the collective bargaining process in the Riverpark school system focus on achieving strategic aims through three phases: (1) prenegotiations planning; (2) contract negotiations; and (3) contract administration. Action in each of these phases is brought to bear on these concerns:

- In the prenegotiations stage, designing a contract aimed at operating the system effectively and efficiently in the public interest and exercising authority to accomplish these aims.

- Establishing as a basis for negotiations the point of view that the strategic aims for the system as a whole, and for the human resource function in particular, can and should be furthered through the process.

- Taking the position that any negotiated contract places improvement of educational quality for every school attendee as an organization imperative.

- Stressing the premise that a negotiated contract represents an exchange in which the system creates conditions for adequate compensation, fairness, justice, opportunities for career development, and life satisfaction. System members, as partners in the exchange, are assumed to meet performance criteria; adhere to the system's code of ethics and loyalty expectations; contribute to resolution of disrupter problems noted below; and commit to realization of individual, group, and organizational goals.

- Providing system members with employment rights such as position information, performance obligations, and supervisor quality; performance assistance, opportunities for career development, and upward mobility; performance recognition; and involvement in the system planning process.

- Employing negotiations to relieve conditions conducive to organizational disrupters such as grievances, lawsuits, strikes, theft, turnover, absenteeism, abuse of benefit provisions, poor morale, alcoholism, drug abuse, and antiorganizational behavior.

- Structuring the bargaining process to enhance strategic aims, including a negotiating team, good faith bargaining, resolving contract disputes, maintenance of a negotiations manual, and continuous monitoring of contract outcomes in relation to established objectives.

FIGURE 10.3   *Illustration of a policy statement of intent regarding the conduct of collective bargaining.*

lective bargaining. Decisions are needed to determine what work is to be done, what mechanisms are needed to perform the work, and what the rules will be for individuals delegated to do the work. As outlined in Table 10.2, one conceptual approach to a collective bargaining organization consists of two mechanisms: a planning committee and a negotiations team. The functions of each group will be examined in turn.

TABLE 10.2
Responsibility matrix for collective bargaining process for the Foxcroft school district.

Collective Bargaining Process Time Structure

Responsibility	Phase 1 Prenegotiations Period —to—	Phase 2 Negotiations Period —to—	Phase 3 Postnegotiations Period —to—
Board of school directors	Creates planning committee and bargaining team. Identifies internal responsibilities and relationships. Approves alternate proposals to be designed and costed.	Approves all variances from negotiations plan. Ensures that all issues are resolved at the required levels. Reviews contract prior to approval.	Ratifies agreement. Incorporates agreement elements into official budget. Directs chief executive to communicate agreement details to appropriate parties.
Chief executive	Coordinates all planning responsibilities. Ensures that preparations are proceeding systematically. Prepares for possible strike. Keeps board informed about negotiations proceedings.	Serves as board liaison agent to planning committee and negotiations team. Coordinates all system activities related to bargaining process.	Coordinates communication of contract details to administrative staff. Coordinates implementation of contract.
Bargaining planning committee	Prepares bargaining strategy and negotiating plan for board review and adoption. Advises board on personnel plans related to negotiations.	Counsels with negotiations team on actual or anticipated negotiations problems, impasses, and disagreements. Appoints ad hoc committee(s) as needed.	Records experiences concerning planning and negotiating the agreement.
Bargaining team	Identifies strike issues for board. Establishes negotiations strategy and tactics.	Continues bargaining process in accordance with planning guidelines.	Communicates short- and long-term implications of contract (chairperson submits written report).
Professional negotiator	Assesses union motivation, strategy, and goals for impending negotiations. Counsels board on impact of union proposal in relation to system goals. Provides analyses of strengths and weaknesses of current contract. Counsels and drafts contract language on request.	Conducts bargaining process in accordance with board objectives. Focuses negotiations on problem solving. Counsels on request. Ensures that all contract items are in legal compliance. Advises board on third-party utilization.	Evaluates and submits in writing report on all aspects of various negotiations (within 45 days). Reviews contract for omissions, errors, and ambiguities. Counsels board regarding contract infractions and disputes about contract interpretation.
Director of business affairs	Provides comparative data on system's standing regarding economics, benefits, and other issues. Assesses impact of settlement costs of optional plans.	Evaluates union proposals relative to settlement costs. Renders general support service to negotiations team.	Transforms agreement into budgetary items. Administers fiscal aspects of agreement.
Director of personnel	Prepares strike manual. Provides current and historical information pertinent to planning. Prepares negotiations handbook. Reviews prior grievance and arbitration decisions.	Furnishes negotiations team with relevant information concerning key issues. Prepares press releases as directed by chief executive.	Records experiences concerning administration of agreement (disputes, infractions, and court decisions).
Secretary	Renders secretarial service to planning committee and negotiations team. Develops minutes, records, and reports for negotiations team.	Provides support service to system negotiations personnel.	Prepares official negotiations documents to be stored in information system.

The Planning Committee

One approach for reducing the number and complexity of potential collective bargaining issues is a central committee that develops recommendations for consideration by the board of education. A major function of this committee is to advise the board on systemwide personnel matters related to collective bargaining, such as compensation, security, promotion, transfer, and other working conditions. A second function of this committee is to advise the board with respect to strategies and tactics that could be adhered to in collective negotiations sessions.

The collective bargaining *planning committee* is one mechanism for strategic planning. It can recommend what proposals the system should make, identify and analyze proposals unions are likely to make, and suggest alternatives to both union and system suggestions. Controlling for this committee is that the system is interested in judging proposals on the merits of their contribution to the strategic aims of the total operation.

Strategic plans will be affected by a variety of factors, including resources of the school system and attitudes of groups who influence plans (unions, boards of education, communities, and administrative personnel). The strategic plan in negotiations really boils down to how the system intends to treat the human resources in its employ. If properly planned, it can be advantageous to all parties.

The planning committee may include representatives from the board of education, the chief executive, line and staff administrative personnel (such as principals, supervisors, and assistant superintendents), legal counsel, and professional negotiators or other consultants. No single model can be suggested for the planning committee. As a generalization, however, it should be noted that the board of education, the immediate superintendency team, and administrative extensions of the superintendency should have representation.

The Negotiating Team

Much attention has been devoted in the literature to the issue of who will represent the board of education at the negotiations table. An adequate answer to this question requires the consideration of many factors. What might be an appropriate answer for a small school district may not be the same answer for a large school district; likewise, what might be an appropriate answer for a school district with a stable union–management relationship may not be the same answer for a school district with a hostile union–management relationship.

Given the fact that most school districts within the United States are relatively small, the predominant managerial collective bargaining team is one comprised of superintendents and school board members. When adhering to this model as the designated negotiating team, it is important to limit the number of board members participating at any one time to be less than a quorum. If a majority of school board members participate in a particular negotiation session, items agreed to within that particular session may by default be ratified because of the majority presence on the part of school board members.

Another common model for a managerial negotiating team consists of using administrators from within the district. Ideally such a negotiating team would be comprised of administrators with job assignments in the business area, student personnel area, curriculum area, building-level assignment area, and human resource area. An advantage of this model is that it preserves the board members' roles as ratifiers of the final contract.

Still other districts employ the services of a professional negotiator to represent the school board at the bargaining table. The advantages associated with a professional negotiator are many and include experience with all phases of collective bargaining as well as knowledge about external market conditions. Major disadvantages include expenses associated with services rendered and with being absent from the system when the contract is being administered.

Regardless of the particular team designated to represent the school board, there are certain prerequisites. These include the following:

- Understanding the operation of the system in all its ramifications
- Possessing the knowledge to conduct negotiations within the established legal structure
- Understanding the needs of personnel groups and the ability of the system to satisfy those needs
- Discerning trends in personnel policies and procedures
- Possessing the ability to retain the confidence of the system and to make decisions on its behalf

Shaping the Human Organization Through Contract Design

By considering the collective bargaining process as a series of stages, one can identify several aspects of Phase 1 (planning) where opportunities exist to develop plans for enhancing both individual and organizational effectiveness. To capitalize on these opportunities, consideration must be given to the existing contract and to the anticipated contract. A vision is needed to guide the school system from where it is to where it should be.

During the time period when the system operated under the existing contract, many changes are likely to have occurred. Board members, administrative staff, and bargaining unit members may have changed, and these changes may be compounded with other changes in the internal and external environment existing when the original contract was ratified. Effective planning in this phase of the collective bargaining process requires considerations of and anticipation for effects of these changes on the upcoming bargaining process.

The actual critique of the existing labor contract can be facilitated greatly through the use of a questionnaire. Intent of the questionnaire is to secure facts as

> A. Are there clauses in the present contract that need modification?
>
> B. What are the reasons for needed modifications? What information has led you to support the need for contract modification?
>
> C. Has the agreement achieved those goals the school system expected to achieve as a result of its formulation and acceptance?
>
> D. Is evidence available to indicate violation of the terms of the agreement?
>
> E. What difficulties have been encountered in administering the agreement?
>
> F. Have desirable items been excluded from the agreement?
>
> G. Does the present agreement permit the flexibility required to administer the school system effectively?

FIGURE 10.4 *Foxcroft school district questionnaire for reviewing current contract provisions.*

well as opinions regarding the functional operation of the existing contract. Contained in Figure 10.4 is an example of some of the questions for which responses are sought.

Reactions to the existing contract should be assessed from a variety of stakeholders. At minimum, these stakeholders include school board members, management level staff, members of the planning committee, and members of the bargaining team. An analysis of these responses provides the initial gist for the bargaining planning process.

Prior to formulating any formal reactions to the existing contract based on the information provided by the stakeholders, the school board should request that the bargaining agent for the employee group submit an initial set of proposals for the new labor contract. Receiving this set of proposals from the bargaining agent affords the school board a strategic advantage within the upcoming bargaining process. That is, the school boards will possess knowledge about what the labor union desires before they reveal what they have to offer.

Such knowledge is particularly important when formulating a negotiating strategy—important in that those areas of managerial prerogatives that failed to be addressed within the confines of a labor contract remain under the exclusive control of the school board. Consequently, it is to management's advantage within the collective bargaining context to limit the scope of bargaining.

Determining the Scope of Bargaining

The scope of bargaining is determined by the types of issues actually negotiated at the bargaining table by the representative of the employees and the negotiation team of the school board. As such, the scope of bargaining is determined, at least in part, by the counterproposals that the school board offers to the union prior to entering the actual negotiation process. Management's initial set of counterproposals should be based on an analysis of the initial contract critique and on an evaluation of labor's initial set of proposals.

Initial proposals submitted by the union for the anticipated labor contract can be evaluated according to three criteria. These criteria originated from the private sector and have been adopted almost universally by the public sector bargaining laws. The criteria are mandatory subjects of bargaining, permissive subjects of bargaining, and prohibited subjects of bargaining.

Mandatory subjects of bargaining are those items that, if requested by either party, must be bargained. Generally, these subjects include hours, wages, and working conditions and/or issues that impact these items. In addition to these basic items, certain states, such as Ohio, have expanded this list to include as mandatory items of bargaining those items in the existing labor contract regardless of the item's former status.

Permissive subjects of bargaining include those items that both parties must agree to bargain if such items are to be actually negotiated at the bargaining table. Examples of permissive items might be the use of district facilities or district equipment for union activities (buildings for meetings, copying equipment, etc.), assignment of teacher aides, classroom changes, and so on. If either party refuses to negotiate a permissive item, then that item is ineligible as a topic for the bargaining table.

Prohibited subjects of bargaining involve those items that if encapsulated within a labor contract are unenforceable. These items involve issues beyond the lawful authority of the employer (e.g., revealing student records to unauthorized sources) or items that impact the legislative rights of employees (e.g., discriminatory hiring). In some instances, prohibited subjects have been declared by state legislation, such as in Minnesota where student class size is declared as a prohibited subject of bargaining and becomes unenforceable even if included within a ratified contract.

In addition to using the legislative classifications involving mandatory, permissive, and prohibited subjects for evaluating proposals submitted by a bargaining agent, other schemes for evaluating these proposals exist. Proposals submitted by a bargaining agent can be evaluated according to organizational concerns, individual concerns, and general concerns. Each of these concerns can provide the board of education with valuable insight when designing a negotiation strategy for upcoming contract talks.

Organizational concerns pertain to those proposals that benefit primarily the bargaining agent. By being able to use school facilities (e.g., buildings for meetings) and school equipment (e.g., copying machines and the mail system for communication) in the conduct of official union business, the administrative cost is decreased and the communication efficiency is increased for the bargaining agent. Whether or not employees are required to pay their fair share (agency shop) for representation has implications for the size of the bargaining agent's coffers.

Individual concerns focus largely on economic items within the proposals. Most important are issues related to the amount of and rate for actual pay. Less important than actual salaries, but still important for individuals, are the levels and types of benefit packages available to them.

General concerns are less of a priority either to the organization as a bargaining agent or to the individual as an employee. Examples of general concerns include personalized parking places or "dress down" days. Although certainly a pleasure to have, individual concerns are unlikely to generate much opposition within the bargaining process if management refuses to negotiate these items.

To determine exactly which items the school board desires to incorporate within its initial proposals to the bargaining agent, both the legislative and functional classification categories can be used to define a negotiation strategy and to restrict the scope of bargaining. Contained in Figure 10.5 is a 3 × 3 matrix whereby each item from the bargaining agent's proposals can be classified. By following this classification, considerable insight can be gained and a plan can be designed to address one of the most difficult aspects of the collective bargaining process.

Indeed, the **scope of bargaining** has been an issue fraught with conflict throughout the history of public sector bargaining. At the core of the matter is the question of bargaining scope, especially as it pertains to noneconomic issues. Unions have sought to extend their sphere of influence into the policy role of organizations by insisting that the scope of negotiations include items traditionally considered to be organizational prerogatives.

It is not uncommon for unions to submit proposals pertaining to the curriculum, the instructional system, the performance appraisal system, and staff development. Expanding the scope of bargaining to include educational policy issues (especially those that are not conditions of employment) is unwise on the part of management. However, in far too many instances, school districts have forfeited the right to manage by bargaining important topics that should not have been discussed at the bargaining table.

	Union Concern	Member Concern	General Concern
Mandatory			
Permissive			
Illegal			

FIGURE 10.5 *Item classification scheme.*

Contract Negotiations

After the initial proposals for the school board have been formulated through pre-negotiation planning (see Figure 10.2), the collective bargaining process is ready to advance to Phase 2. It is within Phase 2 where the actual give and take of bargaining a master agreement between the school board and the employee group begins. As can be observed within Figure 10.2, a series of events take place within this phase of the collective bargaining process.

During the initial meeting between the designated representatives of both management and labor, two major events should transpire. First, management should present the school board's initial set of proposals to the bargaining agent of the employees. Time should be allotted for management to discuss the rationale underlying each proposal, point out the strengths or the weakness within the current operation addressed by the proposals, and explain how the proposals complement the strategic plans of the district.

Focus of the initial presentation is to present and not to negotiate. Actual negotiations should commence at a later stage (discussed later). This presentation is designed to impart information and to answer questions about the school board's position relative to the anticipated contract.

Second, the other order of business in the initial meeting between the parties is to set two specific calendar dates for subsequent activities. The first of these two dates establishes a cut-off point beyond which no new item can be introduced into the bargaining process. This date should allow the union enough time to review management's initial set of proposals and to recast, if necessary, the proposals presented to management prior to the initial meeting of the parties at the bargaining table.

It is important that management enter into the bargaining process only after it is clear what items are to be bargained. By establishing the actual scope of bargaining prior to beginning table negotiations for the anticipated contract, important parameters are set for the negotiation process. Without knowledge of the true scope of bargaining, management enters the negotiation process at a disadvantage.

A second date sought in the initial meeting between labor and management involves the starting time for actual negotiations to begin. This date should follow the first date and should allow management sufficient time to modify the school board's initial proposals and to address any new content, if necessary. It is during this second meeting that the actual negotiations between the school board representatives and the employee representatives actually commence.

Within the second meeting between the representatives for labor and for management the major goal is the establishment of ground rules. Ground rules are formal procedures and processes by which the negotiation process is governed. As such, ground rules should be agree able to by both parties, committed to writing, and signed by both parties.

Some of the most common issues addressed by ground rules are found in Figure 10.6. As can be observed within this figure, ground rules cover the entire

1. Location for Bargaining Sessions
2. Starting Time for Bargaining Sessions
3. Length of Bargaining Sessions
4. Size of Bargaining Teams
5. Method of Record Keeping
6. Process for Establishing Agenda
7. Open or Closed Meetings
8. Order of Ratification Process

FIGURE 10.6   *Example of typical ground rules.*

bargaining process from beginning through ending with the order of ratification. In the event that problems develop during the negotiation process, the ground rules will be controlling were applicable.

During the actual negotiation process, proposals and counterproposals for specific items are submitted and evaluated by labor and by management. When both parties mutually agree to a particular proposal for a specific item, this agreement is acknowledged by what is labeled within the collective bargaining process as a tentative agreement (TA). A TA requires both parties to sign and date the agreed upon proposal, and this proposal is set aside for ratification consideration and not revisited during the bargaining process.

After the bargaining table representatives have tentatively agreed to all proposals, the entire package of proposals is submitted for approval. This approval process, labeled as ratification, requires a majority approval by both constituents. Constituents for management are the school board members and constituents for labor are the bargaining unit members.

However, instances may arise where labor and management fail to mutually agree with respect to a particular item. This can produce a stalemate within the bargaining process and is labeled as an impasse. Impasses can occur in several different ways and are resolved through different types of procedures.

Impasse Procedures

As noted earlier in this chapter, an impasse during the collective bargaining process can occur in one of two different ways. One way for an impasse to occur is when either labor or management refuses to negotiate an item (in essence, the counterproposal is no proposal). The other way for an impasse to occur is that the parties fail to mutually agree on a specific item being negotiated. To resolve these different types of impasses, separate procedures are followed.

When either party refuses to negotiate an item proposed by the other party, a declaratory ruling is sought to resolve this type of impasse. A declaratory ruling determines whether or not the item causing the impasse is a mandatory or permissive subject of bargaining. Declaratory rulings are issued by a state employment relations board (SERB) in those states having such agencies and by mutually agreed to third parties in those states without such boards.

If the item causing the impasse is determined by the proper authority to be a mandatory subject of bargaining, then the parties are directed to negotiate the item. However, being directed to negotiate does not imply that mutual agreement with respect to the item must be achieved. When the item causing the impasse is determined by the proper authority to be a permissive item, the item is excluded from the bargaining process.

For the other impasse situation involving a failure to mutually agree on an item being negotiated, a more elaborate process is evoked than is the case involving a declaratory ruling. This process, in its most advanced form, involves three separate but related phases. These phases are mediation, fact-finding, and arbitration.

Mediation is the first step within the impasse resolution process. The goal of mediation is either to get the parties to agree relative to the contested item(s) or to restart the bargaining process between the two parties relative to the contested item(s). In most instances, mediators rely on the powers of persuasion and the parties fear of the unknown encountered in the advanced stages of impasse resolution.

Fact-finding is the second step in the impasse resolution process. Although the goals of fact-finding are the same as in mediation, the fact-finder has somewhat greater powers of persuasion than the mediator because the fact-finder will issue a formal written report. Even though the report issued by the fact-finder is not binding, it can influence both the public and an arbitrator.

A final step in the sequence of impasse resolution procedures is arbitration. An arbitrator will conduct a formal hearing where each of the parties will present their case and will challenge their opponent's case. Following the formal hearing, the arbitrator will issue a ruling about the contested item(s), and this ruling, in most instances, becomes part of the new labor contract.

Contract Contents

The new labor contract ratified by the school board members and by the bargaining unit personnel stipulates certain terms and conditions of employment that will exist over a specified period of time. Most labor contracts consist generally of three functional categories, each of which serves a specific purpose: (a) organizational security, (b) compensation and working conditions, and (c) individual security. Each of these divisions of the agreement will be discussed briefly in the following text.

Organizational Security

One of the first steps in collective bargaining is to settle the scope of recognition to be accorded bargaining units representing teachers or other personnel in the school system. Security clauses in agreements covering personnel groups negotiating with the school system may include such matters as the description of the bargaining unit, duration of the agreement, degree of recognition of the union or of the association, avoidance of discrimination based on union membership, permissible union activity on school premises, and access to school executives by union officials.

Prerogatives of the school system in the agreement are intended to affirm the rights the system must have to discharge administrative functions with which it is entrusted. Protective clauses in agreements reserve for the system discretion in such personnel matters as size of staff, position content, teaching or work schedules, promotion, transfer, discipline, dismissal, staffing assignments, appraisal, and leaves of absence. In addition, the system may demand clauses stipulating protection of personnel from union intimidation, exercise of good faith in the use of privileges granted, restraint in publishing false or misleading information about the system, and a zipper clause that ensures that negotiations will not be reopened for a specified period of time.

Compensation and Working Conditions

Core to any agreement negotiated collectively between two parties is compensation and working conditions for bargaining unit members. The school system, under the terms of the agreement, agrees to provide certain remunerations and to establish working conditions for employees in exchange for specified services. Capturing these concerns are clauses addressing salaries, wages, collateral benefits, class size, consultation in setting school calendars, lunch and rest periods, adequacy of physical facilities for teachers, transfers, teacher planning time, protection of teachers from physical assault, nonteaching functions, control of student behavior, school closings at noon before holidays and vacations, academic freedom, and recruitment of unqualified personnel.

Individual Security

Clauses in the agreement that cover the security of an individual member are designed generally to protect the employee against arbitrary treatment from the school system, the union or association, other personnel or personnel groups, and community groups. This type of security is of as much concern to the system as to the individual or the bargaining agent. Protection against arbitrary acts by the system is provided by a grievance procedure. Likewise, protection of the individual against arbitrary acts by the union or association is provided by clauses covering the right of an individual to belong or not to belong to the union and to be free from intimidation by the union.

Contract Administration

Following the ratification of the labor contract by bargaining unit members and by school board members, Phase 3 (see Figure 10.2) of the collective bargaining process is entered. Much of the work in Phase 3 rests squarely with the human resource function in the public school setting.

Because each new labor contract contains changes over the previous labor contract, system personnel working with bargaining unit members must be apprised of these changes. To apprise appropriate personnel of the changes, human resource administrators conduct workshops. Within these workshops, hopefully, before the implementation date of the contract, information is contextualized for administrators and supervisors.

After the agreement has been ratified by both parties, each party has a responsibility to make the contract work. Although the rights and obligations of both the system and the union are specified, disputes are certain to arise over the meaning of the language in the agreement, as well as over methods employed to implement the contract. Because numerous disputes arise from the interpretation or application of contractual language, care should have been taken to use language that will minimize misinterpretation.

In spite of the care taken when drafting the agreement, it is likely that problems will arise in the interpretation and/or application of items within the agreement. When problems do arise, the contractual means designed for their resolution is the grievance procedure. A grievance procedure provides the mechanism to challenge what is perceived as a violation, misinterpretation, or misapplication of contractual terms within the agreement.

Most grievance procedures have a series of steps that must be followed, and each of these steps is monitored by the human resource administrator. At minimum, these steps begin with a meeting between the grievant and the immediate supervisor and, if not resolved at this level, are advanced to a system level for adjudication. Failure to obtain a satisfactory resolution at the system level results in either the board of education or an arbitrator rendering a final decision relative to the grievance.

During the life of a labor contract, the human resource administrator is monitoring and appraising constantly the effects of the contract for fulfilling the goals of the strategic plan. Monitoring and appraising includes several activities:

- Recording and reporting to the superintendent of schools progress and problems encountered in administering the contract
- Interpreting the agreement for the administrative staff
- Recording experiences concerning administration of the meeting with union representatives to examine ways of improving the administration of the contract

Review

This chapter is focused on five principal aspects of collective bargaining as it relates to public education in the United States:

- The historical basis and attendant developments of public sector bargaining for education in the 20th century. One development of note at the turn of the century is the potential merger of the National Education Association and the American Federation of Teachers, which would become the nation's biggest and by far the nation's richest union.

• Elements of a model for the collective bargaining process.

• The behavior of three predominant players in public education collective bargaining—employer, employee, and government.

• The important role of the human resource function in coordinating, systematizing, and administering the collective negotiations process.

• Opportunities for the school system to employ collective bargaining to further its strategic objectives.

Discussion Questions

1. How does negotiator behavior differ between collaborative and competitive negotiating modes?

2. Describe the characteristics of an effective negotiating team.

3. What is the role of the informal contract within the contract design process?

4. What factors influence the range of items that fall within the scope of bargaining?

5. Respond to the following statement: "As bargaining costs increase, educational outcomes decrease."

6. Compare and contrast each of the following impasse procedures: mediation, fact-finding, advisory arbitration, binding arbitration.

7. If the right of teacher unions to call a strike is abolished, what alternatives should be considered as viable substitutes?

8. Should collective negotiation sessions for teacher contracts be open to the public?

References

American Federation of State, County & Municipal Employees. (n.d.). *Public sector collective bargaining laws.* Retrieved July 31, 2002, from the American Federation of State, County & Municipal Employees Web site: **http://www.afscme.org/otherlnk/weblnk36.htm**

American Federation of Teachers. (n.d.). *Collective bargaining: Are teacher unions hurting American education?* Retrieved July 31, 2002, from the American Federation of Teachers Web site: **http://www.aft.org/research/reports/collbarg/ifwf/t2.htm**

National School Boards Association. (1996). *The school personnel management system* (Rev. ed.). Alexandria, VA: Author.

Supplementary Reading

Clay, M. V. (1997, March). A collaborative approach to collective bargaining. *American School Board Journal, 3*(54), 19.

Dunlop, J. T., & Zack, A. M. (1997). *Mediation and arbitration disputes.* San Francisco: Jossey-Bass.

Egler, T. D. (1995, July). The benefits and burdens of arbitration. *HR Magazine,* 27–30.

Keane, W. (1996). *Win-win or else: Collective bargaining in the age of public discontent.* Thousand Oaks, CA: Corwin Press.

Lewis, A. (1998, March). Pussycat or tiger? *Phi Delta Kappan, 79,* 7.

Lieberman, M. (1993). *Public education: An autopsy.* Cambridge, MA: Harvard University Press.

Mezzacappa, D. (1998, July 6). Teachers reject union merger. *Philadelphia Inquirer,* A1–A5.

Mezzacappa, D. (1998, July 7). Teachers send a message. *Wall Street Journal,* A16.

Pfandenhauer, D. M. (1998, March). Selecting and using labor and employment. *HR Magazine,* 119–126.

Schrag, P. (1998, May 25). Divided they stand: Merger mania hits the teachers' union. *The New Republic,* 17–19.

Thompson, R. W. (1998). HR issues fill Congress' in box. *HR Magazine,* 70–73.

GLOSSARY

Academic freedom The ability of professional personnel to exercise intellectual independence and to encourage it in the classroom without impediment or undue restraint.

Administrative theory A set of concepts that guides administrative behavior and influences choices from among alternatives for deciding on courses of action.

Adverse impact A management practice that has a disproportionate effect on a protected class group.

Affirmative action Employment practices designed to afford certain protected class persons preferential treatment within the employment process.

Age Discrimination Employment Act Prohibits employment discrimination against persons over 40 years of age regarding selection, compensation, termination, and related personnel practices.

Alternate ranking A norm-based assessment technique used to evaluate jobs and/or individuals by focusing on either the most important job and the least important job, or the highest performing employee and the lowest performing employee.

Americans with Disabilities Act of 1990 (ADA) States that employers may not discriminate against an individual with a disability in hiring or promotion if person is otherwise qualified for position.

Application form An instrument designed to collect preemployment information from applicants.

Application ratio The number of applicants applying for each position (10:1, 20:1, etc.).

Appropriate labor market A policy decision focusing on the identification of comparable organizations.

Arbitration Process that involves an impartial third party who collects pertinent facts from the disputants and proceeds to make recommendations based on the findings.

Archives Storage arrangement for retention of records having historical importance.

Audit A formal review and evaluation of an administrative process.

Authority Empowerment vested in school officials to create and modify formalized conditions of employment and to encourage and uphold adherence by system members.

Base pay The amount of pay generally reflected on a salary schedule for a position, excluding any forms of supplemental pay.

Base rate The percentage of employees who would perform successfully if a predictor were not used to select employees.

Behavior tolerance zones Zones of behavior tolerance that the organization will accept from a system member.

This concept can be illustrated in terms of a continuum arbitrarily divided into two kinds of behavior: productive and counterproductive. The line of demarcation is established to assist the organization in evaluating the acceptability of past, present, and predicted future behavior.

Benefits A form of compensation in addition to base pay that can be either direct or indirect, such as vacation and insurance.

Bona fide occupational qualification (BFOQ) A skill or trait that is absolutely necessary for effective job performance.

Cafeteria benefits plan A benefit plan in which position holders elect benefits they will receive within a specified dollar amount.

Career The sequence of positions experienced throughout an individual's working life.

Career development Activities pursued by individuals based on specific career objectives.

Career ladder Vertical progression from one position to another.

Career path Movement upward, downward, or across levels in the organizational structure.

Career planning Organizational programs to assist position holders in considering their interests, capabilities, personality, and objectives in relation to career opportunities.

Career stages Stages through which a position holder passes from career outset to retirement. These stages have been described as establishment, advancement, maintenance, and withdrawal. Career stages have been compared to life stages, identified as early adulthood, mature adult, midlife, and withdrawal.

Checklist A criterion based job performance assessment technique design to assess either the presence or absence of specific personal characteristics or job behaviors.

Civil rights Individual rights created by federal and state constitutions, statutes, and court decisions, one element of which is employment.

Civil Rights Act of 1964 (CRA) Prohibits all forms of discrimination on the basis of race, color, religion, sex, or national origin.

Civil Rights Act of 1991 (CRA) States that the employer must demonstrate that educational requirements, physical requirements, and so on, are job related.

Cohort A group of individuals having a statistical factor (e.g., age or class membership) in common in a demographic study.

Cohort survival ratio A factor expressing variation in the number of individuals within a cohort from one accounting period to the next. For example, 550 individuals enrolled in Grade 10, having been preceded by 500 in Grade 9 enrolled during the preceding year, would yield a ratio of 550:500, or 1.10.

Collective bargaining The process by which a teacher union and the school system negotiate a contract for a stipulated period of time regarding compensation, benefits, work periods, and other conditions of employment. The terms *collective bargaining* and *collective negotiations* are employed interchangeably in the literature. *Bar-*

gaining generally refers to the total bargaining process, one phase of which is negotiations. At-the-table activities, as well as those directly relevant thereto, are viewed as negotiations.

Collective bargaining process One of the processes in the human resource function embodying three phases: pre-negotiations, negotiations, and postnegotiations.

Comparable worth Refers to discrimination against women through pay practices. Embraces the position that women should receive the same compensation as men for holding positions of comparable worth as well as equal worth. Work assignments not equal in content but providing equal value to the system warrant equal compensation.

Compensation equity Conformity to principles of fairness and impartiality in deciding the economic worth or value of positions and position holders. *Internal equity* refers to equal pay for equal work and performance outcomes under similar working conditions. *External equity* refers to internal compensation that is comparable to that of other school organizations with which the system competes for personnel.

Compensation index A plan for establishing base salaries for administrative and supervisory personnel by transforming responsibility levels into dollar values.

Compensation planning tools These include the position guide, organization chart, structural analysis diagram, and compensation scattergram.

Compensation policy A formal statement that reflects the goals and intentions of the board of education in regard to a system's compensation practices.

Compensation structure Interrelated provisions governing salaries, wages, benefits, incentives, and noneconomic rewards for school personnel.

Compensatory model An empirical procedure for combining information about an employee's performance on each dimension when a minimum level of performance is required on each dimension.

Compression A percentage that reflects the function growth potential associated with a particular salary range.

Computer (a) An electronic machine that, by means of stored instructions and information, performs rapid, often complex calculations or compiles, correlates, and selects data; (b) a programmable electronic device that can store, retrieve, and process data.

Concentration statistics An index that reflects the distribution of protected class persons across different job categories within an organization.

Confidential information Maintenance of information about system personnel within the limits of the Privacy Act of 1974.

Construct validity A type of validity appropriate for assessing abstract concepts such as leadership, satisfaction, or motivation.

Content validity An analytical paradigm for assessing the appropriateness of a measure or process.

Contingency plans Plans established to resolve a possible but uncertain occurrence, such as a budget rejection by the board of education or community, a teacher strike, new legislation affecting the system, a court decision, or a school merger.

Contingent personnel Temporary, part-time, and substitute professional or support personnel. Defined in general terms by the U.S. government as those who work fewer than 35 hours per week.

Continuity process The managerial actions associated with retaining employees by an organization.

Contract administration Day-to-day administrative negotiations between the union and the school system. Grievance machinery is employed to resolve contractual disputes.

Contract design The elements of a written contract proposal concerning system–union relationships, compensation issues, and contractual disputes.

Control Evaluation of the extent to which progress is being made according to plan (objectives). When results deviate from standards, corrective action is initiated to ensure success of the operation. Some form of control is essential to every organizational undertaking, regardless of its scope.

Criterion A standard, benchmark, or expectation by which to evaluate personnel performance, policies, processes, procedures, and organizational outcomes.

Criterion contamination The degree to which job tasks and behaviors are unique to the actual criterion and the predictor.

Criterion deficiency The degree to which job tasks and behaviors are unique to the actual criterion.

Criterion-referenced The level of job performance exhibited by an employee compared to an external standard independent of the level of job performance exhibited by other employees.

Criterion-related validity analysis A set of paradigms used to assess the relationship between a measure of procedure and a known standard.

Criterion relevance The degree to which job tasks and behaviors are reflected by the ultimate criterion, actual criterion, and predictors.

Culture Values shared by system members that produce norms shaping individual and group behavior.

Data (plural of *datum*). (a) Known, assumed, or conceded facts developed to establish a verifiable record of some past happening or event; (b) facts or figures from which inferences are made or conclusions are drawn; (c) individual facts and statistics capable of being converted into information.

Database (a) A collection of organized data, especially for rapid retrieval; (b) mass data in a computer arranged for rapid expansion, updating, or retrieval.

Data processing The conversion of raw data to machine-readable form and its subsequent processing.

Defined benefit A type of retirement system that entitles an employee to a fixed income based on dollar contribution, chronological age, and appropriate job experience.

Defined contribution A type of retirement system that requires a specific amount of contribution for investing and uses investment returns to determine retirement income.

Demotion A job change by an employee from a position of high value to a position of lower value.

Development appraisal Designed to improve performance or potential for performance; identifies areas for improvement or growth.

Development process A process designed to assist position holders to raise their level of performance in present or future assignments to performance expectations.

Discrimination Employment practices that have a disproportionate impact on certain individuals.

Dismissal A personnel action initiated by the system to sever an employment relationship.

Diversity Composition of a heterogeneous work force in terms of position, race, ethnicity, national origin, gender, age, religion, language, skills, disabilities, aspirations, personal idiosyncracies, behavioral preferences, and lifestyles. Diversity management involves what to address and through what human resource functions.

Due process A process that protects system members or union protection against infringement on employment rights. Requires showing of "just cause" and the use of "rules of reasonableness."

EAPs Employee assistance programs. Plans designed to assist members with resolution of personal problems (e.g., alcohol or substance abuse) affecting position performance.

Eclectic model An empirical procedure for combining information about an employee's performance on dimensions of job performance utilizing certain aspects of the multiple cutoff and compensatory models.

EEOC Equal Employment Opportunity Commission. Established as the administrative agency for Title VII (Civil Rights Act of 1964).

Effectiveness The degree to which organizational, group, or individual aims or intended effects are accomplished.

Efficiency Outcomes or results evaluated in terms of organizational resources expended.

Elasticity A percentage that reflects changes over time in the theoretical growth potential of a salary range.

Employee Polygraph Protection Act States that employers are prohibited from requiring or requesting job applicants to take a lie detector test.

Employment communication A two-way exchange or partaking of information between supervisors and subordinates, designed to achieve mutual understanding of roles and relationships underlying position performance.

Equal employment opportunity Employment practices designed to be neutral with regard to the protected class status of an individual.

Equal Pay Act of 1963 A federal law requiring equal pay for equal work, regardless of gender.

Ethics Personal principles and beliefs used to guide decision making or to direct overt actions.

External environment Forces external to the organization over which it has no control, such as federal, state, and local regulations; court decisions; public opinion; economic fluctuations; and political movements or activities influencing system courses of action.

Face validity An unacceptable measure of appropriateness based on unsubstantiated opinion.

Failure analysis The process identifying the factor or combination of factors associated with ineffective performance.

Family and Medical Leave Act of 1993 A covered employer must provide up to 12 weeks of unpaid leave if the employee provides appropriate documentation substantiating the need for leave.

Feedback Information received by position holders and/or administrators regarding position performance or planning outcomes.

Fiduciaries Financial organizations entrusted with managing retirement funds and related assets.

File A collection of papers or documents arranged systematically for reference.

Forced distribution One type of ranking technique used to evaluate either persons or positions.

Form A standardized method of recording data.

Formative appraisal Appraisals aimed at improving the performance of position holders.

Form information Written data provided by individuals through completion of specified request.

Forms management Responsibility for creating, revising, and controlling all school system forms.

Goal structure A hierarchy of assumptions ranging from broad to narrow organizational intent (mission, purpose, goals, objectives, and targets). Developed to identify desirable future outcomes.

Graphic rating A performance appraisal technique for evaluating job performance along a single continuum by denoting the level of performance with an adverb, number, or behavior incident.

Grievance procedure A prescribed series of steps or a line of appeals designed to resolve a disagreement, dissatisfaction, dispute, or conflict concerning conditions of employment.

History A type of threat pertaining to internal validity that relates to the passage of time and suggests external factors other than the desired treatment that influences outcomes in assessment.

HMO Health maintenance organization. The Federal Act of 1973 requires employers to offer an HMO (medical organization) to their employees as an alternative to conventional group health plans.

Human resource function Personnel is one of the major functions of school administration, including these processes: planning, bargaining, recruitment, selection, induction, development, appraisal, compensation, justice, continuity, and information.

Impasse A situation existing when negotiations are deadlocked and the possibilities of reaching common ground for a new contract are unforeseeable.

Incentives Forms of compensation in addition to base salary that link rewards to outstanding performance.

Individual portfolios A performance appraisal technique relying on examples of work compiled by an employee.

Induction A systematic organizational plan to assist personnel to adjust readily and effectively to new assignments so that they can contribute maximally to the work of the system while realizing personal and position satisfaction.

Information Knowledge consisting of facts that have been analyzed in the context of school administration.

Information consists of data that have been refined.

Information policy A procedural document pertaining to the collection, maintenance, and usage of formal records maintained by an organization.

Information process A series of phases used to describe the acquisition, uses, and evaluation of data by an organization.

Information system A systematic plan designed to acquire, refine, organize, store, maintain, protect, retrieve, and communicate data in a valid and accurate form.

In-service education Planned programs of learning opportunities afforded staff members for the purpose of improving the performance of individuals in already-assigned positions.

Instrumentation A type of threat pertaining to internal validity that suggests outcomes are due to changes in calibration of the measuring instrument rather than intended treatment conditions.

Internal consistency A criterion for evaluation of compensation systems that focuses on the interrelationship among positions.

Internal environment Forces within the school system, such as mission, goals, processes, performance culture, and leadership styles, that influence organizational courses of action.

Job A group of positions identical with respect to their major tasks.

Job analysis A formal set of procedures used to identify and define job tasks and behaviors.

Job categories Includes professionals, office and clerical personnel, skilled and semi-skilled operatives, unskilled laborers, and support personnel.

Job content Tasks and behaviors required to perform a job.

Job criteria Actual indicators of tasks and behaviors necessary to perform a job.

Job evaluation The process by which jobs are compared in order to determine compensation value and ensure pay equity.

Job predictors Assessment instruments used to measure tasks and behaviors required for job performance.

Job satisfaction Individual inclination, expression, feeling, or disposition relative to a work assignment and the environment in which it is performed.

Job simulations A set of job tasks designed to approximate actual job behaviors and duties.

Job specification A statement setting forth the personal requirements or capabilities entailed in performing the work of a position.

Justice An inclusive term covering, completely or broadly, organizational maintenance of what is just by impartial adjustment of conflicting claims, rights, misconduct, or system personnel abuses.

Justice system Organizational provisions by which personnel actions (individual and organizational) are determined as right or wrong. Rewards and penalties are allocated impartially according to principles of equity or fairness.

Learning curve A graph depicting proficiency rates over periods of time.

Management by objectives (MBO) A narrative system of performance appraisal that focuses on establishing and assessing goals mutually determined by the employee and employer.

Maturation A type of threat pertaining to internal validity that suggests changes in outcomes are due to biological changes in participants rather than treatment conditions.

Mentor programs Programs established by a school system to enable outstanding experienced teachers to serve as coaches, guides, and/or role models, especially for beginning teachers, teachers changing from one grade position to another or to another school, and to enhance the performance of other experienced teachers. Mentor programs entail special incentives for those serving as mentors.

Minority Part of a population differing from others in some characteristics (cultural, economic, political, religious, sexual, or racial) and often subjected to differential treatment.

Misconduct Deliberate violation of system employment standards relating to felony, insubordination, embezzlement, exceeding authority, misappropriation of funds, drug and alcohol abuse, off-duty conduct, and employment creating a conflict of interest to detrimental effect on the system.

Model A tentative description of a system or theory that accounts for all of its known properties. Models for the human resource function, for example, are conceptual frameworks designed to isolate key factors in personnel programs, processes, or procedures to show how these factors are related to and influence each other. A model helps to visualize or portray plans that cannot be visualized directly or readily before adoption.

Modeling The use of models to create, pretest, diagnose, and monitor various kinds of school system plans (structures, instructional systems, human resource processes, pupil forecasts,

and compensation designs). Models are employed frequently to design and test the reasonableness of new plans or to diagnose the worthiness of those already in operation.

Mortality A type of threat pertaining to internal validity that occurs when participants withdraw their participation because of training conditions.

Motivation Internal or external forces that influence an individual's willingness to achieve performance expectations.

Motivation theories Assumptions regarding determinants that influence personnel to cooperate in putting their abilities to use to further organizational aims. Among those cited in the literature are two-factor, social comparison, consistency, reinforcement, and expectancy theories. Beliefs school officials hold about motivation influence personnel decisions.

Multiple cutoff model An empirical procedure for combining information about an employee's performance on each dimension when a minimum level of performance is required on each dimension.

Narrative systems A family of self-referenced systems that compare different dimensions of job performance as exhibited by a sample employee.

National Health Care Insurance A variety of national health care insurance plans were introduced in the 103rd Congress in 1994 without reaching the enactment stage. These ranged from reliance on tax incentives for individual insurance purchasers, to employer-mandated contributions to health care costs, to establishing a national health insurance system.

Need A discrepancy between an actual and a desired state. Objectives are the counterparts of needs and are employed to translate problems into programs.

Negotiating modes Three common modes of negotiations are generally described in the literature: competitive, collaborative, and subordinative.

Negotiations School system professional contracts are commonly negotiated by a single union and a single employer. In some situations, different contract negotiations are agreed upon for different groups of support personnel.

Negotiations strategy Plans that establish the kinds of educational programs and services the system will make available for its clients, procedures by which these programs and services will be delivered, and means for motivating personnel to cooperate voluntarily in making the delivery system effective.

Norm-referenced The level of job performance exhibited by an employee compared to the level of job performance exhibited by other employees.

Norms Unwritten group rules or values shared by members regarding work behavior. Statistical norms are averages sometimes construed as standards (goals).

Objective theory A theory for recruitment that focuses on the economic incentives associated with jobs/organizations.

Objectives What is to be accomplished, for what purpose and to what extent, by whom, with what resources, and within what time frame. Objectives should be measurable and linked to broad system aims and strategies.

Organization A group of individuals systematically united to achieve a particular method or objective, such as a military, educational, religious, or commercial organization.

Organization chart A graphic representation of functions, accountability, responsibility, relationships, and levels of various positions in the organizational structure.

Organization culture Values, standards, and attitudes of appropriate conduct and fair treatment established and reinforced by the organization and system members.

Organization manual A document (handbook) describing the formal organization structure and related policies, processes, programs, rules, and regulations.

Organization structure A framework for assigning roles, responsibilities, relationships, and decision-making authority among system members.

Organizational development (OD) Most definitions include: a planned, systematic intervention designed to shape organization culture; by improving individual, intragroup, and intergroup attitudes.

Organizational elements Key elements include structure, design of positions, power, and staffing.

Organizational influences: external Among the external, uncontrollable elements influencing the human resource function are the regulatory environment, legal precedents, political climate, federal and state legislation, community population patterns, cultural/social change, technological developments, economic change, school enrollments, and union culture.

Organizational influences: internal Among the internal elements influencing the human resource function are the financial condition of the system, quality of information flow, structural setting, quality and quantity of school personnel, individual behavior, group behavior, and nature of formal and informal organizations.

Organizational manual A doument for describing the formal structure of an organization through the use of flow charts and statements relating to positions.

Paired comparison A norm-based job performance assessment technique that involves dyadic pairings among all employees comprising a work group.

Performance appraisal The process of arriving at judgments about a member's past, present, or predicted future behavior against the background of his or her work environment or future performance potential.

Performance appraisal system Techniques and procedures used by an organization to assess the job performance of employees.

Performance criteria Criteria used to measure or evaluate the position holder's performance. They include trait, behavioral, or outcome criteria or any combination of the three.

Performance culture Established patterns of behavior deemed essential to fulfillment of agreed-on position, group, and organizational values, standards, and attitudes.

Performance effectiveness The level of performance that the position holder is expected to achieve.

Performance effectiveness areas Key results areas or components, specified in a position description, in which the incumbent should be investing time, energy, and talent to achieve position expectations.

Performance objectives A statement containing information relative to what a position holder is expected to accomplish and how well it is to be accomplished.

Personnel administration Refers to the range of personnel activities involved in achieving individual, group, and organizational aims through proper use of the system's human resources.

Personnel continuity process A series of managerial tasks and provisions designed to retain competent personnel and foster continuity in personnel service.

Personnel development needs Development needs that surface at various levels (organizational, unit, and individual), at different times, for varying reasons.

Personnel development process Formal and informal activities aimed at improving the abilities, attitudes, skills, and knowledge of system members.

Personnel information Information about individuals who apply for employment and enter, work in, and leave the system.

Personnel information modules Units of personnel information arranged or joined in a variety of ways with the specific purpose of contributing to administration of the human resource function.

Personnel information process An organizational process through which efforts are made to achieve a desired state relative to personnel information. Steps in the process include diagnosis, preparation, implementation, evaluation, and feedback.

Personnel policy A written statement expressing general aims and intentions of the board of education with respect to working conditions and relationships that are intended to prevail in the school system.

Personnel protection Protection of persons, jobs, income, and staffing.

Phased retirement Opportunities for personnel nearing retirement to reduce their workload through leaves of absence; part-time employment; and reduced work days, work weeks, or work years.

Placement The assignment of an individual to a specific position within an organization.

Planning Deciding in advance of action those objectives to be achieved and developing strategies to achieve them.

Planning tools A set or collection of management mechanisms that belong to or are used together. For example: (a) *mission* refers to the primary purpose for which schools are established; (b) *strategy* refers to the use and allocation of system resources to guide action toward long-range objectives; (c) *policies* are the express system intent and boundaries within which actions are permitted or expected; (d) *aims, goals,* and *objectives* refer to desirable future results; (e) *programs* and *projects* are plans designed to achieve objectives; (f) *procedures, rules,* and *regulations* are specific instructions that guide actions and performance behavior essential to attainment of objectives; and (g) *controls* are management arrangements designed to compare planned and actual results; (h) *budgets, audits, standards, in-*

ventories, and *research studies* are types of controls employed to compare and correct deviations from plans.

Planning vision An idealistic image of the school system or its components in a preferred future state. A vision of the future state of the human resource function, for example, incorporates the long-run changes deemed essential to achieving the desired image.

Policy Broad statements of organizational intent that establish guidelines to govern the scope and boundaries of administrative decisions. There are, for example, compensation policies to govern base pay, addends, benefits, temporary hires, and pay levels comparable with other employers.

Portfolios An assessment technique for evaluating performance that relies on the compilation of work materials and outcomes.

Position A collection of tasks constituting the total work assignment of a single worker.

Position guide A statement describing both position requirements and position holder requirements. Useful in the recruitment, selection, induction, compensation, and development processes.

Position-holder value Economic worth of individuals who occupy positions in the system.

Position value The relative importance of a position in the organization structure. Positions involving greater responsibility and difficulty are valued more highly and should receive more pay than those of less responsibility and difficulty.

Power The degree to which an individual can influence others.

Power bases Five power bases are described as reward power, coercive power, referent power, legitimate power, and expert power.

Practice significance The functional utilization of a process, procedure, or practice to achieve a purpose.

Predictive validity An empirical paradigm for assessing the appropriateness of a measure or process.

Pregnancy Disability Act of 1978 (PDA) Prohibits discrimination in employment practices on the basis of pregnancy, childbirth, or related medical conditions.

Pre-negotiations planning Initial phase of the collective bargaining process, which includes such activities as developing the bargaining structure, analyzing the current contract, anticipating issues, preparing the financial outlook, developing the bargaining handbook, and formulating strategy and tactics.

Privacy Act of 1974 Federal legislation that places limits on the collection and dissemination of personal information of members of affected organizations.

Privacy laws Legislative acts addressing scope of access to personal records of students and employees.

Problem personnel System members who are unable or unwilling to meet organizational standards of performance or behavior.

Procedural justice Refers to organizational procedures employed to arrive at impartial adjustment of conflicting claims, rights, or adherence to employment standards. Focuses on conformity to truth, fact, or reason.

Professionalism The standing practice or methods of a professional as distinguished from an amateur. Involves professional character, spirit, and methods. Expertise is currently assumed to be the defining element of professionalism in areas such as law, medicine, academe, nursing, and teaching.

Professional staff size index The number of professional staff members per 1000 students.

Program structure Parts of an educational program arranged in some way, such as curricula; courses of study; electives; and instructional objectives, outcomes, and practices.

Promotion A job change by an employee from a lower level position to a higher level position.

Protected class status Protection of specific groups of individuals from discrimination in employment on the basis of group characteristics (age, sex, race, etc.).

Psychic income (also referred to as *noneconomic perquisites*). Includes a variety of privileges incidental to regular salary or wages. Granted voluntarily, beyond position requirements, usually in recognition of, in return for, or in anticipation of some service to the school system (recognition, appreciation, status symbols, special commendations, transfers to more attractive work, psychological security, or special arrangements related to work or working conditions).

Psychological contract A conceptual view of an unwritten employment transaction between the system and its members in which the position holder exchanges certain types of position behavior (cooperation, continuity, and adherence to position requirements) in return for compensation and other sources of job satisfaction (rights, privileges, and position control).

Quality of organizational life The extent to which conditions or arrangements in the school system maximize opportunities for the position holder to assume a personalized role conducive to satisfaction of position performance, growth, initiative, and flexibility.

Ranking systems A family of norm-referenced systems that compare the job performance of one employee to the job performance of other employees.

Rating systems A family of criterion-referenced systems that compare the job performance of an employee to external standards.

Rationality Pertains to an expected salary differential between a supervisor and a subordinate.

Recognition procedures Formal process followed by employees to establish and acknowledge by a union.

Record (a) A written entry or memorial for the purpose of preserving memory or authentic evidence of facts or events; (b) accumulation and organization of data regarded as being of more than temporary significance.

Records center A central storage area for school system inactive records.

Records inventory The records the school system maintains, by categories, their location, retention, disposition, and management responsibilities.

Records policy Guidelines for directing, controlling, and auditing the school system's records program.

Recruitment The administrative task performed by an organization to attract applicants for employment consideration.

Recruitment message The communication between an organization and an applicant independent of mode.

Reference Information obtained from external sources about applicants, which can be either professional or personal.

Regression Either a type of threat pertaining to internal validity or a statistical technique used for assessing co-variation.

Regulatory environment Outside forces that govern and influence virtually all personnel processes (e.g., the U.S. Constitution, congressional acts, executive orders, state and local legislation, and judicial systems).

Reinforcement The process of modifying behavior by arranging positive consequences for desired behavior and negative consequences for undesired behavior.

Reliability Refers to those measures that give consistent results either over periods of time or among different raters.

Reports Utilization of records to communicate information.

Resignation A voluntary decision by a position holder to sever an employment relationship.

Retention-ratio projection An estimate of the future number of individuals in a cohort, derived by multiplying an existing number by the mean survival ratio experienced over a selected number of time intervals.

Retroactive enrollment ratio A factor expressing variation in the number of individuals enrolled from the present accounting period to the preceding period. The ratio is derived by dividing enrollment in a grade during a given year by enrollment in the next higher grade during the following year. For example: 500 individuals enrolled in Grade 9, having been succeeded by 550 individuals enrolled in Grade 10 during the following year, would yield a ratio of 500:550 or .91.

Salary Amount of money received for services rendered by employees exempted from the Fair Labor Standards Act of 1938.

Scope of bargaining The substance of economic and noneconomic issues to be negotiated at the bargaining table.

Security process Arrangements designed to protect system members from internal threats and anxieties that occur in organizational life.

Selection The administrative task performed by an organization to choose among applicants for employment purposes.

Selection A type of threat pertaining to interval validity that suggests that outcomes obtained are an artifact of the particular participants rather than the treatment condition.

Self-referenced One dimension of job performance exhibited by a single employee is compared to another dimension of job performance exhibited by the same employee.

Simple ranking A norm-based job performance assessment technique for aligning employees or jobs along a single continuum relative to specified criteria.

Socialization process Formal and informal experiences through which members become adjusted to the values, roles, relationships, and culture of the organization. A formal socialization process (induction) is aimed at assisting

members to make a productive start in their positions.

Span of control Ability to manage a given number of people.

Spreadsheet A computer program used to analyze numbers in a row and column accounting format. Useful in budgeting, collective bargaining planning, forecasting school enrollment, and staff projections.

Staff development Systematic means for continuous development of performance capabilities of system personnel. The philosophical underpinning of staff development is that anyone who keeps a job should keep proving and improving himself or herself every day.

Standard of comparison The criterion to which an employee's level of job performance is compared.

Standards Criteria against which to judge or measure the acceptability of performance or service. These measures include quality, time, cost, and personnel ratios.

Stakeholder One who has a monetary share, personal or emotional concern, or involvement in the well-being of an educational enterprise.

Statistical significance The empirical utilization of a process, procedure, or practice to achieve a purpose within the bounds of certain probabilities.

Stock statistics An index that reflects the degree of utilization of protected class persons relative to their distribution in the labor market.

Strategy Development or employment of overall plans, sometimes referred to as *grand designs*, in order to achieve goals, planned effects, or desired results. Considered a technique of total planning that encompasses the overall aims of the system and establishes functional strategies (e.g., educational program, personnel, logistics, and external relations) to achieve them. Each functional area is broken into individual modules to create an overall strategic plan for the organization.

Stress interview A recruitment-selection technique designed to identify candidates who are capable of reacting in a calm and composed manner in tense, uncomfortable, and pressure-driven situations.

Strike To quit or cease working in order to compel employer compliance with a demand.

Subjective theory A theory for recruitment that focuses on the psychological rewards associated with jobs/organizations.

Summative appraisal Personnel appraisal focused on decisions involving compensation, tenure, dismissal, promotion, and reemployment. Does not occur simultaneously with formative appraisals.

Support personnel Employees who perform work for which no educational certification is required and who do not participate directly in the educational process.

Systems concept A concept that embraces the interdependence among system components and the internal and external environments in which they operate.

Technical rationality Judicious use of techniques, operations, resources, knowledge, and know-how to improve, sustain, and encourage effective performance.

Technology Systematic advancements for improving standard operating procedures within an organization.

Tenure An official status granted after a trial period to a teacher or a member of another covered professional class to protect the individual from summary dismissal.

Termination Severance of an employment relationship.

Termination at will The absolute right to discharge, with or without cause, in the absence of a written contract.

Testing A type of threat pertaining to internal validity that suggests outcomes of an assessment are due to the pre-test rather than to the treatment condition.

Theories of learning Assumptions regarding the process by which new behaviors are acquired.

Theory (a) A proposed explanation to describe or account for a phenomenon; (b) an individual view, speculation, or hypothesis. Theories in the literature describing certain aspects of the human resource function include behavioral, organization, equity, motivation, administrative, and communication theories.

Transfer A job change by an employee from one position to another position within an organization where both positions are of equal value.

Turnover Changes in the composition of the work force due to resignation, transfer, retirement, or behavioral reasons. Generally expressed as the rate of turnover—the number of persons hired within a period to replace those leaving or dropped from the work force.

Uniform guidelines of 1978 Federal guidelines covering employee selection procedures.

Unionism A school system or other organization in which the terms and conditions of employment are fixed by legal forces between employer and teacher union. Modern unions rely heavily upon the political process at all levels of government to realize their objectives.

Validity The degree to which an instrument measures what it is designed to measure.

Values Ideals, customs, and beliefs of system members for which a group has an affectionate regard.

Variable A quantity susceptible to fluctuating in value (e.g., test scores, performance rank, and absentee rate).

Wage Amount of money received for services rendered by employees covered by the Fair Labor Standards Act of 1938.

Work Diaries An assessment technique for evaluating jobs or individuals on the basis of a written narrative compiled by employees.

Work-force analysis Analysis of the composition of the work force with respect to balance in the number and percentage of minority as well as male and female personnel currently employed, by level and position classification.

Work itself theory A recruitment theory that focuses on duties and job tasks associated with jobs/organizations.

AUTHOR INDEX

SUBJECT INDEX